当代国际商务文化阅读丛书

Readings for Modern International Business Culture

希波克拉底誓言

——『商务交际』篇

Hippocratic Oath

Business Communication

【英汉对照】

吴斐 编著

武汉大学出版社
WUHAN UNIVERSITY PRESS

图书在版编目(CIP)数据

希波克拉底誓言:“商务交际”篇:英汉对照/吴斐编著.—武汉:武汉大学出版社,2016.5

当代国际商务文化阅读丛书

书名原文:Hippocratic Oath:Business Communication

ISBN 978-7-307-13995-4

Ⅰ.希… Ⅱ.吴… Ⅲ.国际商务—英、汉 Ⅳ.F740

中国版本图书馆 CIP 数据核字(2014)第 181967 号

责任编辑:郭园园 金 军　　责任校对:鄢春梅　　版式设计:韩闻锦

出版发行:**武汉大学出版社** (430072 武昌 珞珈山)

(电子邮件:cbs22@whu.edu.cn 网址:www.wdp.com.cn)

印刷:武汉中远印务有限公司

开本:880×1230 1/32 印张:10.125 字数:222 千字

版次:2016 年 5 月第 1 版　　2016 年 5 月第 1 次印刷

ISBN 978-7-307-13995-4　　定价:28.00 元

前　言

人类社会进入21世纪后，国家间的商务往来更加频繁，商务交际手段随着互联网的诞生和电子信息的进步日新月异，国际化企业的文化和理念千差万别，商务话题的表达和沟通能力无疑是人们所遇到的最大障碍。在我们熟知的生活英语、学术英语之外，商务英语不仅是我国目前从事或即将从事涉外商务人员英语实际应用能力不可多得的辅助工具，更是商务工作人员在这个国际化的高科技时代商务竞争能力、外贸业务素质和英语水平的重要体现。《当代国际商务文化阅读》（英汉对照）丛书以从事国际商务活动所必需的语言技能为经，以各种商务活动的具体情景作纬，将商务精神和商务元素巧妙融合，展示时尚而又经典的商务文化世界流行风，为广大读者提供一套语言规范、内容新颖、涉及面广、趣味性强、具有实用价值、富于时代精神的读物，既注意解决人们在国际商务环境中遇到不熟悉的专业词汇无法与外国合作者就工作问题交流沟通的难题，又着力解决人们学外语单纯地学语言而缺乏商务专业知识的弊端。

《当代国际商务文化阅读》（英汉对照）丛书由10个单行本组成:《拥抱新欢亚马逊（Embracing Amazon Service）——电子商务篇（E-commerce）》、《华尔街梦魇（Nightmare on Wall Street）——商界风云篇（The Business Circles）》、《路易斯·波森的朋克摇滚（The Punk Rock of Louis Posen）——商界精英篇（Business Elites）》、《希波克拉底誓言（Hippocratic Oath）——商务交际篇（Business Communication）》、《强烈的第一印象（A Powerful First Impression）——商务礼仪篇（Business Etiquette）》、《企业帝国继承权之争（Corporate Empires' Grappling wite Succession）——商务文化篇（Business Culture）》、《紫色血液（The Purple Blood）——商务心理篇（Business Psychology）》、《多米诺骨牌效应（The Domino Effects）——商务知识篇（Business Knowledge）》、《公开的赌注（Public Stakes）——商务演讲篇（Business Speeches）》、《伊斯特林悖论（The Easterlin Paradox）——感悟财富篇（Comprehension of Wealth）》。这套丛书的编写旨在帮助读者在国际商务环境下，能够读懂英文的商务信息和商务新闻，并能对某一商务话题的知识有全面透彻的了解，领悟当代时尚商务文化成长的环境和思维方式，提高在全球化高科技时代的商务竞争能力、外贸业务素质和英语交际水平。丛书中的阅读材料力求做到题材广泛、内容精辟、语言规范，遵循趣味性、知识性和时效性原则，培养读者在商务环境下的英语竞争能力和综合应用能力。丛书融时代性与经典性为一体，内容经得起时间考验，文字经得起反复咀嚼，保证其可读性。读者在阅读过程中接收大量的语言输入，为合理组织和娴熟运用英语语言表达自己的思想打下牢固的基础。丛书的单行本包括以一个主题为中心的30篇文章，每篇文章包括题记、英语原文、汉语译文、生词脚注和知识链接。"题记"用丰富生动的语言点评文章的精髓，对文章的内容起到提炼和画龙点睛的作用。"英语原文"主要摘自当代国际主流报纸杂志，具有语言规范、内容新颖、涉及面广、趣味性和时代感等特点。“汉语译文”力求准确流畅，既关注译文的文化语境及其内涵，也重视译文的外延和现当代标志性语言符号。“生词脚注”的难度把握在大学英语六级和研究生英语词汇程度，以帮助读者及时扫清阅读障碍。“知识链接”根据文章内容，或精解一个专业术语，或阐释一种新的商务理念，或介绍叱咤商界的企业或公司，以帮助读者培养游弋商海、运筹帷幄的能力，具备洞悉中西文化的国际视野。

《希波克拉底誓言》（Hippocratic Oath）——商务交际篇（Business Communication）为读者展示了希波克拉底誓言、重建各国之间的经济之墙、打造卓越的供应链、国际商务的跨文化管理、商业团队中的人际关系、社交网络效益、荣格框架下的成功团队、跨国公司的表演、与“授权予我一代”沟通、马基雅弗利启示和贸易全球化共识等商务交际的策略和技巧。商务交际道德是商界职业活动的行为规范。希波克拉底誓言是一项由希波克拉底制定的医道规范，指古代西方医生在开业时都要宣读的一份有关医务道德的誓词。商界管理版本的希波克拉底誓言创造和维持了一种社区感，以及成员对彼此、对职业的相互责任感，将职业化的管理人员推上了更为严格的知识和能力标准以及道德风险和谋略的平台。商务交际策略是驰骋商场必须具备的一种能力。产品生产和流通过程中所涉及的原材料供应商、生产商、分销商、零售商以及最终消费者等成员通过与上游、下游成员的连接组成的网络结构成为竞争策略的关键供应链，而商业圈的社交网络效益则超越了公司之间的界限，促使“人力资本”的传统观念向“社会资本”的流行概念转换，以博客圈这种物以类聚的生态形式发现商业机会，达到不同族群之间的理解和交流。优秀领导者是商务交际决策能力的操盘手。他们的天才之处在于即时感知环境的变化，做出战略性选择、人力资源选择和在危机情况下做出的选择。优秀领导者既是冷兵器时代的项羽，沧海横流，方显英雄本色，又是互联网时代的乔布斯，用创新和孤独打造超越于产品之上的艺术和人文结合的远见卓识。团队建设是提高企业的应变能力和持续创新能力的基础。成功团队包括四种人：具备理性想象力的魔术师，他们认为新思想或洞察力是唯一可以改变世界的东西；务实而又情绪化的恋人，他们着眼于建设成功的联盟，认为行动应当一致；情感和想象力丰富的君主，他们着眼于大局，根据事情是否能得出他们想要的结果判断一切；既理性又务实的武士，他们只能清楚地看到直接发生在自己面前的事情，认为行动是直接取胜的关键因素。全球经济一体化的跨国经营导致了资本技术的快速流动。跨文化人力资源、跨文化团队建设、跨文化协同作用、跨文化意识培训、海外工作人员的跨文化培训、跨文化谈判、跨文化公关顾问、跨文化语言培训等一系列全面的资源整合，不仅为国际交往创造了理解的桥梁，也为商业成功打开了沟通的渠道。交际战略是公司占据业界制高点的必要手段。保尔森的牌技、整修花旗集团、恶意杀价、熟悉网络的私屋房主与农夫之战、麦凯恩与投资人的合作、欣赏“伟大的威胁者”、信托紧缩危机等经典案例，将欲擒故纵原则、集中兵力原则、目标明确原则、计划与计算原则、创新与应变原则等军事战略思想发挥得淋漓尽致。

　　商务交际的魅力在于让商人在道德的漩涡中变得更像坚守信仰

的政客，在操纵策略的逻辑中变得更像思维缜密的哲学家，在建设团队的过程中变得更像挥斥方遒的领袖，在全球化的跨国重组中变得更像运筹帷幄的建筑师，在充满希望和竞争的市场变得更像足智多谋的勇士。让我们把握商务交际的时代动脉，享受世界流行文化创造的快乐、荣誉、价值和成就感！

作　者

2016 年 1 月

目　录

目　录

目　录

题 记

希波克拉底誓言是一项由希波克拉底制定的医道规范，指古代西方医生在开业时都要宣读的一份有关医务道德的誓词。哈佛大学的两位教授将企业管理人员与医生和律师的职业精神进行对比，提出了现代希波克拉底誓言的商界管理版本。商业的职业化进程首先对传统的工商管理硕士学位提出了挑战：安然公司曾经的首席执行官杰弗里·斯吉林就拥有哈佛大学的工商管理硕士学位；而比尔·盖茨这样一名非传统意义上的成功者无疑缺乏正规的管理训练。所以，商界管理版本的希波克拉底誓言创造和维持了一种社区感，以及成员对彼此、对职业的相互责任感，将职业化的管理人员推上了更为严格的知识和能力标准，以及道德风险和谋略的平台。

Hippocratic Oath

Do bosses need their own Hippocratic Oath? First, do no harm.

Managers of many of the world's leading financial firms have found hope. Now, as the world's economy slows, attention will be turned to managers of non-financial firms, to see if they are any better prepared for the rainy day that was bound to come sooner or later. It will be no surprise if soaring bankruptcies demonstrate that their risk management is just as inept①, and just as focused on maximizing short-term profits and their pay packets without thinking too hard about something terrible that would happen when the good times ended.

Why is this failure so unsurprising? In a new article in the Harvard Business Review, Rakesh Khurana and Nitin Nohria, who teach at the Harvard Business School, argue that the problem is literally a lack of professionalism. Contrasting corporate managers with doctors and lawyers, the authors title their article with their argument: "It's Time to Make Management a True Profession". As they point out, "unlike doctors and lawyers, managers don't need a formal education, let alone a license to

① inept [iˈnept] *adj.* 无能的

希波克拉底誓言

老板们需要立下自己的“希波克拉底誓言”吗？ 首先，这种做法没有伤害性。

许多世界顶级金融公司的经理们已经发现了希望。 现在，由于世界经济放缓，关注度将转向非金融公司的管理人员，看他们是否能更好地迎接迟早要到来的困难时期。 如果不断飙升的破产证明他们的风险管理也同样无能，同样只顾专注最大限度的短期利润和他们的薪酬，对繁荣期终结时将会发生的可怕事件完全不慎重思考，这是毫不奇怪的。

为什么这个失败如此不值得大惊小怪？ 任职哈佛商学院的教师拉凯什·库拉纳和尼汀·诺瑞亚最近在《哈佛商业评论》上发表了一篇文章，宣称这个问题其实是缺乏职业精神。 他们将企业管理人员与医生和律师进行了对比，文章的标题则结合了他们的论点：“是时候把管理当成真正的职业了。”正如他们所指出的，“管理人员不像医生和律师，不必接受正规教育，更不用说行业许可证。 他们也不必坚持普遍和强制性的行为守则”。 即使个体企业制定和执行公司行为守则或价值声明，“也没有一套能被普遍接受、主管团体支持的职业价值，并且主管团体有权惩罚违背行为守则的管理人员”。

这个论点隐含着对工商管理硕士的尖锐批评，拉凯什·库拉纳

practice. Nor do they adhere to a universal and enforceable code of conduct." Even if individual firms write and enforce corporate codes or value statements, "there's no universally accepted set of professional values backed up by a governing body with the power to censure[①] managers who deviate from the code."

Implicit in this argument is a deep criticism of the MBA, a degree that Rakesh Khurana and Nitin Nohria teach, and that many of today's failing managers hold. Indeed, there are already rumblings about the failure of the MBA courses that Wall Street's "finest" took before rising up the ranks of global finance—just as there was after Enron went bust, Jeffrey Skilling, Enron's chief executive, holds an MBA from Harvard.

Yet, as the professors point out, the desire to make management a profession like law and medicine was central to Harvard Business School in the first decades after it was founded 100 years ago. A start would be for management education to "adopt the more stringent[②] knowledge and competency standards required by true professions," they argue. For instance, the Association to Advance Collegiate Schools of Business "could devise and administer an exam that all graduating MBAs would have to pass before they were licensed to practice". Managers could also be required to take top-up courses to retain their licenses.

One question this raises, the authors concede, is just how essential

---

① censure [ˈsenʃə] *vt.* 责难

② stringent [ˈstrindʒənt] *adj.* 严厉的

和尼汀·诺瑞教授的就是这个学位的课程，也是现如今许多失败的管理人员拥有的学位。其实早就有人喋喋不休地抱怨失败的工商管理硕士课程了，华尔街“最杰出”的人士拿到工商管理硕士学位之后，在全球金融界的地位迅速提高。安然破产就是例证，安然公司曾经的首席执行官杰弗里·斯吉林就拥有哈佛大学的工商管理硕士学位。

然而，正如教授们指出的，哈佛商学院成立100多年以来，头几十年的核心是致力于让管理成为法学和医学这样的专业。他们认为，管理教育开始“采取真正的职业所要求的、更为严格的知识和能力标准”。例如，高级商学院协会“可以制定和实施一种考试，所有在读的工商管理硕士必须通过考试，才可获准入行”。管理人员还被要求研修升级课程，以维持他们的行业证书。

作者承认，这也引起了一个问题，即管理教育究竟有多么重要。的确，像比尔·盖茨这样一名非传统意义上的成功者可能表明，缺乏正规的管理训练是成为成功企业家的优势。而在医学界和法律界，未经专业培训即成功登顶的从业人员的例子要少得多，尽管有一些广受欢迎的另类治疗师和埃琳·布劳克维基等新兴的法律英雄。拉凯什·库拉纳和尼汀·诺瑞提议，管理工作应该根据足够的专业培训进行分类，以便市场明确这种培训的价值。但是，很难想象接受大学终身教育的传统企业家已经不再是一种时尚。

也许，对究竟是什么构成职业行为准则取得一致的意见比教育水准更为重要。为此，两位教授提出了希波克拉底誓言的管理版本，所有的管理者都必须照此宣誓。他们主张：“守则创造和维持了一种社区感，以及成员对彼此、对职业的相互责任感。”他们提出

management education is—indeed, the success of iconoclasts① like Bill Gates might suggest that a lack of formal management training was a positive advantage in becoming a successful entrepreneur. Medicine and law have far fewer examples of top practitioners succeeding without professional training—despite the popularity of some alternative healers and upstart② legal heroes such as Erin Brockovich. Rakesh Khurana and Nitin Nohria propose that management jobs be classified according to the amount of professional training required in order to allow the market to make clear the value of such training, but it is hard to imagine the traditional entrepreneur educated in the university of life going out of fashion.

Perhaps more important than an educational standard may be a general agreement on what constitutes professional standards of behavior. To this end, the two professors propose a managerial version of the Hippocratic Oath, to which all managers must swear. "Codes create and sustain a feeling of community and mutual obligation that members have toward each other and toward the profession," they argue. The management oath they propose covers issues including selfishness ("I pledge that considerations of personal benefit will never supersede the interests of the enterprise I am entrusted to manage") and transparency③

① iconoclast [aiˈkɔnəklæst] *n.* 提倡打破旧习的人

② upstart [ˈʌpstɑːt] *n.* 暴发户

③ transparency [trænsˈpɛərənsi] *n.* 透明,透明度

的管理誓言覆盖的问题包括自私（“我保证，个人利益绝不会凌驾于我受托管理的企业利益”）和透明度（“我发誓，精确无误且公开透明地代表企业对相关各方履行职责”）。

这套誓言缺乏医学界“首先，不具有伤害性”的简单透明，主要原因是超难判断一名管理人员的工作是否出色，这要在他或她已经停止工作很久后才能得出结论，即使在那时也不好判断。教授们要管理人员保证：“通过提升企业给社会创造的价值来服务公众的利益。”但是，这是一个很难的判断标准。同行和公众通常把注意力放在他们容易看到的表现尺度上：利润。在企业中，即使一名管理人员忽略了一些活动，既没有使公司的长期利润最大化，也没有援助社会，利润仍然可以连续几年上涨。除休·劳里的才华横溢和愤世嫉俗的虚拟医生和公司以外，反对职业标准的机构并没有在医学界获得成功。

然而，随着越来越多的公众和政界人士由于经济问题而责备企业，职业化的呼声更难以及时得到响应。今天的商界领袖和教育工作者如果明智的话，就会明白，正是他们以开明的利己主义之名认真的采取了职业化的目标，社会才开始恢复了对他们的信任。

知识链接

Hippocratic Oath 希波克拉底誓言。古代西方医生在开业时都要宣读一份有关医务道德的誓词：“我要遵守誓约，矢志不渝。对传授我医术的老师，我要像父母一样敬重。对我的儿子、老师的儿子以及我的门徒，我要悉心传授医学知识。我要竭尽全力，采取我认为有利于病人的医疗措施，不能给病人

("I vow to represent my enterprise's performance accurately and transparently to all relevant parties").

This lacks the simple clarity of medicine's "First, do no harm", largely because it is exceedingly hard to judge whether a manager is doing a good job until long after he or she has ceased to do it, if even then. The professors want managers to pledge "to serve the public's interest by enhancing the value their enterprise creates for society." But this is a difficult standard to judge; peers and the public tend to focus on the measure of performance they can see easily: profit. In business, profit can go up for years even when a manager is overseeing activities that neither maximize the long-term value of the company nor aid society. With the exception of Hugh Laurie's brilliant and misanthropic① fictional doctor, house, going against the norms② of the profession is not the route to success in medicine.

Yet, as the public and politicians increasingly look to blame business for the problems of the economy, the call for professionalism could hardly be more timely. If they are wise, today's business leaders and educators will see it is in their enlightened self-interest to take the goal of professionalization seriously, and thus start to regain society's trust.

(835 words)

---

① misanthropic [ˌmizənˈθrɔpik] *adj.* 憎恶(或蔑视)世人的

② norm [nɔːm] *n.* 标准,规范

带来痛苦与危害。我不把毒药给任何人，也决不授意别人使用它。我要清清白白地行医和生活。无论进入谁家，只是为了治病，不为所欲为，不接受贿赂，不勾引异性。对看到或听到不应外传的私生活，我决不泄露。"这个医道规范的制定者就是希波克拉底。

题　记

物质和精神产品的流动冲破区域和国界的束缚，资本的全球化推动了重建各国之间的经济之墙的步伐。推开历史的厚重之门，中国的郑和引领经济全球化的风骚，但清朝闭关锁国长达五百年之久，令中国的全球化抱负随着郑和的逝去而消失殆尽。英国的工业革命揭开了全球化的崭新篇章，但第一次世界大战将现代全球化的伟大时代带入了杂乱无章的停滞。然而，随着21世纪的到来，全球化强势风靡世界的每一个角落，各国之间的经济往来比以往任何时候都更要频繁。对支持者而言，全球化是一种基于世界大同理想的意识形态；对反对者而言，反全球化是一种基于平等世界理想的意识形态。但请记住：正是中国首开了全球化经济之先河。

Rebuilding of National Economic Walls

At the museum of history in Hong Kong, you could visit an exhibition whose centerpiece was a old, bleached, shaped piece of wood, 11 m long. To be honest, it didn't look much. But it told a tale. For the wood was a rudder① post from a huge Chinese junk built around the time, nearly 600 years ago, when the Chinese eunuch admiral Zheng He embarked on seven epic voyages that took him to Southeast Asia and the shores of India, Arabia, and Africa, trading for spices and fabrics, livestock and raw materials.

After centuries, when Zheng He's exploits were forgotten even in China, he has deservedly entered the pantheon of the world's great explorers. The admiral has been adopted in his homeland as a symbol of an old, outward-looking, adventurous China, all things, perhaps, which it is once more. But the memory that China once traded with the world is not the only lesson of Zheng He's life. Here's another: when he died, so did China's global ambitions. Mandarins② decided that oceangoing voyages

---

① rudder [ˈrʌdə] *n.* 方向舵

② mandarin [ˈmændərin] *n.* 满清官吏

重建各国之间的经济之墙

在香港历史博物馆，你可以参观一间展室，它的中心装饰品是一根陈旧、褪色的成型木条，有11米长。说实话，它看起来没什么特别之处，但是，它却向我们讲述了一个故事。这根木条是一艘巨大的中国平底帆船上的舵柱，该船建造于大约600年以前，当时郑和作为中国宦官的将领乘此船开始了7次长达33年的下西洋航行，他曾到过东南亚、印度海岸、阿拉伯和非洲等地，进行香料、纺织品、家畜和原材料交易。

几个世纪以后，当郑和的功勋即使在中国也逐渐被人们遗忘之时，他却堂而皇之地进入世界伟大探险家的神殿。这名船队司令在他的家乡被认为是古代敢于走出国门、充满冒险精神的英雄。另一个事件令中国的全球化抱负随着郑和的逝去而消失殆尽。清王朝认为，远洋航行既浪费时间又浪费金钱。南京的大型海军造舰船坞很快解体，中国倒退至以己国为中心、闭关锁国长达五百年的时期。这是一个警示录：贸易之波既能够将我们联合起来，也可以让我们随波逐流。约翰·梅纳德·凯恩斯所写的《和平的经济后果》中有

were a waste of time and money; soon the great naval shipyards in Nanjing had been broken up, and China retreated into a self-absorbed attitude of mind that it would not lose for half a millennium. It's a cautionary note, a reminder that the waves of trade that knit us together can ebb as well as flow. There is a famous passage in The Economic Consequences of the Peace, written by John Maynard Keynes, which every student of globalization knows by heart. Keynes describes life as it existed in 1914, when a man in London could travel the world freely, invest wherever he wanted, and "could order by telephone, sipping his morning tea in bed, the various products of the whole earth, in such quantity as he might see fit, and reasonably expect their early delivery upon his doorstep." Not only that, Keynes' Londoner "regarded this state of affairs as normal, certain, and permanent, except in the direction of further improvement." It was not to be. World War I brought the modern world's first great era of globalization to a jarring① halt; trade atrophied②, and legislation like the Smoot-Hawley tariffs passed by the U. S. Congress gave a legislative imprimatur to protectionist sentiment.

Could such a moment be upon us again? Are the walls around national economies being built once more? From the numbers, the argument seems absurd. World trade is growing healthily, by over 7% a year. The U.N. Commission on Trade and Development estimates that the value of global flows of foreign direct investment grew by a remarkable 29% . Yet a quick look around the planet might lead to the impression that globalization is in crisis. Indigenous people in Ecuador intensely protested

① jarring [ˈdʒɑːriŋ] *adj.* 不调和的

② atrophied [ˈætrəfid] *adj.* 萎缩的

一名篇，全球的每一位学生对此谙熟于心。凯恩斯描述了发生在1914年的那段生活，那时伦敦人可以在世界各地自由旅行，在他想投资的地方投资，“躺在床上一边喝早茶一边打电话，根据他认为合适的数量订购世界各地的产品，理所当然地认为他们订购的产品会早早地放在自家门口的台阶上”。不仅如此，凯恩斯笔下的伦敦人“认为除了在方向上需做进一步改善之外，这种状况将会正常、固定和持久”。事实并非如此。第一次世界大战将现代世界的第一次全球化的伟大时代带入了杂乱无章的停滞。贸易萎缩，美国国会通过的《斯姆特-霍利关税法》之类的立法给予保护主义的观点以立法认可。

这样的时刻还会再次降临到我们身上吗？各国的经济之墙还会再次建立吗？根据以下数据，这种疑问似乎是荒谬可笑的。世界贸易正以每年超过7%的速度健康增长。联合国贸易与发展委员会估计，全球的外国直接投资流量价值呈现29%的显著变化。然而，对全球的快速观察或许会给人留下全球化危机的印象。厄瓜多尔的本土居民强烈抗议本国与美国的自由贸易协定提案，他们认为这将导致他们的经济和文化被北方的巨人所染指。在首尔，美国公司的侵入者卡尔·伊坎试图在烟草公司的董事会上占有一个席位，但韩国大学商学院的系主任江海森认为，“这重新激起了反对外国投资者的情绪”。泰国前总理他信将其所拥有的电信公司多数股权卖给了新加坡的国家投资公司淡马锡，这一事件再次引发了反对他信总理的

against a proposed free-trade agreement with the U.S. that they thought would deliver their economy and culture to the colossus of the North. In Seoul, the attempt by U.S. corporate raider Carl Icahn to get a seat on the board of tobacco company has, says Jang Hasung, dean of Korea University's business school, "reignited① anti-foreign-investor sentiment." The sale of a controlling interest in Shin Corp., owner of Thailand's leading telecommunications company, to Temasek Holdings of Singapore has been one of the catalysts for the Bangkok demonstrations against Thai Prime Minister Thaksin Shinawatra, whose family controlled Shin Corp. In France, an effort by the Italian gas company Enel to acquire Groupe Suez appears to have been thwarted by a hastily arranged, government-sponsored marriage between Suez and Gaz de France. The very idea that a state-owned company from Dubai might take over a British company P&O, that controlled six ports in the U.S., gave most members of Congress an attack of the vapors; Dubai Ports World has now said that it will sell P&O's U.S. assets to an American buyer. Even in Britain, where the economy has been "Wimbledonized" for years (London has a great tennis tournament, but no Briton ever wins it) and where, says Robert Wade of the London School of Economics, there is "an unusually deeply held belief in the merits of free trade and free investment," there are limits. When Russian gas behemoth Gazprom started stalking② the British supplier Centrica, officials let it be known that "any new ownership would face robust scrutiny." Put all those straws in the wind and you've got a flying haystack. "We're at a point here," says Kenneth Courtis, vice chairman of Goldman Sachs Asia, "where

---

① reignite [ˌriːigˈnait] *vt.* 重新激起

② stalk [stɔːk] *vt.* 跟踪,追踪

曼谷示威游行。在法国，意大利国家电力公司下属的意大利天然气公司试图收购苏伊士财团，看来已经遭到一场草率安排的、苏伊士财团和法国天然气公司之间的政府资助的联姻拦截。迪拜的一家国有资产公司可能接管一家控制着 6 个美国港口的英国铁行港口公司，正是这种想法给了大多数自吹自擂的国会成员当头一棒。迪拜港口世界公司目前已经宣称，它将把铁行港口的美国资产出售给一位美国买家。伦敦经济学院的罗伯特·韦德认为，即使在英国这样一个“温布尔登化”多年的经济体（伦敦有一个很棒的网球锦标赛，但是从来没有英国人赢得冠军），“对自由贸易和自由投资有着非同寻常的根深蒂固的信念”之地，也还有限制。当俄罗斯的石油天然气巨头俄罗斯天然气工业股份公司开始暗中跟踪英国供应商森特里克时，官员们放风说：“任何新的所有权将面临严厉的审查”。查看所有的这些蛛丝马迹，你就会一目了然。高盛亚洲副主席肯尼斯·库尔蒂声称：“我们正处于一个关键点。如果这只是少许的意外便无可厚非，但若是一种趋势的开始，就值得我们关注。”

自由贸易？全球化的重心是哪个？即使经济学家把它的基本原则作为被披露的真相，也从来没有无可争议吗？谁从贸易中获利？没有人游说立法机关来感谢他们提供的廉价 T 恤。正如 20 世纪 80 年代，日本投资者超额支付从夏威夷海滨酒店到洛克菲勒中心的一切之后，美国的立法者们才开始猛烈地抨击，国内主要实业公司的外国所有者提出了强烈的反对。康提斯说：“很多国家仍然在

if this is just a little pop it doesn't mean very much. But if it's the beginning of a trend, it's big."

Free trade? Which is at the heart of globalization? Has never been uncontroversial, even if economists regard its tenets① as revealed truth? Who gain from trade? Nobody lobbies a legislature to thank them for cheap T shirts. And just as in the 1980s, when U.S. legislators had panic attacks after Japanese investors overpaid for everything from Hawaiian beachfront hotels to the Rockefeller Center, the foreign ownership of key domestic industries is promoting a backlash. "Countries are still trying to keep some poles of industrial strength within their economies," says Courtis. "I wouldn't have any problems whatsoever if the British apparel② industry was taken over entirely by Bangladesh firms," Wade says. But as for "strategic industries" like energy, water, airports and aerospace, he continues, "then you do have to pay much more attention to the consequences of fast-growing foreign ownership."

Among economists, there's a common admission these days that there have been woeful at explaining the benefits of globalization. "We haven't been very good at showing how a lot of new job creation comes through foreign investment, which is often the greatest driver of employment, technological progress, and benefits to consumers," says Ian Goldin, a vice president of the World Bank and co-author of a new book on globalization and development. Columbia University's Joseph Stiglitz, a Nobel prizewinning economist, adds a further thought: nations, he says, want to pick and choose between bits of globalization that benefit them and those

---

① tenet [ˈtenit] *n.* 原则,信条

② apparel [əˈpærəl] *n.* 服装

试图保持工业力量在经济中的某些支撑地位”。韦德说：“如果英国的成衣制造业被孟加拉国的公司完全接管，我也不会有任何问题。”但是关于策略性工业，如能源、水、机场和航空等行业，他继续说道，“你必须对外国所有权快速增长的后果给予更多的关注”。

经济学家们近来达成了共识：对全球化利益的解释不尽如人意。世行的副主席伊恩·戈尔丁认为，“我们不善于展示外国投资到底能够创造出多少新的工作岗位，而这通常是就业、科技进步、消费者福利的最大驱动力”。伊恩也是一本关于全球化与发展新书的合著者。曾获得诺贝尔经济学奖的哥伦比亚大学教授约瑟夫·迪格里兹提出了更深入的思考，他认为，国家总是想在全球化中趋利避害。迪格里兹说：“我们相信出口有利而进口不利。我们相信贸易，但仅限于一个方面，而且如果事物是公平的，我们就会胜过所有人。这里有一种伪善主义。”

也许最重要的是，那些相信无法逃避全球化的人仍然坚持认为，互联网、越来越大的集装箱货运、依赖复杂的物流软件实行跨国商品外包的技术将会继续给世界带来更紧密的联系。但请记住：香港的舵柱装在一艘120多米长船的尾部，是几十年后哥伦布横跨大西洋的小船舵柱的6倍左右。

that don't. "We believe that exports are good but imports are bad," says Stiglitz, "we believe in trade but only on one side, and that if things were fair we'd outcompete everybody. There's a kind of hypocrisy."

Perhaps above all, those who believe in the ineluctable march of globalization insist that technology the Internet, ever-bigger container ships, multi-nation sourcing of goods that depends on sophisticated logistic software will continue to bring the world closer together. But remember: that rudder post in Hong Kong was on the stern of a ship more than 120 m long, or six times the size of the little craft that Columbus sailed across the Atlantic a few decades later.

(1,125 words)

知识链接

Enel 意大利国家电力公司是全球第三大电力公司，也是意大利国内最大的国有公共事业企业。旗下主要有电力和天然气两大业务分支，此外还有电力、能源设备制造、环保设备制造、研究开发、新型能源开发等公司和机构20多个。

Groupe Suez 苏伊士财团(Group Financier Suez)是法国大垄断资本集团。第二次世界大战后以苏伊士通海运河环球公司为中心形成。财团的活动以金融业为主，工业方面以化学、石油、电气设备、纺织、造船、水泥和造纸为重点。

Dubai Ports World 迪拜港口世界是一家阿联酋企业，该公司曾因在2006年斥资68亿美元收购了一个伦敦集团，从而间接获得了对5家美国港口商业业务的控制权。

Gazprom 俄罗斯天然气工业股份公司是世界上最大的天然气公司，总部在莫斯科。它为中欧、东欧和独联体各国提供所需的几乎全部天然气。

题　记

在金融组织承受严重压力、信贷市场的严寒明显地影响全球居民日常生活的大背景下，该轮到美国财长亨利·保尔森出牌了。他首先考虑出手购买美国银行的股份，从而稳定疯狂的市场，并阻止经济的严重衰退；接下来，保尔森将携手一个美国资本结构调整计划在黄金时间亮相；随后，保尔森还决定对相关银行和企业注资。但保尔森的牌技还有待接受市场的考验，实力雄厚的银行抗议政府购买少量普通股本注入值得投资的银行，而只有当财政部长阻止那些让人吃惊的股票投资者时，购买银行股份才能够加快复苏。

Paulson's Playing-card Miracles

It's time for Henry Paulson to show his cards.

The Treasury secretary is considering buying shares of U.S. banks in the government's latest bid to calm frenzied① markets and prevent a deep recession. By easing fears about bank capitalization and creditworthiness, a share purchase could nudge② the money that banks are sitting on back into circulation among consumers and businesses. But if Paulson's latest move is to restore markets to health, equity investors will have to be lured back into the financial sector as well. And before they come back, they will have to have a clearer view of which institutions the government will stand behind, and how much that support will cost.

To date, Paulson has had a rough time painting that picture, instead coming up with ad hoc,inconsistent responses to crises in which a troubled firm might be saved, nationalized or allowed to die. "Investing is playing Russian roulette③ if the government might show up at the door," says Andrew Moloff, chief investment officer at Evercore Asset Managment in New York. "It's not in anybody's best interest to have equity holders running for the hills." No details are yet available on how the U.S. might

---

① frenzied [ˈfrenzid] *adj.* 疯狂的,激怒的

② nudge [nʌdʒ] *n.* 轻推

③ roulette[ru(ː)ˈlet] *n.* 轮盘赌

保尔森的牌技

该轮到亨利·保尔森出牌了。

财政部长正在考虑以政府的最新报价出手购买美国银行的股份，从而稳定疯狂的市场，并阻止经济的严重衰退。股份收购能够推动银行回购的资金在消费者和企业之间的流通，缓解对银行资本和信用等级的恐惧。如果保尔森的最新举措能让市场恢复健康，股市投资者也必将被吸引回金融行业。但他们在回来之前必须要有更清晰的概念：政府部门将会支持哪些机构，这种支持又会耗费多少成本。

到目前为止，保尔森已经艰难地描绘了这样一幅画，他没有提出特别的方案，只是对危机做出了前后不一致的反应，即陷入困境的公司可能获得解救，也可能被国有化，或者允许其消亡。纽约艾菲科资产管理公司的首席投资官安德鲁·莫洛夫认为，“如果政府能在家门口表演，那么投资就是在玩俄罗斯的轮盘赌。让股权持有者碰壁不符合任何人的最佳利益”。没有任何细节表明美国会如何实施解救方案。但是保尔森指出，近期颁布的经济稳定立法给了他“宽泛、灵活的权限”，让他可以采取行动，向规模大小不等的所有金融机构注资。据报道，政府将会在随后几周对美国银行进行优先股投资。

proceed, but Paulson noted that recently enacted① economic stabilization legislation gives him "broad, flexible authorities" to take actions including injecting capital into financial institutions of all sizes. Reports say the government would make preferred stock investments in U. S. banks in coming weeks.

If so, the U.S. plan could resemble one unveiled in London. The U.K. Treasury said it would make 50 billion pounds ($ 88 billion) in funding available to eight big banks, including Barclays, HSBC and Royal Bank of Scotland. Banks that raise the requisite capital, whether in the private market or from the government, will get the bonus of having the Treasury stand behind their debt as they roll over billions of pounds in maturing loans in coming months. An analyst report estimates shareholders could see their investments diluted② by as much as 30% .

But that might not be the worst thing for those investors. By naming the eight participants in its program and saying they must raise an undetermined amount of capital, the U.K. provides the markets with a clear picture and avoids the stigma③ involved in a strictly voluntary plan. In a voluntary plan, banks that tap the government for funding might be seen as riskier than those that sit by and insist, whatever investors might suspect, that they remain well capitalized.

But whatever form its actions take, the feds must make clear what their standards are for determining when firms are eligible④ to receive

---

① enact [i'nækt] *vt.* 制定法律,颁布

② dilute [dai'ljuːt] *vt.* 降低,削弱

③ stigma ['stigmə] *n.* 耻辱

④ eligible ['elidʒəbl] *adj.* 有资格当选的

如果这样的话，美国的计划可能与伦敦公之于众的计划类似。英国财政部称，它将给包括巴克莱银行、汇丰银行和苏格兰皇家银行在内的八大银行发放500亿英镑（880亿美元）的可用资金。银行无论是在私人市场还是依靠政府筹集的必要资金，只要财政部做债务的后盾就会取得红利，因为他们推出去的贷款在未来几个月将滚动为数十亿英镑的到期贷款。据一份分析报告估计，股东可以看到他们的投资被稀释多达30%。

但对于投资者来说，这可能并不是最糟糕的事情。英国通过指定八位项目参与者，并命令他们必须筹集不确定数额的资金，给市场提供了一幅清晰的画面，避免了在卷入严格意义上的自愿计划时出现的耻辱。在自愿计划中，要求政府提供资金的银行被认为比那些袖手旁观和坚守的银行冒的风险更大，不管投资者如何猜想，这些银行仍然维持着雄厚的资本。

但是，不管采取什么样的行动，联邦政府应该弄清楚他们的标准是什么，以决定公司何时有资格接受资金，以及何时的注资是强制性的。了解哪些公司看上去投资不足是关键，因为之前房利美和房地美的国有化，雷蒙兄弟、华盛顿互惠银行的后续破产，美国国际集团的几近崩溃，每一事件都引起了政府的不同反应。

对于美国最大的银行来说，一个良好沟通的美国资本结构调整计划将在黄金时间亮相。美国银行筹集了100亿美元的新基金，帮助偿还不断上升的信贷损失和补足银行金库，以备收购美林公司。但是这家总部位于夏洛特的银行不得不以罕见的最新市场价——高达30%的折扣出售股份。花旗和富国两大银行正在为接管美国银行饱受打击的同城对手美联银行展开竞争，他们也期待在未来几周之

capital, and when capital injections are mandatory. Knowing which firms are seen as undercapitalized is crucial in the wake of nationalization of Fannie Mae and Freddie Mac, the subsequent failures of Lehman Brothers and Washington Mutual and the near collapse of AIG, each of which elicited different responses from the government.

A well-communicated U.S. recapitalization plan could come at a good time for the biggest U.S. banks. Bank of America raised $ 10 billion in new funds to help pay for rising credit losses and to restock its coffers as it prepares to acquire Merrill Lynch. But the Charlotte-based bank had to sell shares at an unusually steep 30% discount to recent market prices. Citi and Wells Fargo, the two big banks competing to take over BofA's stricken crosstown rival Wachovia, are also expected to raise tens of billions of dollars in new capital in coming weeks. There are signs they could use a hand: Citi shares have lost 38% and Wells 27% recently.

Adding to the uncertainty are the ever-shifting evaluations of the firms the government has already intervened with. The Federal Reserve Bank of New York said it would lend as much as an additional $ 38 billion to AIG, the insurer that nearly collapsed after ratings downgrades subjected it to calls for cash collateral it didn't have. The new loan comes just after the Fed offered to lend AIG $ 85 billion to keep it from filing for bankruptcy, and just days after it came to light that AIG had already drawn down $ 61 billion of that loan. AIG's problems may be unique, though the market doesn't seem to think so. Shares of other insurers have tanked over, with Prudential down 56% since stocks started their slide.

An alternative to the targeted injection plan comes from Duke University finance professor Campbell Harvey, who says the government should make small purchases—worth, say, 2% to 5% of the common equity—into all the

内筹集数百亿美元的新资金。有迹象表明，他们可能需要帮助，因为花旗银行和富国银行的股份近期分别下降了38%和27%。

政府已经插手的企业不断变化的估价增加了不确定性。纽约联邦储备银行称，将对美国国际集团追加380亿美元的资金，这是一家接近破产的保险公司，经评级之后遭到降级，有待于交付其并没有的现金抵押。就在联邦政府给美国国际集团提供850亿美元以阻止其申请破产保护之后，新贷款随之而来；就在新贷款曝光几天之后，美国国际集团已经用完了这笔贷款中的610亿美元。美国国际集团的问题可能是独特的，尽管市场并不这么认为。自股票开始下滑以来，其他保险公司的股票价格全面下挫，其中美国保德信金融集团的股价下降了56%。

杜克大学的金融学教授坎贝尔·哈维提出了目标注资计划的替代方案。他认为，政府应该购买少量等值资产，即2%到5%的普通股本，然后全部注入联邦政府认为值得救援的银行。这种做法不仅为资金薄弱的银行提供了资金调整的优势，实力雄厚的银行也可达到同样的效果。

虽然实力较强的机构可能会抗议，他们并不需要货币，也不想让他们的股东任人宰割，对有偿付能力的银行进行全面投资，可以将多余资金交付给实力雄厚的银行，然后他们可以借出，从而推动经济活动。哈维认为，“这才是取得信誉产生机制的最佳方案”。广泛的股权投资优势使他们能够迅速获得回报，而对大、小银行的支持，将有助于扩大贷款，为中小型企业创造就业机会。但是，政府也必须有所判断，哪些机构将会垮掉，从而禁止向该类企业提供资金。

banks the feds deem worthy of saving. Doing so offers the advantage of recapitalizing not only the weak banks but also the strong ones.

And while stronger institutions may protest that they don't need the money and that they don't want their shareholders to have to take a haircut, making an across-the-board investment in solvent banks could pay off by giving the strong banks excess funds that they can then lend out, boosting economic activity. "That's the best way to get credit creation going," he says. The advantage of widespread equity investments is that they can be made quickly and, by shoring① up banks both big and small, should help expand lending to job-creating small and midsize businesses. But the government must also decide which institutions will fail, and must not put funds into them.

He says it's reasonable to expect that hundreds of smaller banks will go under before the cycle turns. The feds must set up a bad bank along the lines of the Resolution Trust Corp. of the 1980s savings-and-loan debacle② to dispose of problem bank assets over a period of years. Japan's failure to recover from an asset bubble that inundated its banking system in the early 1990s shows that clearing out the deadwood is crucial to any economic recovery.

You don't want to be prolonging the inevitable. Buying bank shares could help fuel a recovery, but only if the treasury secretary stops surprising equity investors.

(1,007 words)

---

① shore[ˈʃɔːriŋ] *vi.* 支撑,支持

② debacle [diˈbɑːkəl] *n.* 崩溃

哈维认为，预计几百家规模较小的银行在周期扭转前倒闭是可能的。联邦政府必须建立一个坏账银行，按照20世纪80年代储蓄和贷款危机中清债信托公司的方式，处理一段时期以来的银行资产问题。在20世纪90年代早期，日本没能从资产泡沫泛滥的银行体系中恢复过来，这一事实表明，清除存在已久的一些问题是任何经济复苏的关键。

人们不想延长不可避免的事件。只有当财政部长阻止那些让人吃惊的股票投资者时，购买银行股份才有助于加快复苏。

知识链接

BofA 美国银行(Bank of America)美国银行是全球首要的金融服务机构之一，为美国第二大银行。它致力提供一应俱全的个人及商业银行服务，服务遍及美国21个州、哥伦比亚特区及全球30个国家。

Wachovia 美联银行(Wachovia，又称瓦霍维亚银行)于2001年由美联银行同瓦霍维亚银行合并而成，并沿用了后者的名字，是向零售、经纪与公司客户提供金融服务的最大公司之一。它的四项核心业务是普通银行、资本管理、资产管理和公司与投资银行。

题　记

卓越的供应链是一棵枝叶茂盛的大树：生产企业构成树根；独家代理商则是主干；分销商是树枝和树梢；满树的绿叶红花是最终用户；在根与主干、枝与干的一个个节点，蕴藏着一次次的流通，遍体相通的脉络便是信息管理系统。几乎每一个行业的公司都在谋求转向，越来越多地将优化供应链作为竞争策略的关键，他们正在重点关注如何将产品生产和流通过程中所涉及的原材料供应商、生产商、分销商、零售商以及最终消费者等成员通过与上游、下游成员的连接组成网络结构。印度的未来物流公司通过整个供应链的纵向一体化实现消费者物流的零失误；印度耐克公司的供应链策略的首要目标是赢在精确时刻和产品的集合形式；美国国际商用机器公司通过储备适量的、具备必要技能的人员，建立反应灵敏的供应链。“雨披事件”之类的错失商机的痛苦无疑让商界精英们刻骨铭心。

Building an Excellent Supply Chain

When Martha Stewart, America's diva of décor, was released from federal prison in West Virginia, millions of people around the world saw and read about it. Stewart's first public appearance since being imprisoned five months earlier had an interesting and unexpected aside: It created a new fashion trend.

At the time of her release, Stewart wore a grey-and-white poncho that had been knitted by a prison inmate. That garment① attracted the interest of many women, and over the next few days, Stewart received numerous requests for the pattern and the type of yarn used to make it. Yarn companies and apparel manufacturers were eager to clamber onto Stewart's "prison poncho" bandwagon. The Lion Brand Yarn Company, a leading yarn-maker in the U.S., later said that in the first few days after Stewart's release, more than half a million people downloaded the poncho's crocheted and knitted patterns from the company's website. Apparel and logistics companies, however, ignored the hubbub②. They saw little relation between their business and the emerging wave of business opportunities that the poncho was creating.

Anshuman Singh, chief executive officer of Future Logistics—the

---

① garment [ˈɡɑːmənt] *n.* 衣服

② hubbub [ˈhʌbʌb] *n.* 叫嚷声

打造卓越的供应链

美国“家政女王”玛莎·斯图尔特从西弗吉尼亚州的联邦监狱获释的那一刻，全球数以百万计的人观看或阅读了这则新闻。斯图尔特被关押五个月后的首次公开露面展示了有趣且出人意料的一面：这次公开露面创造了一个新的流行趋势。

斯图尔特出狱时，穿了一件灰白色的雨布织成的衣服，是她在监狱的室友缝的。这件外衣引起了很多女性的兴趣，在接下来的几天，斯图尔特收到了不计其数的咨询，有的询问样品，有的询问这种类型的制衣纱线。纺纱公司和服装制造商心急如焚，紧紧追随斯图尔特的“监狱雨披”潮流。美国领先的纱线制造商狮牌纱厂后来说，斯图尔特获释的最初几天，从该公司网站下载雨布编织式样的用户超过50万。但是，服装和物流公司忽略了这场喧哗，他们没有看到自己的生意与雨披创造的新一波商机之间的关系。

未来物流的首席执行官安舒曼·辛格，在位于海得拉巴的印度商学院（ISB）近期举行的全球供应链峰会上曾谈到玛莎·斯图尔特的雨衣。未来集团是一家快速增长的印度零售商，未来物流是其物流公司。他的观点是，物流企业已经错失了一个巨大的商机。他

logistics arm of the Future Group, a fast-growing Indian retailer—spoke about Martha Stewart's poncho at the recent Global Supply Chain Summit held at the Indian School of Business (ISB) in Hyderabad. His view was that logistics firms had missed out on a huge opportunity. "In the first week after Martha Stewart appeared on her television show wearing this poncho, consumers went wild and demand soared, but neither the apparel companies nor their supply chains were ready," he said. "All around the U.S., there were lost sales." Various speakers at the conference noted that companies in almost every industry are increasingly turning to supply chain excellence as a critical aspect of competitive strategy, and they are focusing on how to maximize the effectiveness of their supply chain networks to deliver business results.

Take retail, for instance. In categories such as fashion, food, general merchandise and home products, retailers have to deal with very small quantities—and even individual pieces. Usually, moving an item from the vendor to the store involves at least six physical transactions. The scenario① gets much more complicated when multiple vendors across several product categories are involved, each with its own requirements of logistics and supply chain set up. Food retail, for instance, has to deal with issues of freshness and perishable② products. Apparel, in contrast, has to operate within a limited fashion time cycle. Household items tend to be either bulky or fragile, and so on.

In countries like India, where most retail stores are located in the heart of the city—where rents are high and storage space is scarce—supply chain management has even more serious business implications. Future Logistics, Singh said, now handles 2.5 million SKUs (or stock

---

① scenario [siˈnɑːriəu] *n.* 方案,事态

② perishable [ˈperiʃəbl] *adj.* 易腐坏的

声称："玛莎·斯图尔特身穿这种雨披在电视台出现后的第一周，消费者几乎疯狂，需求激增，但服装公司与供应链却没有准备好。整个美国都存在这种销售损失。"出席会议的各方发言人指出，几乎每一个行业的公司都在谋求转向，越来越多地将优化供应链作为竞争策略的关键，他们正在重点关注如何达到供应链网络效用的最大化，以输送经营成果。

以零售为例。就时装、食品、日用品和家用产品等类别的商品而言，零售商的交易量极少，甚至是单件销售。通常情况下，一件商品从供应商到商店至少需要 6 次实货交易。当多家供应商的产品涉及几个类别、每个类别各有自己的物流需求和已经建立的供应链时，情况变得更加复杂。例如，食品零售必须解决产品的保鲜和防腐问题。与此相反，服装必须在有限的时尚周期内交易。家居用品往往要么笨重、要么易碎，等等。

在印度这样的国家，大多数零售商店位于市中心，那儿的租金昂贵、存储空间有限，供应链管理具有更重要的商业意义。辛格说，未来物流现在每天可以为未来集团向全国各地的各种零售商运输 250 万件（或库存单位）商品。这一数据有望增加到每天3 000万件以上。辛格估计，即使精确度达到 98%，也有大约 60 万件无法及时发货，每天由此产生的销售损失估计超过4 000万卢比（100 万美元）。

辛格指出，在未来物流公司，零失误的需求将是消费者物流的最重要的推动力。虽然基础设施、技术、自动化、流程和人员都将

keeping units) a day across the Future Group's various retail formats around the country. This number is expected to increase to more than 30 million SKUs a day. Singh reckons that even with 98% accuracy, some 600,000 pieces will not be delivered correctly, resulting in an estimated sales loss of more than Rs. 40 million ($ 1 million) a day.

At Future Logistics, the biggest driver in consumer logistics will be the need for zero defect. While infrastructure, technology, automation, processes and people will all play an important role, zero defect can only be achieved through vertical integration across the entire supply chain—from raw material supply, production, wholesale and retail. The different parts of the supply chain will no longer be able to work in silos as they do today, Singh noted.

Manufacturers, for their part, have realized that while they may have the best production facilities, compelling products, strong brands and great distribution networks, all of these mean nothing if the products are not available in stores when and where the customers want them. Ravi Kallayil, director of operations at Nike India, said: "Supply chain is one of the most critical aspects of Nike's corporate strategy. The primary goal of our supply chain strategy is to win at the moment of truth. This means that, as a manufacturer, we have to ensure that our products are in stock where and when the consumer shops."

At Nike—which has $ 16 billion in revenues today with the goal of getting to $ 23 billion by 2015—process excellence is a key component of the company's supply chain strategy. According to Kallayil, Nike's three businesses—footwear, apparel and equipment—have some similarities since most of the products are made in Asia and sold to similar customers worldwide. Their production processes, though, are completely different. Much of this has to do with the fact that it has never owned a factory but has chosen to work through contract manufacturing. Said Kallayil: "We

在其中发挥重要作用，但零失误只能通过整个供应链的纵向一体化来实现，即从原材料供应、生产、批发、再到零售。供应链的不同环节不再可能存在目前的筒仓工作状况。

就制造商而言，他们已经意识到，即使他们可能拥有最好的生产设备、引人注目的产品、强大的品牌和巨大的分销网络，如果产品不能在顾客随时随地需要时出现在商店里，这些都毫无用处。印度耐克的业务主管拉维·卡拉伊说："供应链是耐克运营策略最重要的方面。我们供应链策略的首要目标就是赢在精确时刻。也就是说，作为一个制造商，消费者无论在何时何地购货，我们必须确保产品的供货。"

耐克 2015 年的收入目标是 230 亿美元，而目前达到 160 亿美元，流程卓越是公司供应链策略中的关键组成部分。卡拉伊认为，耐克的三大业务，即鞋类、服装和设备，均具有一定的相似性，因为大多数产品在亚洲制造，然后销售给世界各地的同类消费者。当然，它们的生产过程完全不同。这与耐克的运营现实有很大关系，耐克从来不设自己的工厂，而是采用外包生产的方式。卡拉伊说："我们试图通过标准化建立卓越流程的实力。我们运用精益制造的概念实现这个目标，丰田汽车使这种做法广受欢迎。"

耐克公司还在运作它称之为的"投送精度"。卡拉伊解释说，耐克构思了产品的集合形式。一个集合包括上衣、裤子、鞋、包、帽子等。这也是消费者通常喜欢的购买方式。虽然耐克设计的这些产品都是一个集合中的一部分，每个类别的商品却是在不同的地

are trying to build our strength in process excellence through standardization. We are doing this through the concept of lean manufacturing, which Toyota has made popular."

Nike is also working towards what it calls "delivery precision." Kallayil explained that Nike conceives its products in the form of collections. A collection could consist of a top apparel, a bottom apparel, shoes, bag, cap, etc. This is how customers usually like to buy products. While Nike designs these products as part of one collection, each category of items is made in different locations. As a result, if supply chain execution goes awry①, these products are not available as complete collections, and that leads to loss of sales. "Getting this streamlined is extremely challenging because it involves changing the way contract manufacturers work," said Kallayil.

Information technology services firms have found that key concepts used in conventional supply chains such as demand management, strategic sourcing, inventory management, supply synchronization, project management, use of technology and so on, are also applicable in the services environment. Take inventory, for instance. Clifford Patrao, a senior managing consultant at IBM Global Business Services, pointed out that inventory in services is really "stored capacity" in people. A services organization needs to ensure that it has the right number of people with the necessary skills to build a responsive supply chain without overloading and adding costs. At IBM, if people are on the bench waiting for projects to come in, they spend their time upgrading their skills through e-training courses.

(1,058 words)

---

① awry [ə'rai] *adj.* 出错的

方制造出来的。所以，如果供应链执行出现差错，这些产品就不能组成完整的集合，会造成销售损失。卡拉伊说："采用这种流线型的方式极具挑战性，因为它改变了合同制造商的工作方式。"

信息技术服务公司发现，用于传统供应链中的主要理念，如需求管理、战略采购、库存管理、供应同步、项目管理、技术运用等，也适用于服务行业。以库存为例，美国国际商用机器公司全球业务服务部门的高级管理顾问克利福德·帕特雷奥指出，服务的库存实际上是人才"储备能力"。服务机构需要确保其储备适量的、具备必要技能的人员，以建立反应灵敏的供应链，既没有冗余又不增加成本。在国际商用机器公司，如果人们一旦成为即将到来的项目的候补人员，他们会花时间通过电子培训课程提高自己的技能。

知识链接

Future Logistics 未来物流公司是印度企业未来集团旗下的物流及供应链管理子公司，提供全球性货运代理业务的服务。

Toyota 丰田汽车公司(Toyota Motor Corporation)是一家总部设在日本爱知县丰田市和东京都文京区的汽车工业制造公司，隶属于日本三井财阀。丰田汽车公司自2008年始逐渐取代通用汽车公司而成为全世界排名第一位的汽车生产厂商。其旗下品牌主要包括凌志、丰田等系列高中低端车型。

题　记

“荣格框架下的成功团队”从精神分析和心理分析的独特角度，阐述了大局意识、协作精神和服务精神的团队精神。荣格框架下的成功团队包括四种人：具备理性想象力的魔术师，他们认为新思想或洞察力是唯一可以改变世界的东西；务实而又情绪化的恋人，他们着眼于建设成功的联盟，认为行动应当一致；情感和想象力丰富的君主，他们着眼于大局，根据事情是否能得出他们想要的结果判断一切；既理性又务实的武士，他们只能清楚地看到直接发生在自己面前的事情，认为行动是直接取胜的关键因素。苹果的产品是当代魔术大师乔布斯变出的一只只兔子，微软的产品是勇敢的武士比尔·盖茨占领全球市场的利器，风靡世界的卡通是迪士尼王国及其君主的娱乐霸业。拥有荣格框架下的成功团队你就可以征服世界。

A Winning Team in the Jungian Framework

Volumes of articles and books have been written on the topic over the years, offering advice on how to avoid the dysfunction① that often renders teams ineffective. We have all been part of groups that failed, either because of hidden agendas or personalities that didn't quite mesh②. In my experience as an executive and a consultant, I've come to believe the personal style of team members has the greatest influence on a group's success. More important than any technical skill a team member brings is the ability to work closely together, free of backbiting③ and political maneuvering. The key is having the right mix on your team.

By and large, there are four archetypes of people in companies: magicians, warriors, sovereigns④, and lovers. You can easily define them using the Jungian framework introduced by psychologist Robert Moore and mythologist Douglas Gillette.

---

① dysfunction [dis'fʌŋkʃən] *n.* 垮掉

② mesh [meʃ] *vi.* 紧密配合

③ backbite ['bækbait] *vi.* 背后诽谤

④ sovereign ['sɔvrin] *n.* 元首

荣格框架下的成功团队

多年来，大量的文章和书籍已经涉及这个话题，提供了如何避免通常导致团队合作效率低下的障碍。我们都是失败团队的成员，或是因为别有用心的动机，或是因为缺乏紧密配合的个性。根据我的经历，作为一名行政主管和顾问，我逐渐认识到，团队成员的个人风格对团队的成功影响最大。在工作中紧密配合的能力、远离诽谤和政治操纵比团队成员带来的任何技能都更为重要。关键在于正确的团队组合。

总的来说，公司里的人可归纳为四种类型：魔术师、武士、君主和恋人。你可以使用心理学家罗伯特·摩尔和神学家道格拉斯·吉列引入的荣格框架，轻松地阐释他们的基本特征。

魔术师。在你的公司，他们是理性但富有想象力的灵魂。他们认为，新思想或洞察力是唯一可以改变世界的东西。事实上，他们无法摆脱创意。他们给团队提供的帮助是从帽子里拉出一只兔子。这种类型的人认为，对于思想的纯粹争论等同于行动。

恋人。对他们来说，一切都归结为人与人之间的关系。他们既务实又情绪化。他们着眼于建设成功的联盟。他们痴迷的不是思想，而是情感。他们认为行动应当一致。

君主。他们属于情感和想象力丰富的一类人。他们着眼于大

Magicians. They are the rational yet imaginative souls in your organization. They think a new idea or insight is the only thing that can move the world. In truth, they're obsessed by ideas. Their answer to feeding the troops is to pull a rabbit out of a hat. These types of people think a mere argument over an idea equals action.

Lovers. For them, everything comes down to human relations. They're pragmatic but emotional. They focus on building the winning coalition. They are obsessed not by ideas but by feelings. They consider agreement an action.

Sovereigns. They are the emotional and imaginative types. They focus on the big picture and judge everything on whether it leads to where they want to go. They redefine what people consider is possible. They are obsessed by beliefs. And they consider direction and form of action.

Warriors. They are rational and pragmatic. They're focused on the next battle and can only see clearly what's directly in front of them. They hold people accountable to systems and the fairness of those systems. They're obsessed by facts. For them, action is finding the critical factor to get something immediately accomplished.

Apple's Steve Jobs is clearly a magician. Watching him introduce a new product on stage is like watching a master magician pull a rabbit out of a hat. Microsoft's Bill Gates, with all his competitive juice to dominate his industry, is a warrior. IBM's Tom Watson, who plastered the walls of Big Blue with "Think" signs, was a magician. Could anyone think of GE's Jack Welch as anything other than a warrior? Indeed, one of the most fascinating campaigns in all of business is the attempt by Welch's successor to transform a warrior company like GE into a hothouse of ideas.

局，根据事情是否能得出他们想要的结果判断一切。他们重新定义人们认为可能的事。他们痴迷于信念。他们考虑的是行动的方向和方式。

武士。他们既理性又务实。他们关注下一场战争，只能清楚地看到直接发生在他们面前的事情。他们支持对制度负责的人和这些制度的公平性。他们痴迷于事实。对于他们来说，行动是直接取胜的关键因素。

苹果公司的史蒂夫·乔布斯显然是一位魔术师。看着他在台上介绍新产品的过程犹如看魔术大师从帽子里变出一只兔子。微软的比尔·盖茨是一名武士，他用全方位的竞争能量主宰他所处的行业。美国国际商用机器公司的汤姆·沃特森是一位魔术师，他在墙上贴满了带有“思考”标志的蓝色巨人。你能认为通用电气公司的杰克·韦尔奇根本算不上一名武士吗？事实上，所有交易中最迷人的战役之一是韦尔奇的继任者把通用电气这样的武士公司转化成一个思想的温室。杰夫·伊梅尔特拓展了通用公司的视野，提倡“工作中的想象力”，与韦尔奇时代彻底分道扬镳。他的高级团队如果不拥有更多的魔术师，他就会陷入困境。

显然，这只是一个简化了的框架，但对任何一位组建团队的领导人来说，它都具有逻辑上的意义。最有效的团队通过拥有各种健康的、不同类型的关键角色维持平衡，因为每种类型都具有做不同事情的优势。一个拥有魔术师、武士、恋人和君主的团队可能是你的最佳团队。当一种类型占主导地位时，摩擦和冲突可能会发生：丧失创造力，缺乏灵活性，规避风险和瘫痪。这就是为什么最有效的领导人了解自己是谁，周围会有一些能与他们能量互补、抵消他

Jeff Immelt, whose "imagination at work" vision for GE is an extreme departure from the Welch years, will have a hard time of it without more magicians on his senior team.

Obviously, this framework is a simplification, but there are logical implications for any leader assembling a team. The most effective teams maintain a balance by having a healthy variety of types in key roles because each type is good at doing different things. A mix of magicians, warriors, lovers, and sovereigns will get you the best team possible. When one type dominates, friction and conflict can occur: a fall-off of creativity, a lack of flexibility, risk aversion, and paralysis. That's why the most effective leaders know who they are and surround themselves with people who complement their strengths and offset their weaknesses. The warrior needs a magician, a sovereign, and a few lovers. What often happens in organizations is you get a group of warriors, and they don't like the magicians so you don't have any of them on your team.

Clearly, there is beauty in balance. That is the place where individual team members become more sensitive to each other's needs. Too many magicians and your team will be pondering opportunities all the time, but will lack decisive action, even though the thinking will be excellent. Why? Because magicians are more concerned with having it done "right," rather than having it done. They're especially vulnerable to pursuing superior technology at the expense of something that customers would buy. And a group of them in a room will look more like a debating society than a high performance team.

Too many lovers and you have another set of problems. These employees value consensus to the detriment of results. They hold far too

们弱点的人。武士需要一位魔术师、一位君主和少量的恋人。公司经常发生这样的事：你带了一群武士，他们不喜欢魔术师，所以你的团队一位魔术师也没有。

显然，平衡是一种美的境界。单个的团队成员在平衡中对相互的需要变得更加敏感。太多魔术师的团队面对机会始终苦思冥想，但缺乏果断的行动，即使他们的思考无可挑剔。为什么？因为魔术师更关心做“正确”的事，而不是采取行动。如果为了追求卓越的技术而损害顾客可能购买的东西，他们会尤其敏感。一群魔术师在一个房间里看上去更像一个正在辩论的社团，而不是高效率的团队。

太多恋人的团队也会有其他的一系列的问题。这些雇员们看重一致性而不顾后果的危害。他们举行了太多的会议。他们说得太多，但做得太少。恋人过分依赖外部的建议，往往看上去就缺乏竞争力和优势。

另一方面，如果外界环境发生变化，太多武士的团队会遇到困难。他们不会主动适应，从而错过竞争对手可以利用的机会。他们就像一队接受检阅的士兵，会受到创新的挑战。

太多的君主往往使公司一次面临太多的方向，或往往从根本上改变公司的方向。君主占统治地位的团队没有重心，许多尚未解决的业务问题始终得不到解决。他们显得分崩离析，缺乏沟通，他们往往在策略和方向上苦苦挣扎。

尽管如此，一些公司需要一种类型或另一种类型的占主导地位的人，有效地贯彻某些策略和价值。魔术师最适合创新为主的公司，发现是这些公司成功的关键。武士在观念上适合竞争激烈的环

many meetings. They do too much talking and not enough acting. The lover excessively relies on outside advice and often appears to lack both competitiveness and edge.

Too many warriors, on the other hand, will experience difficulty if anything in the environment changes. They won't be proactive and will consequently miss opportunities competitors may exploit. They appear as a parade of soldiers, and they can be innovation-challenged.

Too many sovereigns will often pull an organization in too many directions at once, or will radically change direction often. Sovereign-dominated teams will have no center of gravity and will keep many unresolved business issues up in the air all the time. They appear fragmented, with poor communication, and they often struggle with strategy and direction.

That said, some companies require a predominance of one type or another to effectively pursue certain strategies or values. Magicians are the best fit for innovation-based companies in which discovery is crucial to success. Warriors are ideally suited for highly competitive environments that demand a conquering-the-world mindset.

Do you have the right mix on your team?

(908 words)

境，这种环境需要征服世界的心态。

你拥有正确组合的团队吗?

知识链接

Big Blue 美国国际商用机器公司(IBM)一直被人们称为蓝色巨人，表示信任、可靠。而可口可乐的标识是红色与活力。这些热情的颜色不仅仅作为这些公司的标识，也显示着人们对这些品牌的理想化认可。

题　记

在全球经济一体化的跨国经营中，不同形态的文化氛围给公司的组织结构和管理机制造成了各种障碍。国际商务跨文化管理的当务之急是在管理过程中寻找超越文化冲突的公司目标，以维系不同文化背景的员工共同的行为准则，从而最大限度地控制和利用企业的潜力与价值。因此，跨文化咨询公司和跨文化咨询顾问应运而生，有针对性地提出了一系列的跨文化解决方案，包括跨文化人力资源、跨文化团队建设、跨文化协同作用、跨文化意识培训、海外工作人员的跨文化培训、跨文化谈判、跨文化公关顾问、跨文化语言培训等各个方面。这种全面的资源整合不仅为国际交往创造了理解的桥梁，也为商业成功打开了沟通的渠道。

Cross Cultural Management for International Business

Globalization, the expansion of intercontinental trade, technological advances and the increase in the number of companies dealing on the international stage have brought about a dramatic change in the frequency, context and means by which people from different cultural backgrounds interact. Cross cultural solutions to international Business demands are increasingly being viewed as a valid and necessary method in enhancing communication and interaction in and between companies, between companies and customers and between colleagues.

Cross cultural consultancies are involved in aiding companies to find solutions to the challenges cross cultural differences carry. International and national Businesses are ultimately the result of people. As with incompatible① software, if people are running on different cultural coding, problems can occur. Cross cultural consultancies therefore concentrate their efforts on interpersonal communication. Different

① incompatible [ˌinkəmˈpætəbl] *adj*. 不协调的

国际商务的跨文化管理

全球经济一体化、洲际贸易的扩大、技术进步以及越来越多的公司在国际舞台上伸展拳脚，这一切使不同文化背景的人在相互交往的过程中次数、范围和手段都发生了巨大的变化。国际商务需求的跨文化解决方案正越来越多地被认为是一个有效的和必要的方法，它可以加强公司内部、公司之间、公司与客户以及同事之间的沟通与交流。

跨文化咨询公司参与并帮助企业寻找方案，以解决跨文化差异带来的挑战。国际和国内贸易最终都是人们活动的结果。如果人们用不同的文化编码，就如同使用不兼容的软件一样，会产生问题。因此，解决人际沟通问题是跨文化咨询公司首当其冲的重任。不同的文化和文化背景造成了高度多元化的员工之间的障碍、挑战和困难。跨文化差异一般表现在行为、礼仪、规范、价值观念、表现形式、团队工作和非言语交流等领域。这些跨文化差异也相继出现在管理风格、企业文化、营销、人力资源和公关等高层次领域。

cultures and cultural backgrounds between a highly diverse staff base brings with it obstacles, challenges and difficulties. Cross cultural differences manifest in general areas such as in behavior, etiquette, norms, values, expressions, group mechanics and non-verbal communication. These cross cultural differences then follow on through to high level areas such as management styles, corporate culture, marketing, HR and PR.

In order to overcome potential pitfalls①, specialist attention is required in the form of a cross cultural consultant. As one would approach a doctor for a medical diagnosis or an accountant to examine finances, cross cultural consultants offer the expertise, experience and know-how to diagnose problems and provide solutions to interpersonal cultural differences. Within companies there are many facets in which cultural differences manifest②. Some key areas which cross cultural consultants deal with include the following:

Cross Cultural HR: HR covers a wide range of Business critical areas that need cross cultural analysis. Consultants may offer advice on a number of areas including recruitment, relocation, international assignments, staff retention③ and training programs.

Cross Cultural Team-Building: in order to have a well functioning Business unit within a company, communication is critical. Cross cultural consultants will provide tools and methods to promote staff integration, reduce cross cultural conflicts and build team spirit. This is essentially done

---

① pitfalls [ˈpitfɔːl] *n.* 陷阱,圈套

② manifest [ˈmænifest] *vt.* 清楚表示,显露

③ retention [riˈtenʃən] *n.* 保留

跨文化咨询顾问通常以专家的身份帮助人们克服潜在的隐患。正如人们找医生做医疗诊断或找会计师审查财务一样，跨文化咨询顾问可以提供专业知识、经验、专业技能来诊断问题，并对人与人之间的文化差异给出解决方案。公司内部的文化差异表现在许多方面。跨文化咨询顾问处理的问题包括下面一些主要领域：

跨文化人力资源：人力资源广泛覆盖企业需要跨文化分析的关键领域。跨文化咨询顾问可以在若干领域提供咨询意见，包括招聘、重新安置、国际派遣、工作人员留用和培训方案。

跨文化团队建设：为了在公司内部保持运转良好的业务单位，相互交流非常重要。跨文化咨询顾问可以提供工具和方法，促进员工的团结，减少跨文化冲突和建立团队精神。这实质上是通过强调差异和建立优势来完成团队建设，以保证他们积极地使用文化差异。

跨文化协同作用：国际兼并、收购和合资企业需要不同文化背景的人共同协调才能取得成功。跨文化咨询顾问可以对组织机制、交流风格、规范、价值观念和一体化进程给出建议。

跨文化意识培训：与来自不同文化背景、不同的宗教信仰、价值观和习俗的同事、消费者或客户打交道，有时会带来一些问题。跨文化意识培训通常是对文化、国家、地区或宗教的概括介绍，目的是使学员具备足够的知识，能够巧妙处理不同文化背景的人之间的关系，避免误解和错误。

through highlighting differences and building on strengths to ensure they are used positively.

Cross Cultural Synergy①: international mergers, acquisitions and joint-ventures require people from different cultural backgrounds to harmonize in order to succeed. Cross cultural consultants counsel on group mechanics, communication styles, norms, values and integration processes.

Cross Cultural Awareness Training: working with colleagues, customers or clients from different cultural backgrounds, with different religions, values and etiquettes can occasionally lead to problems. Cross cultural awareness training is usually a generic② introduction into a culture, country, region or religion. The aim is to equip the trainee with the adequate knowledge to deal comfortably with people from different cultures, avoiding misunderstandings and mistakes.

Cross Cultural Training for Expatriate③ Relocation: staff that travel overseas need to understand the cultural basics of the host country or region. Knowledge of the country's history, culture, laws, traditions, business practices and social etiquettes all help to minimize the impact of culture shock and hence smooth their transition overseas.

Cross Cultural Negotiations: equipped with their knowledge of the two or more cultures that can be meeting around the negotiation table, a cross cultural consultant advises on areas such as negotiation strategies, styles, planning, closure and etiquette in order to increase the chance of a

---

① synergy [ˈsinədʒi] *n.* 企业合并后的协力优势或协合作用

② generic [dʒiˈnerik] *adj.* 一般的

③ expatriate [eksˈpætrieit] *n.* 侨民

海外工作人员的跨文化培训：远赴海外的工作人员需要了解所在国或地区的文化基础。掌握该国的历史、文化、法律、传统、商业惯例和社交礼仪等知识有助于将文化冲击的影响降低到最低限度，从而实现在海外的平稳过渡。

跨文化谈判：为了具备两种或更多可能在谈判中遇到的文化知识，跨文化咨询顾问提供谈判策略、风格、规划、结束和礼仪等方面的咨询意见，以便增加获得成功结果的机会，避免误解、猜疑和跨文化交际的全面失败。

跨文化公关咨询：公司一旦脱离了本国的背景，就必须对品牌形象、公共关系和广告等所有领域小心谨慎。品位和价值观在不同的大陆会发生重大的变化。关键是要了解品牌名称、形象或广告活动是否适用于目标国的文化。跨文化咨询顾问要检验文字、图像、图片、色彩和符号，以确保它们与目标文化相吻合。

跨文化语言培训：语言培训是公司投资很少的领域，其实它存在着巨大的商业优势。语言知识可以在很多方面弥合文化差异和促进交际顺畅。跨文化咨询公司对业务员提供语言培训，帮助他们适应身处其中的商业环境。

总而言之，跨文化咨询顾问的作用和专长对当今的国际商务显然非常重要。公司目前存在的跨文化差异潜在陷阱涉及面很广。跨文化咨询顾问的主要目标本质上是整合资源。这种同事、客户和

successful outcome, free from misunderstandings, suspicions and general cross cultural communication breakdown.

Cross Cultural PR Consultancy: brand image, public relations and advertising are all areas companies must be careful of when moving out of the national context. Tastes and values change dramatically from continent to continent. It is crucial to understand whether the brand name, image or advertising campaign is culturally applicable in the target country. Cross cultural consultants examine words, images, pictures, colours and symbols to ensure they fit well with the target culture.

Cross Cultural Language Training: Language training is an area where little investment is made by companies, but where the business advantages are great. Linguistic knowledge goes a long way in bridging cultural gaps and smoothing lines of communication. Cross cultural consultancies provide language training to business staff, molding their learning to the Business environment in which they work.

In conclusion, clearly the role and expertise of cross cultural communication consultants is important for today's international business. The potential pitfalls cross cultural differences present to companies are extensive. In essence a cross cultural consultant's primary objective is integration. This integration, between colleagues, clients and customers is crucial for Business success. Equipped with experience, knowledge and above all objectivity, a cross cultural consultant creates bridges of understanding and opens lines of communication.

(767 words)

消费者之间的资源整合对商业成功至关重要。跨文化咨询顾问可以运用经验、知识和上述所有的客观现实，创造理解的桥梁和打开沟通的渠道。

知识链接

HR 人力资源(Human Resources)。人力资源指在一个国家或地区中，处于劳动年龄、未到劳动年龄和超过劳动年龄但具有劳动能力的人口之和。

PR 公共关系(Public Relations)。公共关系指一个社会组织用传播手段使自己与相关公众之间形成双向交流，使双方达到相互了解和相互适应的管理活动。

题　记

就在花旗集团公布维克拉姆·潘迪特出任集团首席执行官之后，管理与领导力专家丹·钱帕和迈克尔·沃特金斯发表了一封写给他的公开信。信中提供了一些管理的指导性建议，列出了识别关键联盟、尽快让称职的高层团队就位、争取旗开得胜、为有效沟通奠定基础、塑造愿景、组建和利用均衡的咨询网络等“放之四海而皆准”的管理真谛。建立“金融超市”一直是花旗集团的雄心壮志。它通过巨额收购和之后的缩减成本逐步建立起庞大的金融帝国，但对利润的渴求也驱使着花旗集团不断地扩展自己的版图，膨胀的成本、过时的技术以及内耗使之成为一片片独立而分散的诸侯王国。接掌全球最大金融机构之一的花旗帅印的潘迪特，如果完全指望用这些“行动指南”来整修花旗，很可能竹篮打水一场空。

Transforming Citigroup

Dear Mr. Pandit,

The decisions you will make during your first few months on the job will have a decisive impact on whether you ultimately succeed or fail. Your transition period is a time of opportunity, but also great vulnerability, in part because you are expected to change Citigroup in fundamental ways. Based on our research and experience working with CEOs in transition, we have developed the following set of guidelines for that will help you to create momentum① during your transition.

Identify the critical alliances. To transform their organizations, new CEOs must gain the support of powerful internal and external constituencies②. Influential players must perceive it to be in their interest to help realize your goals. You must therefore begin to identify them and at least begin to gain their support during the transition. Doing so lays the groundwork for building coalitions③ to drive key initiatives. It also will enable you to decide not only whom you can count on, but also who you need to invest in winning over—and who you need to confront. Usually, a relatively small percentage of managers will be either very supportive or

---

① momentum [məu'mentəm] *n.* 动力

② constituency [kən'stitjuənsi] *n.* 选民

③ coalition [ˌkəuə'liʃən] *n.* 联合

整修花旗集团

亲爱的潘迪特先生：

上任最初数月作出的决策，将对你最终成功与否产生决定性的影响。转型期既是一个充满机遇的阶段，也是一个非常脆弱的时期，部分原因是你肩负着从根本上改变花旗集团的重任。根据我们的研究和与转型期的首席执行官们一起工作的经验，我们已经开发出以下一组指导方针，希望能帮助你在转型期内开创良好的势头。

识别关键联盟。新任首席执行官要想重组机构，必须在公司内外获得强有力的支持。有影响力的玩家必须意识到重组机构关系到自身的利益，可以帮助自己实现目标。所以，上任伊始就必须识别盟友，至少在转型初期获得他们的支持。这种行为可以为建立联盟打下基础，推动重要举措的实施。这也可以使你做出判断，认识到哪些人可以依靠，哪些人需要投资才能俘获，还有哪些人需要你与其直面抗争。通常，采取非常支持或非常反对态度的管理人员在初期比例较小，大多数人处于两极之间。无论是死心塌地的支持者还是顽固不化的反对者，他们都会犹豫不决，可以接受劝导。

尽快让称职的高层团队就位。和许多新任首席执行官一样，你将接手一批资深的经理主管。他们中的一些人具有知识、技术和背景，能满足公司向前发展的需要；而另一些则没有。一些人原本在

very opposed at the outset. Most will lie between these extremes. Neither dedicated supporters nor implacable opponents, they will be undecided and, hence, persuadable.

Get the right top team in place—fast. Like most new CEOs, you will inherit a group of senior executives. Some will have the knowledge, skills, and background needed to drive the business forward. Others will not. Some may have aspired to the CEO slot, perhaps even have been told that the job was virtually theirs in the past. Others may have hidden agendas because you represent a potential threat to their positions and power. All-too-often, new CEOs find that "senior team" is less than descriptive of reality. If your assessments are negative, you will confront the dilemma of either staying with people who are less than what you need or making a change early in your tenure. The decision to remove a senior-level manager is among the most serious and complicated that any leader makes. But among the most common regrets CEOs have is not replacing senior-level people once it becomes clear they are not the right fit for the situation and for the CEO's style or vision. Don't let it happen to you.

Secure early wins. To create momentum, you must secure some early wins. Bringing the wounded SIVs onto Citi's balance sheet may be a start. But by the end of the first six months, at the most, you must have made substantial progress in addressing some of Citigroup's most pressing problems. This means marshalling resources to focus on issues that meet three criteria: (1) they yield tangible financial benefit, (2) they address issues that employees understand to be important, and (3) results can achieved early in the new leader's tenure. New CEOs secure early wins by identifying substantial problems that can be tackled in a reasonable period of time and whose solutions result in tangible operational and financial, not just behavioral / attitudinal, improvements in performance. Critically,

觊觎首席执行官一职，甚至曾在过去被告知，这个位子就是他们的。其他人则可能因为你对他们的职位和权力造成了潜在的威胁，暗藏自己的幕后动机。新任首席执行官时常会发现，所谓的“资深团队”并不像现实中所描述的那样。如果你的评估是消极的，你就会陷入进退维谷的两难境地，不知道是继续容忍那些达不到要求的员工，还是在上任伊始就进行人员变动。开除高层管理人员的决定是任何领导者所做的最严肃、最复杂的决定之一。某些高层工作人员并不适合某个职位，或者并不具备首席执行官的风格或形象，一旦问题显现出来，当初没有进行人员调整就会成为首席执行官们最遗憾的一件事。希望这种遗憾不会发生在你身上。

争取旗开得胜。为了造势，你必须保证在初期获胜。找到花旗资产负债表上伤痕累累的结构性投资工具只是一个开始。但最迟在半年之后，你一定要在解决花旗的紧迫性问题上取得实质性进展。这意味着要对资源进行整合，集中解决符合以下三项标准的问题：(1)他们能产出有形的财政利润；(2)他们能解决员工们认为重要的问题；(3)能在新领导上任初期取得成效。要保证早期的胜利，新任首席执行官们必须能够分清实质性的问题，并在合理的期限内解决，弄清这些问题的解决会给有形资产运营和财政改善带来哪些影响，而不仅仅是行为或态度上的支持。至关重要的是，你在为早期胜利制定行动方案时，应当把注意力集中在极少数重要的问题上，而这些问题处于你日程的中心。在此过程中，你不仅仅要追求结果，而且要设定正确的基调，激励员工的热情。

为有效沟通奠定基础。新任首席执行官未能优先传递信息时，就会准备越轨传达他们自认为重要的价值观，或者详细说明预期目

your early-win initiatives should focus attention on the vital few issues that you believe to be central to your agenda. In doing this, you should seek not only to get results, but also to set the right tone and to energize employees.

Lay the groundwork for effective communications. New CEOs prepare for derailment① when they fail to get their messages about priorities across, to convey the values that they hold as important, or to clearly define expectations. As a result they create vacuums of understanding and emotional connection that undermine their effectiveness. Why? Because no one associated with the organization views your transition with indifference. Everyone is parsing your actions and words closely and critically, hunting for signals of direction, purpose, motives, and, especially, for the answer to "who is this person?" Leaders lay the seeds of their own destruction when they fail to gain control of the communication processes of the company. As a result, do not effectively get their messages across to the people whom they most want to influence; nor do they shape the mood or morale of the organization.

Shape your vision. The term "vision" has been watered down to the point where is can mean everything or nothing. Often it is used to describe the overarching objectives leaders want to achieve, or the organization's mission statement. All too often these are mere slogans or lists of desired objectives or "values" that are put up on the wall and left on coffee tables in executive waiting rooms, but have little impact on behaviors and attitudes in the organization. What we mean by vision is a vivid mental image that depicts your view of the desired future state of the organization in an inspiring way. It is not a statement of mission, a set of objectives, or a list of values. It is a picture of what will be seen, heard, and felt when the

---

① derailment [di'reilment] *n*. 出轨

标。结果，他们造成了理解和情感交流的真空，降低了效率。为什么呢？因为公司的相关人员没有谁会对你的转型活动漠不关心。每个人都在密切并谨慎地分析你的一言一行，寻找有关方向、目的、动机，尤其是回答“谁是合适的人？”的信号。当领导者没能成功地控制住公司的沟通渠道时，他们就给自己播下了毁灭的种子。结果，他们不能有效地将信息传递给自己最想影响的人，也不能塑造公司的情绪或斗志。

塑造愿景。“愿景”这个词已经被淡化了，它既可以意味所有，抑或什么都不是。通常，它被用来描述领导者想要达到的包罗万象的目标，或机构的使命陈述。这些预期目标或价值观常常以口号或列表的形式出现，或挂在墙上，或放在执行官候客室的咖啡桌上，但他们对公司行为或态度的影响却微乎其微。我们所说的愿景，是一幅鲜活的精神图像，它用一种振奋的方式描述了你对公司未来的期待和展望。愿景不是一种使命表述、一组目标或者一系列的价值观，而是机构在履行使命和达到这些目标时，你可以看到、听到、感觉到的真实图景。它与期望的文化有关，或许还包含着传统价值观的回归。对机构的领导者和关键人物来讲，如果它没有鼓舞人心的力量，那么，它就不能称之为愿景。

组建和利用均衡的咨询网络。最后，或许是最重要的，你必须建立和利用合理的建议和咨询网络。没有哪个领导者是一片孤岛。新任首席执行官们很难独自克服接管庞大机构的复杂、有时甚至是混乱的挑战。你从前任手中继承了遗留的、已知的和正在出现的问题与错误。鉴于你刚从外部进入本领域，这些问题或错误可能远非那么明显。事情往往与表象千差万别。所以，找到合适的方式，

organization fulfills that mission, and achieves those objects. It's about the desired culture, perhaps including embracing a return to traditional values. If it's not inspiring, for the leader and for key people in the organization, then it's not a vision.

Build and use a balanced advice network. Finally, and perhaps most important, you have to build and use the right kind of advice and counsel network. No leader is an island. New CEOs cannot succeed alone in overcoming the complex and sometimes chaotic challenges of taking over large organizations. You have inherited problems and mistakes, known and yet to emerge, left over from your predecessors. Given that you are coming in from outside, these problems and mistakes may be far from obvious; things rarely are what they appear to be. So is essential that you find ways to accelerate learning about markets, products, technologies, organizational capabilities, team, politics and culture. Identifying and leveraging the best advisors—internally and externally—is the most effective way to do this.

While adhering to these guidelines is of course no guarantee of success, the failures of new CEOs usually can be tied to violating one or more of them. Don't let it happen to you!

Sincerely,
Dan Ciampa and Michael Watkins

(1,040 words)

加快了解市场、产品、技术、组织能力、团队、政治与文化至关重要。识别并利用内部的和外部的最佳咨询网络，是达到这种目标的最有效的方式。

尽管以上的这些方针并不能确保你一定成功，但新任首席执行官的失败往往与违背其中的一条或者几条密切相关。希望这种事情不会发生在你的身上！

丹·钱帕和迈克尔·沃特金斯

知识链接

SIVs 结构性投资工具(Structured Investment Vehicle)是银行支持的一种投资业务，主要销售商业票据等短期债券，购买次贷债券等长期债券，其利润所得主要来自短期债券和长期债券之间的利差。

题　记

互联网拉动了世界金融市场的经济链环，也推动了商业圈社交网络效益的流行。存在的社交网络超越了公司之间的界限，允许留下的员工与以前的同事保持联系，获取他们在新公司得到的知识，从而使知识通过社交网络的流动关系产生逆向迁移。人们开始在商业社交圈摒弃“人力资本”的传统观念，不再认为员工的流失即是知识的流失；他们更多地关注“社会资本”的流行概念，积极参加专家会议、交换电邮、常用的博客网站、甚至是业余社交等非正式的活动。“六度空间理论”奠定了商业圈社交网络的基础，即地球上任何地方的任何人都能够通过六个人的关系找到自己想找的人。这种典型、深刻而且普遍的自然现象以博客圈这种物以类聚的生态形式展现出来，形成了新的商业联系工具，使人们更容易在全球找到和自己有共同志趣的人，更容易发现商业机会，更容易达到不同族群之间的理解和交流。

The Social Network Benefit

It's always been assumed that one company's loss is another's gain when an employee jumps ship. Just think of the knowledge, experience and connections that go out the door along with a person's boxes and office belongings.

But now a new study suggests that losing an employee, at least in a high-tech field, is not necessarily as bad as it seems. "Firms can wind up learning when employees leave their firm, which is contrary to the conventional wisdom that firms learn by hiring away employees," says Wharton management professor Lori Rosenkopf. She and Wharton doctoral student Rafael A. Corredoira present their conclusions in a paper titled, "Learning from Those Who Left: The Reverse Transfer of Knowledge through Mobility Ties."

The two researchers came up with their silver-lining finding by studying the effects of "outbound mobility" on semiconductor firms in the United States and abroad. By analyzing patent citations, they were able to show that companies can benefit from a reverse flow of knowledge that results when an engineer or other technical expert moves on. Why? Because, according to Rosenkopf, there are social networks that transcend companies and allow the employees left behind to gain access to the knowledge being generated at their colleague's new place of business. She

社交网络效益

人们普遍认为，员工跳槽是一家公司的损失、另一家公司的收获。想想看，员工离开公司带走的不仅是个人的盒子和办公用品，还有他的知识、经验和关系网。

但是，目前一项新的研究表明，失去一名员工，至少是在高科技领域，并非如看上去那样糟糕。沃顿管理学院的教授罗利·罗森科普夫指出："与传统的观念相反，员工流失反而会刺激公司不断地学习，即公司向挖走的员工学习。"她与沃顿管理学院的博士生拉菲尔·科瑞多拉在题为"向离职者学习：知识通过流动关系的逆向迁移"一文中陈述了他们的观点。

这两位学者研究了美国和境外多家半导体公司的"员工溢出效应"，提出了他们的"绝望中见希望"的发现。通过分析专利引用，他们能够证明，当工程师或其他的技术专家离职后，产生的逆向知识流动可以给公司带来收益。为什么？根据罗森科普夫教授的研究，原因是存在的社交网络超越了公司之间的界限，允许留下的员工与以前的同事保持联系，获取他们在新公司得到的知识。罗森科普夫教授解释说，这并非涉及"商业间谍"活动，而是在相同领域工作的技术专家之间的思想和信息交流。她由此得出结论，他们的发现"对员工的流失即是知识的流失等传统观念提出了挑战"。

is not talking about corporate spying, but rather the flow of ideas and information among professionals who work in the same field. Their findings, she concludes, "call into question the conventional wisdom that losing employees means losing knowledge."

Other studies have looked at the opposite phenomenon—"inbound① mobility"—documenting the transfer of knowledge that comes with hiring. When people are viewed strictly as "human capital," the departure of an employee results in the former employer's loss of that person's intellect and talent, and the corresponding gain of those same valuable attributes for the company doing the hiring. "The belief has been that if you lose an employee, that's a bad thing for you," Rosenkopf says. Even common lingo②—that a company is losing a worker to another firm—implies that there is nothing good that could possibly result.

But Rosenkopf says the picture is different when employees are viewed in terms of "social capital". Workers aren't just silos③ of knowledge and skill onto themselves, but rather are part of social networks of workers from various firms who talk about what's going on in their field. Those networks may involve formal arrangements, such as strategic alliances, but they may also be informal, involving professional conferences, e-mail exchanges, common blog sites or even after-hour socializing. "The social capital approach would predict that the firm losing an employee would gain access to the new employer's knowledge, while the human capital approach would not," the researchers suggest in their paper.

---

① inbound [ˈinbaund] *adj.* 向内的

② lingo [ˈliŋɡəu] *n.* 行话

③ silo [ˈsailəu] *n.* 载体

其他的研究观察了相反的现象，即“引进员工”，记录随雇佣而来的知识迁移。当人们被严格当做“人力资本”时，一名员工的流失导致前雇主对该员工的智慧和才能的损失，而招聘该员工的公司却相应地获得了同等价值的属性。罗森科普夫教授说：“人们一向认为，失去一名员工对你来说是件糟糕的事。”即便是常用的行话，即一家公司向另一家公司输送员工，也暗示了不可能有什么好结果。

但罗森科普夫教授认为，当人们从“社会资本”的角度看待雇员时，画面就不尽相同了。工人不只是向自己灌输知识和技能的载体，也是社交网络中的一部分，他们来自不同的公司，讨论各自领域正在发生的事情。这些社交网络涉及战略联盟等正式安排，但他们也可能有非正式的活动，包括专家会议、交换电邮、常用的博客网站、甚至是业余社交。研究者们在论文中指出：“社会资本法预言，公司流失的员工会给新雇主带来知识，而人力资本法却做不到这一点。”

社交网络概念并不新鲜，但无论是在商业世界还是在日常生活中，它现在引起了人们越来越多的关注。美国广播公司万众期待的新剧“六度分离”就基于这一流行的概念，即地球上任何地方的任何人都能够通过六个人的关系找到自己想找的人。这是一个有趣的思想，尽管还没有被证明。

在商界，关系网长期以来一直是聘请董事会成员的重要标准。人们选择董事会成员并非一定要求他们对特殊行业和体制有多么了解，而是认为他们有影响力和优越的社会关系。换句话说，你认识

The concept of social networks in not a new one, but it's getting more attention these days, both in the business world and in everyday life. ABC's much-anticipated new drama, " Six Degrees," is based on the popular notion that anyone, anywhere on the planet can be connected to another person by way of a chain of six people. It's an intriguing① thought, though not a proven one.

In business, networks have long factored into who is picked for a board of directors. Board members aren't necessarily selected for what they know about a particular industry or organization, but rather because they are seen as influential and well connected. In other words, whom you know does matter. On a lower level, inner-office networks play a role in how information flows around a company. The corporate organization chart only tells so much. Who chats with whom around the office and who is the person that people go to for advice also matter.

The value of networks is also well recognized in medicine and science, with researchers routinely reporting their research results and clinical experiences at conferences and in journals. The open sharing of knowledge is considered part of the scientific process.

The technological world may be different.Some previous research has drawn a distinction between the transfer of knowledge that takes place in science and the knowledge flow in high-tech industries. Some researchers believe that there isn't much exchange of ideas and information among tech companies because they compete with one another and want to make

---

① intriguing [inˈtriːgiŋ] *adj.* 引起兴趣的

谁也很重要。在较低的基层组织，办公室内部的关系网决定信息如何在公司传播。公司的组织关系图就很好地说明了这个问题。谁和谁在办公室聊天，以及人们去谁那儿寻求建议也都很重要。

在医药和科学领域，人们也充分意识到了关系网的价值。研究者们例行公事地在会议上和期刊中报告他们的研究结果和临床经验。知识的公开共享被认为是科学进程的一部分。

科技领域可能不同。一些先前的研究在科学领域发生的知识传递和高科技产业的知识流动之间划分了明显的界线。一些研究人员认为，技术公司之间并没有多少观点和信息的交流，因为公司之间互相竞争，都想赚钱。但是，罗森科普夫教授考察了手机行业，发现非正式网络，如参加职业和贸易协会的工程师们，引导战略联盟的构成。研究结果表明，在同一地域范围内，尤其是像硅谷这样聚集了很多半导体企业的地方，也许已经有现成的知识共享机制。这将意味着工人跳槽到另一家公司的影响可能不会那么明显。

这篇研究论文考察了员工离职引起知识逆向流动的各种原因。其中一个原因是新的交流渠道可以在原公司和新公司之间形成，也就是说，工人与他的前同事和朋友保持交流。员工离职还能使公司更近距离地观察其他公司。他们还指出，这些发现不应该被视为促使员工离职的动因。仍然有方法帮助公司体验员工溢出流动，并从这些事件中受益。最后，员工离职时公司需要保持积极的态度。公司应该寻求在员工离职时尽可能友好，培养尽可能多的关系。

至少在高科技公司，离职员工不再仅仅只是一块蛋糕。

money. Rosenkopf, however, has looked at the cellular[1] industry and found that informal networks, such as engineers taking part in professional and trade associations, lead to the formation of strategic alliances. The findings suggests that within a region, especially places such as Silicon Valley where there are many semiconductor firms, there may already be mechanisms in place for the sharing of knowledge. That would mean the effect of a worker moving to another firm would not be as pronounced.

The research paper looks at various reasons why knowledge flows back when a worker leaves. For one, new communication channels may be established between the old firm and the new firm—in other words, a worker keeps talking to his former colleagues and friends. The departure of a worker may also cause a company to take a closer look at what's going on elsewhere. They also suggest that the findings shouldn't be seen as promoting the departure of workers. Still, there are ways for the firm experiencing outbound mobility to obtain benefits from these events. Finally, firms need to keep things positive when a worker leaves. Companies should be looking for making that parting as amicable[2] as possible, to cultivate those ties as much as possible.

The going-away party—at least at high—tech firms-is about much more than sheet cake.

(934 words)

---

① cellular [ˈseljulə] *adj.* 多洞的

② amicable [ˈæmikəbl] *adj.* 亲切的

知识链接

Human capital 人力资本。人力资本指体现在人身上的资本，即对生产者进行教育、职业培训等支出及其在接受教育时的机会成本等的总和，表现为蕴含于人身上的各种生产知识、劳动与管理技能以及健康素质的存量总和。

Social capital 社会资本。社会资本指个人在一种组织结构中，利用自己的特殊位置而获取利益的能力。一个人能从亲戚、朋友、同学、老乡等关系中获取的利益越高，那么他的社会资本就越高。

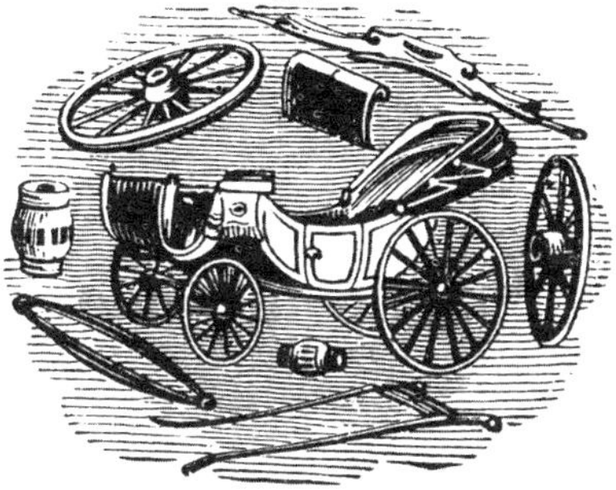

题　记

美国漫画家斯考特·亚当斯创造的系列漫画《呆伯特》，既道尽了小小上班族被老板欺压的无奈，也画出了上班族不时使点小坏、与冷酷的管理层反抗、与勾心斗角的同僚冷幽默的苦与贱。呆伯特在某种意义上已经成为现代商业团队中的搞好人际关系的代言人。职场管理原则的基础是发展人际关系，实现老板和领导者的角色转换；而搞好人际关系的基本原则是真诚，一定要远离职场上拉帮结派的政客、互斗心机的心理学家，以及奉迎打压的语言学家。服务意识和组建多功能型团队是职场伟大领导者的标志，而有效沟通和创建舒适的氛围则是实现职场人际关系多元化发展的途径。呆伯特创造的职场哲学再次阐明了美国著名的成人教育家戴尔·卡耐基的主张：一个人事业的成功只有15%是由于他的专业技能，另外85%要靠人际关系和处世技巧。

The Relationships in the Business Team

In a recent conversation I was told, " Leadership is about managing time and getting things done." I couldn't disagree more.

In my role at the Free Articulator, I manage and lead writers and editors every day. It has been said in the past that trying to manage artists, and all of our writers are, is a very difficult task. I can't honestly disagree with that. The following is a recount of the experience I've gained thus far in building teams that do the work. My response to the aforementioned person was this: leadership is about giving your people the tools to succeed.

Developing relationships is the right foundation. I have met, and worked for, people who believed that a certain level of separation between themselves and their employees will make a better work environment. Apparently, it gives the impression that they really are the " boss" .

Do you want to be a boss or a leader? Bosses give instructions and people follow them out to avoid a short meeting with the human relations director. If the financial need to hold onto the job disappears or another offer comes up, employees quit. The perfect example is the Pointy-Haired Boss from Dilbert. If you're like that boss, your employees hate you and make witty cynical jokes about you all day. Managers and leaders who forge relationships with employees are in a much better position. Many

商业团队中的人际关系

在最近的一次谈话中，有人告诉我："领导能力就是管理时间和安排事务。"我非常同意这种观点。

我在《自由喉舌报》的作用就是每天管理和领导作家和编辑。据说，过去管理艺术家和我们所有的作者是一项非常艰巨的任务。我真的不能否认这一点。下面的阐述是我迄今为止在组建团队、开展工作的过程中获得的经验。我是这样回答前面提到的那个人的：领导能力就是给你的员工获得成功的工具。

发展人际关系是正确的基础。我遇到并为其工作过的人认为，他们自己与员工之间有一定程度的隔阂会创造更好的工作环境。显然，这样做能让人们明白，他们是真正的"老板"。

你想成为老板还是领导者？老板发出指令，员工不折不扣地执行指令，这样员工就可以在短期内避免人事关系总监的传唤。如果经济上不再需要保住这份工作，或者出现了更好的工作机会，员工就会辞职。"呆伯特"中见识短浅的老板是最好的例子。如果你是这样的老板，你的员工会讨厌你，整天和你讲诙谐、冷嘲热讽的玩笑。与员工建立良好关系的管理人员和领导者工作比较顺利。即使有更高报酬的工作机会出现，许多员工也会选择留下，当然前提是报酬比较合理。更重要的是，见识短浅的老板手下的雇员按指令

employees are likely to stick around even if a job with better pay comes up-within a reasonable margin①, anyway. Better yet, where the employees of a Pointy-Haired Boss do the absolute minimum as ordered, those employees you have relationships with are likely to go a step further and provide you with the best outcome they can.

Rule #1 of relationships is being genuine. The people who work for or with you, are not stupid. Yes, there are exceptions to the rule, but it goes without saying: develop genuine② relationships. If you were to apply this advice and forge human relationships with your staff, but couldn't manage to be real about it, then they'll see right through it as a false attempt to care. Frankly, if you can't care about your staff in a real way, you're not management or leadership material. Unless you are part of the cast of Dilbert. If you're in charge of hiring the people you work with, you've got a great advantage here!

Personal relationships set the tone. I work with people who can tell me about both their successes and failures in Business and personal life. They don't do it to shirk their duties, they always get the job done, barring factors that simply make it impossible. Personal relationships do set the tone for their time working with you.

The greatest management oxymoron rests with leaders serve. Here's another Pointy-Haired Boss trait: the power trip. Never get on the power trip. Never think that your position makes you more important. Your position and role is to serve everyone else. You provide direction and you provide assistance in getting the job done. You can't do your employee's jobs for them, but as the go-to person you can make sure that the daily operations are actually contributing to big picture goals. If you're a Pointy-

① margin [ˈmɑːdʒin] *n.* 差额,赚头

② genuine [ˈdʒenjuin] *adj.* 真诚的

的最低标准完成工作，而与你关系良好的员工则会更进一步，尽其所能，按最高标准完成工作。

搞好人际关系的首要原则是真诚。为你工作或与你一起工作的人一点都不傻。当然，这条原则也有例外，但发展真正的人际关系则是不言而喻的。如果你套用这个原则与员工建立关系，但不能以真诚的态度待人，那么他们就会看穿你的把戏，将你的关心当成虚假的企图。坦率地说，如果你不能以一种真诚的方式对待你的员工，那么你就不是管理者或领导者的材料。除非你以“呆伯特”的形象示人。如果你负责招聘和你一起工作的员工，在这方面你有很大的优势！

人际关系奠定了基调。和我一起工作的人告诉我他们在工作和个人生活中的成功与失败。他们这样做并不是推卸责任，他们总是完成工作，除非出现使之变得不可能的因素。人际关系决定了他们和你在一起工作的时间。

最大的管理矛盾在于领导者的服务意识。见识短浅的老板还有另一个特点，就是炫耀权力。决不要炫耀权力。决不要认为你的位置使你显得比较重要。你的位置和作用要服务于其他人。你只是提供完成工作的指导和帮助。你不能替员工工作，但作为核心人士，你可以确保日常运转实际上在为实现整体目标做贡献。如果你是一位见识短浅的老板，你就不可能成为核心人士。你身处圈子之外，雇员欺骗你，而不是与你讨论，公司凝聚力的缺乏会导致更多的问题，并且需要更多的时间达到整体目标。所以，你需要为员工服务。你有义务帮助员工完成工作，而不是只告诉他们怎么做。“整体目标”一词也同样重要。如果你的团队不能看到最终的结

Haired Boss, you're not the go-to person. You're kept out of the loop, employees deceive you rather than discuss with you, and a lack of company cohesion① means more problems and more time involved in attaining those big picture goals. So, you serve your staff. You're there to help them get their job done, not to just tell them to do it. The term "big picture" is important, too. If your team cannot see the end result, the reasons why, the motivations, emotions and outcomes poured into and desired from a project, then their small-time thinking will be a demotivator. Show them the road ahead, and they'll travel there.

The trademark of great leaders is functional teams. Teams are selected from a pool of people with different skills, viewpoints, attitudes and desires. Good teams are not chosen before the project is, because it takes a certain person, and a certain set of people, to attain different goals. But selecting the right set of people is the easy part. Making them work together is hard.

Don't confuse roles. There are times when you don't see your team working well together and you look for ways to solve this and resolve on the easiest thing you can find: artificial② situations. Asking your e-commerce programmer to look over a design with the graphic artist is an artificial situation③. You can't get relationships and communication lines to grow this way, since both individuals will be peeved with the interruption that's not beneficial to either of them. If good relationships don't grow naturally, the least you can do is look for natural situations to promote them; get the copywriter to go through their content with the graphic④ artist, and discuss how the visual feel of the page should reflect

---

① assistance [əˈsistəns] *n.*帮助

② cohesion [kəuˈhiːʒən] *n.* 凝聚力

③ artificial [ɑːtiˈfiʃəl] *adj.* 虚假的

④ graphic [ˈgræfik] *adj.* 绘画的

果、不能了解为什么一个项目需要投入大量的动机、情感和结果，那么他们无关紧要的思维将会成为一种抑制积极性的因素。告诉他们前方的道路，他们会到达那里。

伟大的领导者的标志是组建多功能型团队。所有入选团队的人都具有不同的技能、观点、态度和欲望。良好的团队不是在项目实施之前选定的，因为项目需要特定的个人、特定的一组人，从而达成不同的目标。但是，选择一组合适的人是容易的事，让他们在一起工作却很艰难。

不要混淆角色。有些时候，你认为你的团队没有很好地工作，于是你开始寻找解决这个问题的方法，你可以找到最简单的解决方案：创造人工环境。要求你的电子商务程序员审查绘画艺术家的设计是一种人工环境。你不能用这种方式培育人际关系和沟通链，因为双方会愤怒地中断，不利于任何一方。如果良好的关系不能自然成长，至少你可以做到寻找自然环境，对他们加以促进；让撰稿人与绘画艺术家一道审查内容，讨论页面的视觉效果如何传达文本的思想。

有效沟通。首先，当人失去了特性、成为角色和号码时，沟通就会失败。人有名字，而不是名称。处理电子邮件地址时要牢记这一点。其次，不要向所有人抄送和提醒所有的事情。再者，电子商务程序员没有必要或想要了解网络布局中影像压缩文件的低质量问题。你也许认为，向员工传送这些备忘录会使他们感觉受到了重视，但这种做法实际上阻塞了信息沟通。

创建舒适的氛围。再次提到人际关系话题，你试图用你的团队打造人际关系，但这并不意味着做同样的事让他们彼此会感到安

the copy.

Make communication work. First, communication fails when people aren't people, but roles and numbers. People have names, not designations. Bear this in mind when handing out e-mail addresses. Second, don't CC or memo everyone on everything. Again, the e-commerce programmer doesn't need to or want to know about the low quality of the JPEGs in a web layout①. You might think sending these memos to everyone makes them feel like their part of something, but what it does is clog up information lines.

Build a comfortable atmosphere. Still on the relationships topic, just because you try to forge them with your team doesn't mean they'll feel safe doing the same with each other. Eliminate the stuffy suit-and-tie atmosphere. I don't mean necessarily change the dress code, but don't be too formal; use it where necessary, especially when communicating with external publics, but promote a relaxed, fun yet productive environment internally. It is safe, free-flowing communication that produces results, not forced communication. Remember that if someone has a reason not to communicate, they probably won't. Find the barriers and shove them off a cliff when nobody's looking.

I've only been doing this for a few years, but that's my experience of building effective, cohesive and long-term teams. If you have a high turnover or low employee efficiency problem, give these tips a try. Through trial and error, they worked for me.

(1,074 words)

---

① layout [ˈleiaut] *n.* 布局

全。消除沉闷的西装革履的气氛。我并不是要求必须改变着装，但不要太正式。当需要时，尤其是与外部人员沟通时才穿正装，但要提倡轻松、愉快但高效的内部环境。这是安全、自由沟通产生的结果，而不是强迫性的交流。请记住，如果有人有理由不愿沟通，他们或许是不会沟通。找出障碍，在无人关注时将它们推下悬崖。

我在这方面还只做了几年，但这是我组建有效、有凝聚力和长期团队的经验。如果你有高流动率或员工效率低下的问题，不妨尝试一下这些建议。通过反复实验，它们对我有效。

知识链接

Dilbert 呆伯特是美国作家和漫画家史考特·亚当斯(Scott Adams)根据自身办公室经验和读者来信为本创作的著名职场卡通人物。系列漫画《呆伯特》(Dilbert)描述了一个倒霉的技术职业者呆伯特与一只愤世嫉俗的狗“狗伯特”(Dogbert)的生活经历。方脸、戴翘领带的计算机工程师呆伯特，是全球最有名的上班族，他的身边总是有陷害他的上司和一群神经质的同事。众多上班族读者在这部漫画中看到了自己生活的影子，因此它获得了巨大的共鸣和支持，在 20 世纪 90 年代风靡全球 39 个国家、拥有超过 1.5 亿名读者。现在，“呆伯特”这个漫画角色在职业管理界已经成为一种职场定律。

题　记

自石油大亨洛克菲勒通过“破坏性降价”和“毁灭性竞争”策略来保护他的商业帝国伊始，行业统治者们一直在试图获得汇集稀缺利润并使法令失效的权力。英特尔公司企图利用其市场影响力将另一家芯片制造商AMD挤出市场的例子，就是现代托拉斯的经典再现。为了耗尽竞争对手AMD的收益，英特尔利用持有现金储备的优势，将产品售价降至成本以下。一旦竞争者AMD出局，英特尔的短期损失利润便以更高的价格得到加倍补偿。虽然英特尔拒绝掠夺性价格指控，但它对公司实施的商品捆绑销售模式和回扣销售模式却无法自圆其说。这两种销售模式可以使英特尔这样具有市场主导权的企业仰仗自己确定的市场份额立于不败之地。垄断企业心态与垄断膜拜操纵的市场让财大气粗的商家对弱势竞争对手露出了狰狞的嘴脸，初次遭遇反垄断的AMD面对的将是一场艰难的诉讼之旅。

The Unkindest Cuts

Discounting that promotes competition is hard to distinguish from predatory① pricing.

Before he won the Nobel prize for economics in 1991, Ronald Coase wrote an essay decrying the poor state of research in industrial organization, the discipline in which he established his reputation. The field, he complained, was devoted to the study of monopoly and antitrust policy. That, he said, made for bad scholarship: an economist faced with a business practice that he cannot fathom②, according to Mr. Coase, "looks for a monopoly explanation".

A lot has changed in the 37 years since that lament. The broader research effort for which Mr. Coase called has fostered a richer understanding of how firms respond to customers and rivals. Monopoly explanations now compete with theories that see the same behavior as helpful to consumers. That has made it harder to sort malign③ from benign④ business practices. The antitrust finding against Intel, a maker of computer chips, is a case in point. After a long investigation, ending in a

---

① predatory [ˈpredət(ə)ri] *adj*. 掠夺的

② fathom [ˈfæð(ə)m] *vt*. 看穿;彻底了解

③ malign [məˈlain] *adj*. 恶意的,恶性的

④ benign [biˈnain] *adj*. 良性的

恶意杀价

很难区分刺激竞争的行为和掠夺性定价。

罗纳德·科斯在获得1991年诺贝尔经济学奖前，写过一篇文章，谴责了糟糕的产业组织研究状况，使他在该学科领域建立了自己的声望。他曾经抱怨该领域总是致力于垄断和反垄断政策的研究。他认为这种做法只会影响学术研究，按照科斯先生的意思，经济学家遇到无法理解的商业行为时，只会“使用垄断来解释”。

科斯发出那番哀叹至今已有37年，其间发生了很多变化。科斯先生呼吁的更广泛的研究使人们对企业如何应对客户和竞争对手有了更加丰富的理解。垄断解释现在与某些理论针锋相对，这些理论认为同样的行为有利于消费者。这就更难从良性商业行为中界定恶性商业行为。对英特尔电脑芯片生产商的反垄断调查是一个很好的例子。经过长时间的调查，英特尔案的判决书厚达524页，欧盟对英特尔罚款10.6亿欧元（14.4亿美元），因为英特尔非法利用自身的影响力，将其竞争对手、另一家芯片制造商AMD挤出市场。英特尔拒绝掠夺性价格指控，计划到法院上诉。其律师团声称，已经准备好一整套理论来支撑此次辩护。

掠夺性定价的主张有着悠久的历史。美国竞争政策的基石、1890年制定的谢尔曼反托拉斯法部分是为了应付投诉的小企业，他

bulky 524-page verdict, the European Union fined Intel € 1.06 billion ($ 1.44 billion) for illegally using its muscle to price AMD, a rival chipmaker, out of the market. Intel rejects the charge of predatory pricing and plans a court appeal. Its lawyers have a block of theory on which to build a defence.

Allegations of predatory pricing have a long history. The Sherman Antitrust Act of 1890, the foundation of America's competition policy, was partly a response to complaints by small firms that larger rivals wanted to drive them out of business. Trustbusters need to be wary of such claims. Low prices are one of the fruits of competition: penalising business giants for price cuts would be perverse. But in rare circumstances, a big firm with cash in reserve may cut prices below costs in order to starve smaller rivals of revenue. The profits sacrificed in the short term can be recouped by higher prices once competitors are out of the way.

Establishing that a firm is guilty of predation is difficult. If rivals stumble or fail, that may be down to their own inefficiency or poor products, and not because they were preyed upon. Proving that a firm is pricing below its costs is tricky in practice. Even where a reliable price-cost or profit-sacrifice test is feasible, failing it need not imply sinister intent. There are often pro-competitive reasons to forgo short-term profits. Firms with a new product, or a new version of an existing one, may wish to pick a loss making price to defray the cost to consumers of switching, or because they expect their own costs to fall as they perfect the production process (video-game consoles are a classic example). Losses would then be a licit investment in future profits.

Predation is even trickier to uncover when goods are sold together. A firm that enjoys fat profits on one good may "bundle" it with another on

们抱怨那些规模更大的竞争对手想要把他们挤出市场。联邦反托拉斯检察官需要对这样的诉求持谨慎的态度。低价是竞争的结果，惩罚企业巨头恶意杀价并不明智。但在极少数情况下，为了耗尽较小对手的收益，持有现金储备的大企业将售价降至成本以下。一旦竞争者出局，短期损失的利润便以更高的价格得到加倍补偿。

很难裁定一家公司犯有掠夺性定价之罪。竞争对手如果亏损或破产，可能是自身效率低下或产品拙劣，并非受害于掠夺。实际上，要证明一家公司的定价低于其成本相当棘手。即使采用可靠且可行的价格成本测试或利润损失测试，也不能排除竞争对手的险恶用心。企业往往是为了提升竞争力而放弃短期利润。企业在推出新产品或现有产品的新版本时，通常希望以较低的价格来吸引顾客更新换代，或者希望自己的成本随生产过程的完善而下降（游戏机就是典型的例子）。在这种情况下，损失成为未来盈利的一种合法投资。

当商品捆绑销售时，掠夺性定价会更难发现。企业或许会将利润丰厚的商品和利润较低的商品“捆绑销售”。如果捆绑商品的打折力度够大的话，其他公司就很难提供同等诱人的报价。欧盟叫停了通用和霍尼韦尔的并购提议，就是担心二者联手后有可能采取捆绑式折扣排挤其他竞争厂商。美国政府指定的一个反垄断专家委员会，提出了一项检测捆绑销售是否具备掠夺性的测试。首先，假设折扣只适用于低利润的商品。如果每种商品售价 10 美元，而捆绑后的商品售价 16 美元，4 美元的折扣就归于更有竞争力的商品。接下来，应用价格成本测试，即如果商品的成本高于 6 美元，那么这种捆绑就具有掠夺性。

which margins are lower. If the discount on the bundle is hefty enough, other firms may struggle to offer as enticing a deal. The EU blocked a proposed tie-up between GE and Honeywell for fear that the merged firm might use bundled discounts to squeeze rival suppliers. A committee of antitrust experts appointed by the American government proposed a test for whether bundling is predatory. First, assume the discount applies solely to the low-margin good. So if each good sells for \$10 separately and \$16 as a bundle, allocate the \$4 discount to the more "competitive" product. Next, apply a price-cost test: if the product costs over \$6 to make, the bundle is predatory.

That check seems neat, but sound business practices may still fall foul of it. It may be cheaper for a firm to sell the two goods together, because of cost savings on distribution. Firms also often use bundling as a way of charging high-demand users more. Thin margins on sales of printers, for example, can be made up by bundling in more profitable toners. This kind of "metering" is an efficient way of recovering fixed costs such as research.

Another ambiguous tactic is to offer rebates to customers that reach certain sales targets. Bulk buyers generally pay lower unit prices to reflect suppliers' economies of scale. Rebates can also help align① incentives. Suppliers want retailers to promote their products, offer in-store information and keep plentiful stocks. The trouble is, retailers bear all the costs of such sales efforts but reap only some of the benefits. Rebates provide incentives for retailers to drive sales, as profits are bigger once the target is met.

---

① align [ə'lain] *vt.* 使结盟;使成一行

这种检验方法似乎很简单，但合理的商业行为依然与其大相径庭。由于经销成本减少，把两件商品绑定销售对公司来说可能更划算。公司也经常利用捆绑销售的方法从高需求的顾客身上赚更多的钱。例如，售卖打印机的薄利可以通过绑定利润更高的墨盒一起销售而得到弥补。这种“计量”方式可以有效弥补研究之类的固定成本。

另一种模糊策略是给客户提供回扣，以达到一定的销售目标。总体来说，大宗购买者支付的单价较低，这也反映了供货商的规模经济。回扣也可以帮助协调激励机制。供应商希望零售商销售他们的产品，提供店内信息和保持充足的库存。问题是零售商尽力承担全部的销售成本，但仅获得一些好处。回扣刺激零售商推动销售，因为一旦达成销售目标，利润也会更大。

欧盟认为，英特尔采用的这种回扣销售方式极具杀伤力。只要超出目标端，多卖出的商品价格可以是负值，这正是回扣销售方式的本质。也就是说，如果每次销售 9 件商品，公司收费 1 美元；而销售 10 件商品或更多，单价则是 80 美分（返 20%），第 10 件商品的价值就是负 1 美元，因为 9 件商品的价格是 9 美元，而 10 件商品的价格仅为 8 美元。英特尔这样具有市场主导权的企业就可以仰仗自己确定的市场份额立于不败之地，业内称之为“保底”。

英特尔公司的行为当然值得商榷。如果客户把自己生意的 80% 至 90%交给英特尔，就可以拿到回扣。这种回扣制度看上去是对 AMD 公司竞争威胁的一种回应。然而，欧盟的反托拉斯官员并不太相信自己。英特尔的竞争对手依然活力十足，尽管其投资计划可能已经受挫，潜在的入市者望而却步，AMD 公司并没有被市场扫地

The EU reckons that Intel's use of such rebates was nefarious①. It is in the nature of rebates that, just above the target threshold, the price of each additional purchase can be negative. If, say, a firm charges $1 for each sale of up to nine units, and a unit price of 80 cents (a rebate of 20%) for sales of ten items or more, the price of the tenth sale is minus $1, since nine units cost $9 and ten units costs only $8. A dominant firm like Intel can rely on a certain market share, an "assured base" in the jargon.

Intel's conduct was certainly worth investigating. Its rebates kicked in if customers gave the firm between 80% and 100% of their business. The schemes looked like a response to a competitive threat from AMD. Yet the EU's trustbusters cannot feel too sure of themselves. Intel's rival is still alive and kicking: AMD has not been excluded from the market, though its investment plans may have been thwarted and potential entrants② deterred. Moreover, such a complex case, with a bulky ruling which is still not in the public domain, does not offer much guidance on what sort of rebate schemes might be deemed predatory.

Trustbusters have moved away from the practice that so concerned Mr. Coase in the early 1970s—of being too quick to condemn big firms on the basis of crude judgments. But they are unlikely to find a robust and simple rule to put in place of the old presumption that firms with market power are always suspect.

(1,033 words)

---

① nefarious [niˈfeəriəs] *adj*. 邪恶的;穷凶极恶的

② entrant [ˈentr(ə)nt] *n*. 进入者

出门。此外，英特尔案非常复杂，大宗的裁决仍未公之于众，所以它对判定何种回扣方式具有掠夺性并不能提供太多的指导。

反托拉斯的检察官们已经摒弃了科斯先生在20世纪70年代早期担忧的那种行为，即根据草率的判断迅速给大公司定罪。但是，他们也不太可能找到一个强势而简单的法则来替代陈旧的定律：有市场支配力的公司往往是嫌疑犯。

知识链接

AMD 美国AMD公司是一家业务遍及全球的集成电路供应商，专为电脑、通信及电子消费类市场供应各种芯片产品，其中包括用于通信及网络设备的微处理器、闪存以及基于硅片技术的解决方案等。AMD除了在世界各大城市设有办事处之外，还在美国、欧洲、日本及亚洲其他国家设有生产中心。AMD创办于1969年，总公司设于美国硅谷，超过70%的收入来自国际市场。

题　记

黑格尔说过："世界上没有完全相同的两片叶子"，同样也没有完全相同的两个人，没有完全相同的领导者和领导模式。而5P领导概念则从一个全新的角度诠释了领导者艺术。"关注重要的事情"运用意大利经济学家帕累托创造的80/20法则，告诫领导者抓住事物的本质，有所为，有所不为。"赞扬你要继续的事"鼓励领导者让变化多端的赞扬达到最佳效果，员工可以采取积极的行动为公司效力。"惩罚你想停止的事"期待奖励良好的行为，按比例惩罚非正义的行为。"为你想要的结果付酬"是看得见、摸得着的另类赞扬形式，薪酬和赞扬是公司引擎持续运转的动力。"提升带来你想要的结果的人"对公司的奖励和晋升系统提出了质疑。不论你身在何处或从事怎样的工作，5P领导概念永远是恒定不变的领导原则。

The Five Ps of Leadership

There are whole libraries full of things that tell you what to do about leadership and how to remember what's important. Here's another short edition to that library-the 5 P's of leadership. They are: Pay Attention to What's Important, Praise What You Want to Continue, Punish What You Want to Stop, Pay for the Results You Want, and Promote the People Who Deliver Those Results.

Pay Attention to What's Important

Time management courses, strategy books, and management gurus① all will tell you that there's not a lot that's really important. Your job as a leader is to concentrate on what's most important so that it gets taken care of. Then let the rest of the stuff take care of itself.

If you're a perfectionist, that's going to be hard for you to do. But there's not P for perfectionism in this scheme of things. We recognize that there are limited resources of time, energy, people, and money. Because those resources are limited, you want to go for the big stuff first. What you're after is the 20% of stuff that gives you the biggest bang for the buck. What underlies all of this is something called Pareto's Law. Vilfredo

---

① gurus[ˈguruː] *n.* 权威

5P 领导概念

一座又一座的图书馆装满资料，告诉你当领导该做什么和如何记住重要的事情。本文是献给图书馆的另一个简短版本，即 5P 领导概念。他们包括关注重要的事情、赞扬你要继续的事、惩罚你想停止的事、为你想要的结果付酬和提升带来这些结果的人。

关注重要的事情

时间管理课程、策略书籍和管理权威都会告诉你，真正重要的事并不是太多。作为领导人，应该关注最重要的事，使之受到重视。其他的事情顺其自然即可。

如果你是完美主义者，这种做法对你来说很难将就。但是，在这个方案发展的过程中没有完美主义的 P。我们意识到时间、精力、人才和资金等资源有限。就因为这些资源有限，你必须首先做最重要的事。你追求的是 20% 的利润，这才是货真价实的最大成功。所谓的帕累托定律是构建这一切的基础。维弗雷多·帕累托是 19 世纪后期意大利的经济学家和社会学家。他用公式阐述了一条法则，他称之为“结果不平衡分配法则”。你可能知道它就是 80/20 法则。所有的 80/20 法则认为，做 20% 的事让你获得 80% 的

Pareto was an Italian Economist and Sociologist in the late 19th century. He formulated something he called "The Law of the Unequal Distribution of Results." You probably know it as the 80/20 rule. All the 80/20 rules says is that there's 20% of the stuff you do that gets you 80% of the results. The trick is finding that 20% . Once you've found it you then have to pay attention to it. Pay attention to it in your written and oral communications. Restate the key themes over and over. Don't undervalue repetition, repetition makes for memory and memory makes for action. Pay attention to it in your casual contacts. John Kotter, in his book to general managers, pointed out that effective general managers make great use of the random contacts they have with people. Those contacts could be in the hallway, at the water cooler, in the elevator, or walking down the street. The seize on those moments to talk about the things and ask the questions that are important to their leadership agenda. You should do that too.

Organize your day, your communications, your organizational structures, your reward systems and everything else to pay attention to what's important and then do that with unremitting diligence①.

Praise What You Want to Continue

Praise is your best training tool. In technical terms, praise is a positive consequence that follows a positive action. It's a reward for something done right. Use praise to get people to continue to do things or to take positive action. That's where it's best used. Remember, too, that praise is a tool that is most effective when it's used inconsistently. Used consistently, praise tends to loose its force. So, don't worry so much about praising

① unremitting diligence [ˌʌnriˈmitiŋ] [ˈdilidʒəns]不懈的努力

结果。诀窍在于发现那20%。一旦找到，你就必须对它关注。在书面和口头交流中要关注它。一遍又一遍地重申关键主题。不要低估重复，重复生成记忆，而记忆导致行动。在随意的接触中关注它。约翰·科特在写给总经理的书中指出，有效率的总经理会充分利用他们和别人的随机接触。这些接触可以是在走廊里，在冷水器旁，在电梯里或是走在大街上。抓住这些时机谈事情和提问，这些都是他们管理日程上的重要内容。你也应该这么做。

让你的时间、交际、组织结构、奖励系统和其他所有事情有条有理，以便关注重要的事情，然后坚持不懈、勤奋努力地完成这些重要的事。

赞扬你要继续的事

赞扬是你最好的培训工具。赞扬这个术语是一次积极行动后的积极结果，它是对有所作为的回报。运用赞扬的方式使人们继续做事情或采取积极的行动，这就是对它的最佳使用。也请记住，赞扬是一种工具，变化多端的赞扬使其达到最佳效果。千篇一律的赞扬易于使其失去魅力，所以，不要太在意赞扬人们正确做过的每一件事，但确实要为赞扬操心。寻找机会赞扬他人，这一点很重要，因为我们大多数人生活在一个对他人缺乏足够赞扬的世界里。

惩罚你想停止的事

惩罚是赞美的镜像，它是一次消极行为后的消极结果。它遵循一种原则，一位我过去的学员用圣经术语对它进行了阐述。她说："良好的行为应当给予奖励，非正义的行为应该按比例受到惩罚。"

everything that people do right, but do worry about praising. It's important to seek out opportunities to praise others, because most of us came up in a world where we didn't praise enough.

Punish What You Want to Stop

Punishment is the mirror image of praise. It's a negative consequence that follows negative behavior. It follows a principle stated almost in biblical terms by one of my past trainees. She said: "the good shall be rewarded and the unjust shall be punished in proportion to their deeds." Punishment-negative consequences-is the tool you use to get people to stop stuff. If you figure out what's most important for people to quit doing in your organization, rig up some kind of negative consequence for them if they do it. Be careful though, because you may fall prey to the hot stove guideline. It was Mark Twain who said, "A cat who sits on a hot stove will never sit on a hot stove again". But he won't sit on a cold stove either.

The management lesson here is that if you zap people too much with negative consequences, they don't just quit doing the stuff that you don't want them to do. They quit doing pretty much everything. That's why "rule by fear" and "controlled ferocity①" cultures have a devil of a time getting people to take initiative. They've been zapped so often they're just not willing to risk it.

Pay for the Results You Want

Years ago when I was managing distribution and customer service centers I happened to compliment one of the customer service reps. She immediately turned around to me and said, "Don't just tell me, show me,

① ferocity [fə'rɔsəti] *n.* 凶猛;残忍;暴行

惩罚换来消极的后果，它成为你阻止他人做事的手段。如果你断定，最重要的是让人们停止在你的组织里的工作，若他们坚持要做，就让他们承担某种类型的负面后果。但是要谨慎，因为你可能掉入火炉准则陷阱。马克·吐温曾说过：“坐过火炉的猫绝不会再次坐上火炉。”但它也不会坐冷炉。

这里得到的管理教训是，如果你对那些做了消极事情的人打击过多，他们不只是退出那些你不希望他们做的事，他们几乎停止做所有的事情。这就是为什么“恐惧统理规则”和“有控制的残暴”文化让人们在主动进取时吃尽了苦头。他们常常饱受打击，不再愿意冒险。

为你想要的结果付酬

数年前，我主管分销和客服中心，偶然表扬了一名客服代表。她立刻转过身来对我说：“别光口头表扬了，来点实惠的，发薪日是星期五。”

薪酬是你可以用来奖励人们做好工作的有形方式之一，它是另一种形式的赞扬：看得见、摸得着。但不要让你的思维局限于付钱这种方式，可以用放假、赞誉、选择任务的机会、小礼品和特别红利等方式鼓励你所希望的行为。我有一个客户，当他在他的货运公司巡视时，常常随身携带一满口袋的餐厅礼券。当他发现有人正在做他想鼓励做的事时，他很可能会迅速拿出一张礼券当场交给他。这种行为引起了一种戏剧性的效果，确保了良好的沟通，并且鼓励了积极的行为。我的另一个客户做了类似的事。她是德克萨斯州

payday is Friday."

Pay is one of the tangible ways you can reward people for doing good stuff. It's another form of praise in visible, tangible form. Don't limit your thinking about pay to just money, though. Pay people with time off, recognition, choice assignments, small gifts, and special bonuses to encourage the behavior you want. One of my clients used to carry around a pocket-full of restaurant gift certificates as he wandered around his trucking company. When he found somebody doing something that he wanted to encourage he was likely to whip out a gift certificate and hand it to them on the spot. It created the kind of event and drama that makes for good communication, and it encouraged positive behavior. Another client of mine, a police chief this time, did something similar. She was a police chief in Texas, and, as you might expect, she talked like a Texan. She had little slips made up with one of her favorite phrases on them. It was, "preciate ya." When she heard something about one of her officers that was positive, she sent them one of her ' preciate ya, slips. When she caught somebody done something she wanted to encourage she handed one out. Officers collected the slips and when they got enough, they got recognition in the department newsletter and some extra time off.

Look for ways to pay for the results you want. Pay and praise are the things that get the engine of progress going.

Promote People Who Deliver the Results You Want

This one just makes sense. The problem is that lots of organizations forget about it. They maintain reward and promotion systems that reward the old behavior, even while they're trumpeting the new behavior in memo's, meetings, and executive retreats.

一个警察局的局长，如你所想的一样，她像德州人一样说话。她有一叠小纸条，上面写着一个她喜欢的短语，这就是“感谢您”。当她听到有人表扬她的警员时，她就发给这些人一张“感谢您”的纸条，当她发现有人在做她鼓励要做的事情时，她就给他一张。警员们收集这些纸条，积攒得足够多时，他们就会在部门的通讯报道上得到表扬，还可以得到额外的休息。

为你想要的结果寻找支付方法吧，薪酬和赞扬是让引擎持续运转的动力。

提升带来你想要的结果的人

这条原则很有意义，问题是许多公司忘记了这一点。虽然他们在备忘录里、在会议上和主管度假点大肆宣扬新方案，但是他们仍然维持着奖励过时做法的奖励和晋升系统。

当我刚开始做咨询的时候，一位更有经验和智慧的咨询顾问对我说：“当你第一次进入一个机构时，注意一下他们提升谁。听一听普通员工告诉你的有关谁获得提升和奖励的故事以及其中的原因。这将告诉你这个机构优先考虑的事情是什么，你需要了解这一点。”在你的公司，同僚们在讲什么样的故事？他们在讲老板的什么故事？你希望这些故事都是正面的，他们的老板做了些了不起的事情。如果所有的故事都是负面的，老兄，你就有麻烦了。你的同僚怎样评价那些得到提升的人？他们觉得这些人的提升是因为业绩优异，还是因为他们只是恰好“认识某个人”，或者更糟？

5P 领导概念将帮助你继续行进在公司积极变革的轨道上。请记

When I was just starting out in consulting, a much more experienced and wiser consultant said to me, "When you first go into an organization, pay attention to who it is they promote. Listen to the stories that folks tell you about who gets promoted and rewarded and why. That will tell you just about everything you need to know about what the real organizational priorities are." What are the stories that your people tell in your organization? What are the stories they tell about their bosses? You want those stories to be positive about great things their bosses have done. If all the stories are negatives, buddy you've got a problem. What do your folks say about the folks who are promoted? Do they feel they got promoted on merit because of their performance or because they just happened to "know somebody" or worse.

The five P's of leadership will help you stay on track to positive organizational change. Remember to pay attention to what's important, praise what you want to continue, punish what you want to stop, pay for the results you want, and promote the people who deliver those results and you'll help your organization be the very best that it can become.

(1,276 words)

住关注重要的事情、赞扬你要继续的事、惩罚你想停止的事、为你想要的结果付酬和提升带来这些结果的人，你将帮助你的机构成为它可以成为的最好机构。

知识链接

80/20 Rule 80/20 法则。它是时间管理和人生规划中最重要的概念之一，由意大利著名经济学家维尔弗雷德·帕累托于 1895 年发现，因此，这一法则也被称为"帕累托法则"。帕累托注意到，几乎所有的经济活动都受 80/20 法则的支配。根据这一法则，20%的努力产生 80%的结果，20%的客户带来了 80%的销售额，20%的产品或者服务创造了 80%的利润，20%的工作能够体现 80%的价值，等等。这意味着，如果你有 10 件工作要做，其中 2 件的价值比另外 8 件加起来还要大。

题　记

汽车产业的全球化趋势，导致了激烈的竞争和行业的整合。通用汽车、雷诺汽车和日产汽车等三家公司的结盟，让本就躁动不安的行业又掀起了新的波澜。法国雷诺与几近崩溃的日产汽车达成合作协议，采取一系列的措施拯救后者于破产的边缘。通用汽车基于对填补汽车业务亏损的渴望，期待联手雷诺和日产扭转主营业务上的颓势。但已结盟的雷诺和日产拒绝为新的三方结盟向通用汽车支付额外费用，导致谈判陷入僵局。当法国雷诺还在寻找北美合作者之际，在激烈的竞争压力下挣扎的福特汽车不失时机地步入谈判圈。三方的谈判游戏瞬间转换成四方的竞争和博弈。是采取温和的方式避免摩擦和冲突，还是运用强硬的战术战胜对方，抑或既不温和也不强硬的态度？最终的决定权还在汽车市场。

Lost in Negotiation

Carlos Ghosn, the chief executive of Renault and Nissan, joked that when he wants to talk privately with General Motors Chief Executive G. Richard Wagoner, they can always speak in Portuguese. Both executives, after all, have spent ample time in Brazil. But when it comes to discussing a possible alliance between their three companies, it seems Ghosn and Wagoner have been speaking different languages.

Ghosn envisions① broad cooperation between the three companies, resulting in billions of dollars in savings. Wagoner, apparently, sees less benefit to GM—so much so that he thinks Renault-Nissan should pay GM several billion dollars to compensate for the greater value it would bring to such an alliance. The two executives met in Paris for an update on the two-month-old alliance talks and to try to reconcile their differing views on the potential benefits of a deal.

A source close to the situation said that while the companies have identified many areas in which cooperation could make sense, "there is a fundamental disagreement" over the potential savings to be gained from combining their worldwide purchasing efforts. GM is the world's largest automaker and thus already enjoys considerable economies of scale. GM

---

① envision [inˈviʒn] *vt.* 想象

迷失在谈判中

雷诺和日产的首席执行官卡洛斯·戈恩开玩笑地说，当他与通用汽车首席执行官理查德·瓦格纳私人会晤时，他们总是可以讲葡萄牙语，毕竟，两位执行官都在巴西待过足够长的时间。但是，当提到他们三个公司之间正在讨论的结盟可能性时，戈恩和瓦格纳似乎分别在用不同的语言讲话。

戈恩设想在这三家公司之间开展广泛的合作，这样就会产生数十亿美元的资金节余。瓦格纳显然认为此举对通用来说受益不大，以至于他认为雷诺-日产公司应该支付通用几十亿美元的额外费用，以补偿它给此次结盟带来的更大价值。两位首席执行官在巴黎会晤，为已经组合两个月的结盟举行新一轮的谈判，试图就存在于交易潜在利益上的不同观点达成一致。

知情人士透露，虽然两家公司在很多合作领域已达成共识，但他们对从世界范围内的并购尝试中获得的潜在收益仍“存在根本的分歧”。通用是世界上最大的汽车制造商，并因此已享有相当大的经济规模。通用也相信，一旦其最大的供应商特尔斐破产成为事实，通用将不再需要人为地为零部件支付高价，只会进一步减少购买成本。所以，通用坚信，来自三方结盟的大部分采购效益将会流向规模较小的雷诺和日产。而另一方的戈恩则认为，三家公司都将

also believes that once the bankruptcy of its largest supplier, Delphi is resolved, GM will stop paying artificially high prices for components, thus reducing its purchasing costs even further. Most of the purchasing benefits from a three-way alliance, thus, would flow to the smaller Renault and Nissan, GM believes. Ghosn, on the other hand, believes all three companies would benefit greatly from joint purchasing efforts.

With the two camps so far apart on such a critical issue, the companies decided to continue talking, at least until their original deadline, to see if either side comes around. Over dinner with reporters later evening, Ghosn said the meeting at least clarified the sticking points between the companies. "When there is a discrepancy①, the question is why are we looking at the same facts with different eyes?" he said. "If I felt this was going nowhere, we could have stopped today. The more we have meetings, the more we understand each other."

Yet Ghosn flatly dismissed the idea of an up-front② payment to compensate GM for joining the alliance. "If you start talking about compensation even before you've discussed the synergies③, it's nonsense," Ghosn said. People won't be motivated to look for savings if they know that they'll be paid by their partner for doing nothing. "If you reward them for standing still, it kills the spirit of the alliance," Ghosn said.

The suggestion that GM deserves something akin to a dowry④ for teaming up with Renault and Nissan underscores how far apart the

---

① discrepancy [disˈkrepənsi] *n.* 分歧

② up-front 预先付款

③ synergy [ˈsinədʒi] *n.* 协合作用

④ dowry [ˈdauəri] *n.* 嫁妆

从联合采购中获益良多。

由于两个阵营在这个关键问题上存在如此大的争议，两家公司决定至少在原定日期截止前继续谈判，看是否有一方愿意做出让步。在记者后来参加的晚宴上，戈恩认为，会面至少可以澄清两家公司之间的关键问题。戈恩说：“分歧是存在的，问题是我们为什么会用不同的眼光看待同样的事实。如果我觉得这样做没有结果，我们今天就可以停下来。我们见面越多，就更能互相理解。”

但是，戈恩断然拒绝了为结盟而对通用实施预先补偿性支付的想法。戈恩说：“在讨论企业合并的协同优势之前就开始为补偿支付谈判，真是毫无意义。”如果人们知道他们即使什么也不做，合作伙伴照样会给他们支付报酬，就不会考虑成本的节余。戈恩认为，“如果他们什么也不干就给他们报酬，这将会扼杀结盟的精神”。

有人提议，通用联手雷诺和日产应该得到类似于嫁妆的报酬，这也强调了两家公司之间的差距是多么之大。戈恩在巴黎与瓦格纳会面后不久，声称即使他与通用的谈判破裂，也仍然抱定决心要寻找一名北美的合作者。虽然他说他会足够耐心，但戈恩还是很自然地决定把扩大联盟计划的目光集中在福特汽车身上，福特像通用一样，在激烈的竞争压力下挣扎。据说福特汽车的总裁威廉·福特已经与戈恩接触，一旦戈恩与通用的谈判陷入僵局，即商讨结盟事宜。

戈恩说：“我从一开始就强调，在北美扩大结盟具有意义。这里存在着巨大的商机。”日产是美国市场的主要参与者，但雷诺在20世纪80年代后期将其在美国汽车的股份卖给克莱斯勒后退出市场。由于克莱斯勒现在是德国戴姆勒-克莱斯勒公司的一部分，所以

companies are. In a speech in Paris shortly after his meeting with Wagoner, Ghosn said he is still intent on seeking a North American partner, even if the talks with GM don't pan out. Although he said he can be patient, Ghosn's determination to expand the alliance naturally shifts attention to Ford Motor, which, like GM, is struggling under intense competitive pressure. Ford Chairman William C. Ford Jr is said to have contacted Ghosn about forming an alliance should the talks with GM falter[①].

"I said from the beginning that the expansion of the alliance in North America makes sense," said Ghosn. "There is a lot of value there." Nissan is a major player in the American market, but Renault withdrew in the late 1980s after selling its interest in American Motors to Chrysler. With Chrysler now part of the German Daimler-Chrysler , Ford is the only potential domestic partner for Nissan and Renault in North America.

Ghosn added, however, that Renault and Nissan will continue to focus the talks on GM for now. "We will not divide ourselves on many fronts. We will pursue this discussion. I think the opportunity is there and there are a lot of synergies there that you can unlock," said Ghosn.

He added that while Renault currently has no plans to resume car sales in the U.S., if its alliance with Nissan is expanded to North America, then of course it will create a lot of opportunity. "I always said if you want to be a global player, you must be represented in all markets," Ghosn said.

(733 words)

① falter [ˈfɔːltə] *vi.* 犹豫，支吾

福特只是日产和雷诺公司在北美的潜在国内伙伴。

戈恩补充说，无论如何，雷诺和日产将会继续专注与通用目前的谈判。戈恩认为，“我们不会让自己分成多条阵线。我们将继续这场谈判。我认为机会是存在的，你可以找到很多协同优势”。

他补充说，雷诺近期没有在美国恢复汽车销售的计划，如果与日产的结盟扩大到北美，当然会创造出很多机会。戈恩声称：“我总是说，如果你想成为一名全球参与者，就必须成为所有市场的代表。”

知识链接

Renault 法国雷诺公司。是一家法国车辆制造商，成立于 1899 年，由名叫路易雷诺、马塞尔雷诺和费尔南雷诺的三个兄弟所创。雷诺生产的车辆种类有小型车、中型车、休旅车、大型车等。雷诺的图形商标是四个菱形拼成的图案，象征雷诺三兄弟与汽车工业融为一体。

Nissan 日产汽车公司创立于 1933 年，总部位于日本东京。它是日本三大汽车制造商之一，也是世界十大汽车公司之一。目前日产旗下拥有众多高级轿车品牌，诸如 INFINITY（无限）、CEFIRO（风度）、CEDRIC（公爵）等。车坛有“科技的日产、销售的丰田”之说法。

题　记

制约公司发展的羁绊在于面对新的经济政策和企业危机时，人们总会根据自身的文化背景做出不同的解读。美国公司董事会受《萨班-奥西利法案》的影响，为避免企业重蹈安然公司和世通公司破产的覆辙，着手推行董事长-总裁的职责分工制和废除董事会的“交错董事任期”。但改变职业经理人和公司所有人之间的权力平衡并非一蹴而就之事，缓慢的进展让人仿佛雾里看花，不知是进是退。韩国政府处心积虑向外国人推销本国最混乱不堪的大公司。它诱导通用汽车公司购买已经破产的大宇汽车公司。但急需现金的存储类芯片巨人海力士公司的董事会又断然拒绝了美国美光科技公司的收购建议。这种欲进又退的踯躅是政府夺人眼球的炒作，还是企业欲擒故纵的策略，让期待海外并购重燃行业希望的市场充满揣测和幻想。

One Step Forward, One Step Back

The annual review of American company board practices by Korn/Ferry, a firm of headhunters, is a useful indicator of the health of corporate governance. The recent review shows that the Sarbanes-Oxley act, passed to try to prevent a repeat of corporate collapses such as Enron's and WorldCom's, has had an impact on the boardroom-though at an average implementation cost that Korn/Ferry estimates at $ 5.1m per firm.

Two years ago, only 41% of American firms said they regularly held meetings of directors without their chief executive present; this year the figure was 93% . But some things have been surprisingly unaffected by the backlash① against corporate scandals. For example, despite a growing feeling that former chief executives should not sit on their company's board, the percentage of American firms where they do has actually edged up, from 23% last year to 25% this year.

Also, disappointingly few firms have split the jobs of chairman and chief executive. Another survey of American boards published by A. T. Kearney, a firm of consultants, found that last year 14% of the boards of S

① backlash [ˈbæklæʃ] *n.* 强烈反对

进一步，退一步

猎头公司“光辉国际”推出美国公司董事会年度评论是了解公司治理状况的有效指南。近期发表的年度评论表明，据光辉国际估算，虽然每家公司的平均执行成本达 510 万美元，但《萨班-奥西利法案》的通过对董事会已经产生了的影响，该法案旨在避免企业重蹈安然公司和世通公司破产的覆辙。

两年前，只有 41%的美国公司承认，他们会在首席执行官不在场的情况下定期举行董事会；今年这一数字达到了 93%。但令人惊异的是，对公司丑闻的强烈反对却没有影响到某些事情的发展。例如，虽然越来越多的人认为前任总裁不应该继续留在董事会里，但美国公司董事会中前任总裁的比率不降反升了，从去年的 23%升至今年的 25%。

另外，将董事长和总裁的职务区分开来的公司很少，这一点令人颇为失望。“A. T. 卡尼”咨询公司发布的另一份对美国董事会的调查发现，去年标准普尔 500 强公司中，有 14%的董事会已经进行了职务分工，另有 16%的董事会表示计划这么做。但今年总体只有 23%的公司采取了行动。麦肯锡公司的咨询师早些时候发布的一项调查发现，70%的美国董事和投资人支持职责分工制的想法，而这在欧洲早已是行业惯例了。

&P 500 firms had separated the roles, and a further 16% said they planned to do so. But by this year only 23% overall had taken the plunge. A survey earlier by consultants at McKinsey found that 70% of American directors and investors supported the idea of splitting the jobs, which is standard practice inEurope.

Another disappointment is the slow progress in abolishing "staggered" boards—ones where only one-third of the directors are up for re-election each year, to three-year terms. Invented as a defence against takeover, such boards, according to a new Harvard Law School study by Lucian Bebchuk and Alma Cohen, are unambiguously "associated with an economically significant reduction in firm value".

Despite this, the percentage of S &P 500 firms with staggered boards has fallen only slightly—from 63% last year to 60% this year, according to the Investor Responsibility Research Centre. And many of those firms that have been forced by shareholders to abolish the system are doing so only slowly. Merck, a pharmaceutical① company in trouble over the possible side-effects of its arthritis drug, is allowing its directors to run their full term before introducing a system in which they are all re-elected annually. Other companies' staggered boards are entrenched② in their corporate charters, which cannot be amended by a shareholders' vote. Anyone who expected the legislation to bring about rapid change in the balance of power between managers and owners was, at best, naive.

The government is desperate to sell the most troubled ofSouth Korea's

---

① pharmaceutical [ˌfɑrməˈsutikl] *adj.* 制药学的

② entrench [inˈtrɛntʃ] *vt.* 确立,牢固

另一件令人失望的事情就是董事会在废除“交错董事任期”方面进展缓慢，即每年只改选三分之一的董事，而每一届董事的任期是三年。依据吕西安·贝布查克和阿尔玛·科恩的一份最新哈佛法学院研究，这种为了防止公司权力被接管而发明的董事会显然“与公司价值在经济上的显著下降有关”。

尽管如此，标准普尔500强公司中有交错董事任期的董事会比例只略有下降，“投资人责任研究中心”的数据显示，该比率仅从去年的63%降至今年的60%。许多被股东施压要求放弃这一制度的公司现在只是缓慢地着手这一工作。默克制药公司允许其董事任期到届满，然后再引入每年将所有人重新选任一遍的制度。该公司曾因其生产的关节炎药物可能有副作用而陷入困境。其他公司根据公司章程确立交错董事任期董事会，股东投票不能改变他们的身份。如果有人期望立法会迅速改变职业经理人和公司所有人之间的权力平衡的话，那么他未免太天真了。

韩国政府处心积虑向外国人推销本国最混乱不堪的大公司。部长们认为，这是一种最佳的方式，能够加快经历亚洲金融危机之后的公司调整结构，为更加稳定持续的经济增长扫清障碍。经过与外商断断续续的数月谈判，政府的计划向前跨了一大步，随后又退了相同的一大步。

通用汽车公司（GM）签署了一份合同，购买已经破产的大宇汽车公司。但是，急需现金的存储类芯片巨人海力士公司的董事会断然拒绝了美国的一家竞争对手——美国美光科技公司的收购建议，此举令市场大为震惊。美光科技公司曾出价约34亿美元购买海力士公司的核心芯片业务，并在非存储类芯片业务占少数股份。分析

big companies to foreigners. This, ministers believe, is the best way to accelerate the corporate restructuring begun in the wake of the Asian financial crisis, and to clear the way for more sustainable economic growth. After months of on-off talks with foreign suitors, the government's plans moved a big step forward, and then an equally big step back.

General Motors (GM) signed a contract to buy the bankrupt Daewoo Motor. But the board of Hynix, a cash-strapped memory-chip giant, shocked the markets by rejecting a proposed takeover by Micron Technology, an American competitor. Micron had offered to pay about $3.4 billion for Hynix's core memory business, and to take a minority stake① in the non-memory arm. Analysts predict that the government will put pressure on creditors to rescue a deal with Micron or seek a new buyer.

GM's deal with Daewoo Motor marks the end of an even longer and more painful process. Ford almost bought the car maker two years ago, but pulled out after deciding that Daewoo would be too hard to turn round. GM had been talking with Daewoo for over a year. It has agreed to buy two of the company's four domestic car plants, a factory in Vietnam, a parts unit in the Netherlands and nine overseas sales arms (all in Europe except one, in Puerto Rico of all places). Between them, the two domestic factories can churn out② a combined 530,000 cars and 30,000 commercial vehicles a year.

GM has struck a good deal. Together with various undisclosed

---

① stake [steik] *n.* 股份,尤指金融股

② churn out (以自动方式)大量产出

人士预测，政府将对债权人施压，以拯救与美光公司的这笔交易，或者另辟蹊径，寻找别的买主。

通用汽车公司与大宇汽车公司的交易结束了一段甚至更长、更痛苦的过程。两年前，福特公司差点就购买了这家汽车制造厂，但发现很难使大宇汽车公司起死回生后知难而退。通用汽车公司与大宇汽车公司进行了一年多的谈判。通用公司同意购买大宇公司四家国内汽车制造厂中的两家、位于越南的一家工厂、位于荷兰的一家零配件制造厂和九家海外分厂(除波多黎各一家制造厂外，其余的都在欧洲)。它们中，国内两家制造厂每年可生产53万辆组合汽车和3万辆商用汽车。

通用汽车公司做成了一笔大买卖。它将与各种不愿透露身份的合作伙伴一起拥有新公司，暂时命名为通用-大宇公司，并持股67%。这家美国汽车制造商将为其拥有的42%的股份支付2.51亿美元，但它也将承担大宇汽车公司5.73亿美元的债务。此项收购是通用汽车公司全球扩张战略的关键部分。在相当一段时期内，通用公司一直试图巩固它在亚洲的地位。人们普遍认为，购买韩国现存的一家公司是通用公司的当务之急，因为每年的汽车进口量只占国内销售总量150万辆的3%。通用公司希望利用大宇公司的生产线制造廉价汽车，并用大宇商标在大部分市场销售。

但是通用汽车公司还要做大量的工作，才能重塑大宇汽车被损坏的形象，并重建国内市场份额。大宇原先的市场份额在以前达到37%的高峰后，一直停留在10%左右。通用汽车公司英国子公司沃克斯豪尔跑车部前任首席执行官、目前已被任命但尚未上任的通用-大宇公司首席执行官尼克·赖利认为，既然已经敲定了这笔交易，

partners, it will hold a 67% stake in a new company, tentatively named GM-Daewoo. The American car maker will pay $ 251m for its own stake of 42% , but it will also assume $ 573m of Daewoo Motor's debts. The acquisition is a key part of GM's global expansion. The company has been trying to strengthen its foothold in Asia for some time. Buying a presence in South Korea was seen as particularly urgent, since imports account for only 3% of the 1.5m cars sold in the country each year. GM hopes to use Daewoo's production lines to make budget cars that will be sold under the Daewoo brand in most markets.

But GM has much work to do to rebuild Daewoo's damaged brand image and domestic market share, which hovers around 10% after reaching a high of 37% before. GM has to fill holes in product lines by introducing sport-utility and multi-purpose vehicles, says Nick Reilly, former chief executive of Vauxhall, GM's British subsidiary, and chief-executive-designate of GM-Daewoo now that he has sealed the deal. His management team can expect trouble from South Korea's aggressive unions along the way. In a sign of things to come, the signing ceremony was moved to a secret location after a group of union activists occupied the hotel where it was due to take place.

(910 words)

通用公司就必须填补生产线的空缺，引进运动赛车和多功能汽车。赖利的管理团队预期会遭遇来自韩国工会的强烈攻击。 在签署相关文件时，一群工会激进分子占领了仪式签署所用宾馆，签署仪式被迫转到一个秘密地点。

知识链接

Hynix 海力士半导体公司成立于1983年，是韩国一家以生产和提供像电脑和移动产品等IT设备必需的DRAM和NAND闪存为主力产品的企业，占据世界第二大内存芯片市场，并提供世界最小、最高速、最低电压的内存半导体。

VAUXHALL 沃克斯豪尔汽车公司，1903年开始制造汽车，1925年被美国通用汽车公司收购，为通用在英国的子公司。目前是英国产量较大的轿车厂商之一。

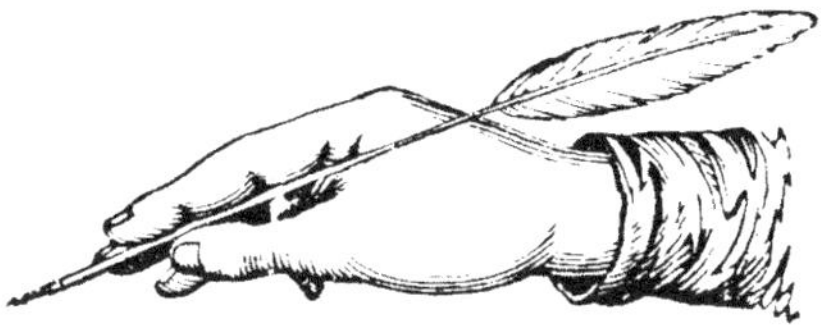

题 记

在股票市场下跌、信贷市场冻结以及不断增长的全球经济危机挤压之下，中小企业因为融资难、税负高、生产成本不断增加，面临着举步维艰的生存困境。小企业主们绞尽脑汁，求助美国联邦中小企业管理局，希望尽早选择最合适自己的脱困路径，实现自身的突破和转型。银行贷款数量的大幅下降使小企业主们人心惶惶，但他们仍然战战兢兢地等待着需要好几个月的时间才能生效的紧急救助和贷款风险补偿。小企业主们也在精打细算，削减无关紧要的开支，重新评估营销预算，并创造性地使用现金流。小企业主们还在试图突破前所未有的生存瓶颈和竞争压力，闯关海外市场，驾驭全球化这盘棋。平民化和个性化、灵活性与专业性、创造力和责任感造就了地球上适应能力最强的动物——小企业主。

How Small Business Owners Can Cope with the Crisis

Don't wait for that bailout[①] to take effect. Manage your credit, watch costs, think globally, and hang on until a recovery materializes. Record financial bailouts are followed by historic stock market drops, frozen credit markets, and a growing global economic crisis. Each day seems to bring a new round of bad news, and there's no end in sight. How will small companies be affected by the bailout that passed last week—and by this week's events? And how should they respond?

Chad Moutray, chief economist at the U. S. Small Business Administration, says small business owners are scared like everyone else. "A lot of them are sitting on their hands at this moment, which is no different from what we've seen all year long in surveys. When asked what they're going to do during the next three months, small business owners are saying: 'Not hiring, not investing in the business, and not expanding.' I suspect this will continue to be the case."

---

① bailout [ˈbeilaut] *n.* 紧急援助(尤指经济上的援助)

小企业主如何应付危机

不要等待紧急救助。管好你的银行存款，关注成本，放眼全球，并坚持到正在实现的经济复苏。创纪录的金融救助之后，出现了历史性的股票市场下跌，信贷市场冻结，以及不断增长的全球经济危机。每一天似乎都带来了新一轮的坏消息，这种状况的改变遥遥无期。上周已经实施的救助和本周的活动将对小企业产生怎样的影响呢？他们又应该如何应对？

美国联邦中小企业管理局的首席经济学家查德·穆特雷认为，小企业所有者和其他人一样吓得要命。“此刻他们很多人都束手无策，这与我们在年度调查中看到的没有什么不同。当问起他们在未来三个月内会做些什么时，小企业主们说：‘不雇人，不做商业投资，不扩张。’我怀疑这种状况会一直持续下去。”

小企业发展中心协会的主席唐纳德·威尔逊认为，企业家们都在与全国各地的企业开发中心联系，请求帮助以获得贷款，或管理他们现有的商业贷款，但做到这一点并不容易。威尔逊说：“仅本财政年度，中小企业管理局的贷款数量就大幅下降，用于这些贷款的美元数量跌至11%到15%。坦白地讲，我们的客户都很害怕，特

Donald Wilson, president of the Association of Small Business Development Centers, says entrepreneurs are contacting SBDCs around the country to ask for help getting loans or managing their existing business loans, butit's not easy. "Just this fiscal year, the number of SBA loans are down substantially and the dollar volume on those loans is down 11% to 15%," Wilson says. "Frankly, our clients are scared, particularly the retailers who are realizing they'll probably see very minimal growth—if any-this holiday season."

Bailout results will take months. With credit still very tight, Wilson says, "our counselors are telling them to look at cutting extraneous① expenses, reevaluate their marketing budgets, and get creative with their cash flow. If consumer spending is down, and you have a normal inventory request every few months, maybe you don't have to order as much now, based on your historical economic data." Many people are confused about why credit is still frozen, given that Congress just approved such a massive federal bailout package. But it will not have an impact until implemented, Moutray says, which is likely to take months.

Of course, not all small business lending has stopped. Eric Aanes, principal of Titus Wealth Management, a financial planning firm based in Larkspur, Calif., says local banks have been advertising that they are still making loans to established businesses. "I went down to try it out and when they looked over my application, they wanted to give me

---

① extraneous [ikˈstreiniəs] *adj.* 无关的

别是零售商，他们意识到今年假日旺季如果有增长的话，也很可能微不足道。”

紧急救助的结果需要好几个月的时间才能生效。威尔逊认为，信贷仍然非常紧张，“我们的顾问告诉他们，要削减无关紧要的开支，重新评估营销预算，并创造性地使用现金流。如果消费者的开支下降，那么每隔几个月就会有正常的库存需求，可以根据公司历史上的财政资料做出统计，也许不用现在就预定这么多”。许多人都很困惑，既然国会刚刚通过了这样一个大规模的联邦紧急援助方案，为什么信贷仍然不能解冻。穆特雷认为，在实施救助前它不会产生影响，这可能需要几个月的时间。

当然，并非所有小企业的贷款都已停止。泰特斯财富管理公司的总裁埃里克·安尼斯认为，当地银行已经打出广告，宣布他们继续给地位稳固的企业贷款。泰特斯财富管理公司是一家总部设在加州拉克斯珀的财务规划公司。他说：“我前去试了一下，他们审查了我的申请之后，答应给我10万美金。所以它还是起作用的。”

安尼斯还表示，他的许多小企业客户都做得很好。他说：“一个客户售出了40万美元的锯，还接到了来自欧洲的新订单，所以他们是没有问题的。我的客户名单里还有一家代理经营的小服装公司，也做得还不错。”

但是，对那些公司受到损害或者迫切需要贷款的小企业主来说，可能会有一段时间度日如年。一位多年的企业家及麻省理工学院斯隆管理学院的管理学教授霍华德·安德森说，这些企业家可能

$ 100,000," he says, "so it does work."

Aanes also says many of his small business clients are doing well. "One client sells $ 400, 000 saws and they're seeing new orders fromEurope, so they're not having issues. And I also have in my client list a small apparel company that factors and they are doing fine," he says.

But for small business owners whose firms are suffering—or whose loans have been called-times may be tough for a while. Howard Anderson, a long-time entrepreneur and management professor at Massachusetts Institute of Technology's Sloan School of Management, says those entrepreneurs may need to live by an old New England adage①: "Use it up, wear it out, make it do, or do without." Small businesses, squeezed all year between rising expenses and reduced demand, are likely to be the first to cut employees and growth—sometimes foolishly. "We often take it in the chops when our bigger customers delay their payments," he notes. "At times like these, the most important person in your company is your credit manager. And if you don't have one, you've got to become one yourself."

Entrepreneurs are most likely to sleep well when no single client represents more than 10% of their business, notes Anderson: "If one of your big clients catches cold, you could get pneumonia② and die." It's tempting to rely on one large customer to make most of your sales, says Ron Adair, a partner at the Resource Group, a Glendale Calif.-based

---

① adage [ˈædidʒ] *n.* 格言

② pneumonia [njuːˈməunjə] *n.* 肺炎

需要一句老式的新英格兰格言来维系生存："用完它，用尽它，让它做，没有它也要做。"小企业一年到头受到费用不断上升和需求减少的挤压，在裁员和增速放缓方面首当其冲，这种做法有时很愚蠢。他指出："我们往往在大客户延迟还款时裁员。在这种时候，公司里最重要的人就是信用部经理。如果你没有信用经理，那么你就只能自己担任这个角色。"

客户代表的业务一个都不超过10%时，企业家极有可能睡个好觉。安德森指出："如果你的大客户患了感冒，你就可能感染肺炎，乃至死亡。"资源集团的合伙人罗恩·阿代尔认为，依靠大客户完成大部分销售极具诱惑。他的公司位于加州的格兰岱尔市，主营财务规划，为许多小企业主提供服务。"这样做容易开发票，容易订货，容易控制仅有的一个关系。但是，如果有一个客户掌控了你的经营，那么一旦这个客户陷入困境，你也会跟着倒霉。"

那些没有拿到新贷款或贷款已被缩减的小企业主们可能需要在公司投入更多的股权。安德森说："首要和唯一的规则是确保公司不会耗尽资金。减少库存、扩展支付条款、加快应付款的结算、缩减未来的计划开支，这些都是你必须做的。"

中小企业管理局的穆特雷认为，这也许是重新审视企业的时候："在出口市场上有很多的机会。要么进军国际贸易，要么勒紧你的腰带，也许就在此一举。在接下来的几个月或几年中，只要抓住若干机会，事情一定有所好转。要确保你到时能处于有利的位置，及时采取行动。"

financial planning firm that serves many small business owners. "It's easy to invoice, easy to do the books, and easy to control just one relationship. But if you have a client that has a controlling position over your business and that client experiences some hard times, you'll really be suffering."

Small business owners who can't get new credit or whose credit has been reduced may need to put more of their own equity into their companies. "Your first and only rule is to make sure your company doesn't run out of money," Anderson says. "Reduce inventory, extend terms you pay out, speed up payables, cut future plans—do what you have to do."

The SBA's Moutray says this may be the time to reevaluate your business: "There are opportunities out there in the export market. It may be time to look at international trade, or it may be time to tighten your belt. Just know that at some point in the next few months or years, things will turn around. And you want to make sure you're in a position to act then."

Anderson is certain that most small business owners will persevere, despite the difficult times. "Small businessmen are very adept and they are total pragmatists. Having run a business for 30 years, I can say that the small business owner is the most resilient① animal on earth."

(887 words)

---

① resilient [riˈziliənt] *adj.* 不屈不挠的

安德森相信，尽管处在困难时期，大多数小企业主仍然锲而不舍。“小商人都非常精明，他们是不折不扣的实用主义者。根据我经营企业30年来的经验，我可以说，小企业主是地球上适应能力最强的动物。”

知识链接

The U. S. Small Business Administration 美国联邦中小企业管理局(简称SBA)于1953年创建，1958年被美国国会确定为“永久性联邦机构”。局长由总统任命，直接向总统负责和汇报工作，全国10个地区局的负责人也全部由总统任命。中小企业管理局的主要任务是听取中小企业的意见及需求，及时向总统报告，并就保护中小企业的权益向联邦政府提出政策建议，促进小企业的健康发展。美国中小企业管理局总部设在华盛顿，在美国十大城市设有分局，有69个地区办公室，17个分支办公室，960多个服务点，员工总人数超过4 000人。

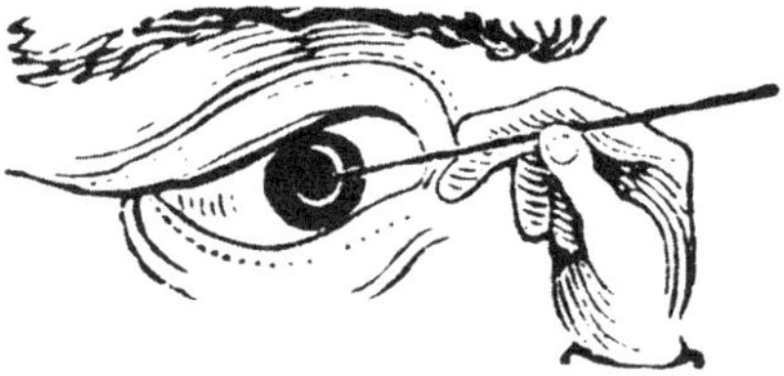

题 记

互联网超越了时间和空间的限制，将现代商战推向了新的网络平台。能源公司可以在过去装扮成农夫，不费吹灰之力将农民的土地掠为己有，而面对熟悉网络的私屋房主，只能是落荒下马，苟延残喘。私屋房主们采用了适于网络的商战策略：统一指挥原则，即建立网站，帮助人们了解自己的选择权；集中兵力原则，即在主网站上设立分板块，提高网络的点击率；目标明确原则，即他们仍然拥有深埋在马塞勒斯南段的天然气矿藏开采权；计划与计算原则，即在网站放置谷歌地图的特写，显示最新的租赁信息、被提议的矿井地点和基础设施的位置；创新与应变原则，即主动扩大链接，和更多的人在网络平台交流，让他们关注后院天然气井的影响情况。网络俨然成为商战中才华横溢的智谋之士，带领一批熟悉网络的私屋房主在捍卫自己财产的阵地上冲锋陷阵。

Web-Savvy Homeowners vs. Landmen

In the pantheon① of American mythology, the oil company "landman" is legendary. The archetype is Daniel Day-Lewis as the ambitious, conniving② Daniel Plainview in There Will be Blood, a smooth-talking, seemingly friendly fellow who, in the short space of time it takes to sip a cup of coffee on the front porch, persuades a dirt farmer to sell his mineral rights for a song. But those kind of landmen exist only in the movies nowadays. There is no sweet-talking your way into a deal in these times. Today's energy company landmen must deal with Texas soccer moms with their own websites and Pennsylvania dairy farmers/bloggers, all armed with Google maps and Excel spreadsheets. The domestic gas-exploration business has undergone a revolutionary face-lift.

For example, landmen showed up late last year in Wayne County, Pa., lured by the possibilities of huge gas reserves in the Marcellus Shale. But Ron Stamets, a website developer who moved to the country from urban New Jersey because he liked the rural lifestyle, heard about it and helped set up a quickie website to help his neighbors understand their options. No

① pantheon [ˈpænθiən] *n.* 万神殿

② conniving [kəˈnaiviŋ] *adj.* 纵容的;默许的

熟悉网络的私屋房主与农夫之战

在美国神话的万神殿里，石油公司的“农夫”是个传奇。丹尼尔·戴·刘易斯是《血色将至》里那个雄心勃勃、城府颇深的丹尼尔·普莱恩维尤扮演者，影片中的丹尼尔·普莱恩维尤谈吐优雅、表面上为人友善，他利用在前门走廊上品尝咖啡的短暂片刻，说服了一个自耕农为一首歌而出售了自己的采矿权。但是，这种农夫目前只可能出现在影片中。在当今这个时代，甜言蜜语的方式根本做不成生意。能源公司的农夫们现在要与自己有网站的得克萨斯州中产阶级的妇女们打交道，与宾夕法尼亚州的奶农或博主们做生意，而他们全都配备了谷歌地图和 Excle 电子表格。国内天然气勘探行业已经发生了翻天覆地的变化。

例如，受马塞勒斯页岩可能存在大量天然气储备的诱惑，农夫去年晚些时候在宾夕法尼亚州韦恩县现身。但是，由于喜欢乡村生活而从新泽西州城区搬来此地的网站开发者罗恩·史塔曼兹听说之后，匆忙建立了一个网站，帮助邻居了解他们的选择权。这儿的交易变得不容易了。马塞勒斯的租赁价格暴涨，从一英亩 20 美元涨到好几百美元。史塔曼兹说，他的网站 www. pagaslease. com 点击率也是一样，飙升到每天 10 万次。这个网站还创办了好几个“子板块”，关注天然气勘探引起的经济、环境和税收影响。大部分成员

easy deals here. Marcellus lease prices ballooned, from $ 20 to hundreds of dollars an acre. So have the hits on his website, www.pagaslease.com, with as many as 100,000 a day, Stamets says. The site has also given birth to several "child boards" that focus on detailed tech talk about the economic, environmental and tax implications of gas exploration. The goal for most members is twofold: What's in it for me, and how am I going to protect the other resources that I've enjoyed for so long?

That kind of knowing, if not calculating, the market by landowners is what the energy industry faces, especially now when many of their rigs are going up in suburban and even urban areas like Fort Worth, Texas, or places like the rolling farmland of western Pennsylvania, where East Coast city dwellers have summer homes or send their kids to camp. And one need not be an urbanite① or a suburbanite to profit from the Web support. In neighboring West Virginia, landowners have discovered, thanks to Stamets and others, that just because their fathers and grandfathers may have signed away coal rights, they still maintain mineral rights to natural gas deep within the southern section of the Marcellus. Similar knowledge, once out of reach, has sparked leasing frenzies in Michigan, Louisiana, Arkansas, Colorado and West Virginia.

What do the websites provide their users, be they hungry to sell or angling② to fight off landmen? Stamets offers information on pricing and leasing, and even photographs of drilling rigs to illustrate just what a well next door to the dairy barn might mean. The site also has a Google map

---

① urbanite [ˈɜːbənait] *n.* 都市人

② angling [ˈæŋgliŋ] *n.* 钓鱼;钓鱼术

只有两个目的：我在里面会获得什么，以及我该如何保护我已经享受了这么久的其他资源？

如果不算计这种心照不宣，土地所有者的市场就是能源行业面临的市场，尤其是现在，很多钻探设备正在向郊区发展，已经到达得克萨斯州沃思堡这样的城市，抑或宾夕法尼亚州西部连绵起伏的农田，东部沿海城市的居民在这些地方有避暑的房屋，或者送孩子来此露营。人们无需在意他是城里人还是郊区人，都能在网络的支持下盈利。在西弗吉尼亚周边地区，土地所有者已经发现，即使他们的父辈和祖辈也许已经签字放弃了煤炭开采权，他们仍然拥有深埋在马塞勒斯南段的天然气矿藏开采权，真得感谢史塔曼兹和其他熟悉网络的人。类似的消息一旦失控，就在密歇根州、路易斯安那州、阿肯色州、科罗拉多州和西弗吉尼亚掀起了租赁狂潮。

网络给用户提供了什么呢？他们是想迫切的卖掉土地还是利用像钓鱼一样的手段来击败农夫？史塔曼兹提供了价格和租赁信息，甚至张贴了钻探设备的图片，用来说明与牛奶场相邻的矿井意味着什么。网站放置了一张谷歌地图的特写，显示最新的租赁信息、被提议的矿井地点和基础设施的位置。史塔曼兹认为，这是一个可以在全国范围内使用的模型。在过去，确定何人于何处拥有何物，意味着花大量的时间查询县法院的地图册。史塔曼兹说："有人告诉我，我们吓得石油公司魂飞魄散。"

史塔曼兹声称，他和宾夕法尼亚州的奶农邻居们根据沃思堡周边的经验正在采取行动。得克萨斯州的石油开发商很早以前就知道了特页岩，但是从达拉斯-沃思堡地区有3.5亿年历史的石头底下提炼约2.5万亿英尺深的天然气，直到上世纪水平钻法技术的出现才

feature that shows up-to-date lease information, proposed well sites and infrastructure locations. It is a model that could be used countrywide, Stamets says. In the old days, locating who owned what and where meant hours of pouring over tract maps at the county courthouse. "Someone told me we are scaring the heck out of the oil companies," Stamets says.

Stamets says what he and his Pennsylvania dairy-farmer neighbors are doing is based on the experiences of Fort Worth neighborhoods. The Barnett Shale site has long been known to Texas oilmen, but extracting what is estimated to be some 2.5 trillion cu. ft. of natural gas from the 350-million-year-old rocks beneath the Dallas-Fort Worth area only became feasible in the last decade with the advent of horizontal drilling techniques. Thirty-five years ago, Fort Worth attorney Bob West helped West Texas landowners negotiate royalty agreements, but he sees a world of difference in contract talks between one or two West Texas landowners and the energy companies back in the 1960s and today's urban explorers. The Internet, particularly blogs, has proved to be a "fabulous① tool" in today's royalty negotiations, West says, empowering landowners and enabling them to form alliances.

There are a significant number of bananas②. Don Young went from being a full-time glass artist to spending 50% of his working hours battling the energy companies via his website, FWcando.org, Fort Worth Citizens against Drilling Ordinance. He first became alarmed at the exploration boom when a prairie reserve near his old, cherished Fort

---

① fabulous [ˈfæbjuləs] *adj.* 难以置信的

② bananas [bəˈnaːnəs] *adj.* 疯狂的，糊涂的

变得可行。35年以前，沃思堡的律师鲍勃·韦斯特帮助西得克萨斯州土地所有者就特许开采权协议进行谈判，但他发现有一个或两个西得克萨斯州土地所有者与能源公司之间的合同谈判在20世纪60年代和现在的城市开发者有极大的不同。韦斯特认为，网络，尤其是博客，在现代谈判中已经被证明是一种“令人难以置信的工具”，它使土地所有者拥有了权力，而且使他们能结成联盟。

有很多著名的网络疯狂人士。邓恩·杨原本是一位全职的玻璃制品艺术家，现在他用50%的工作时间在他的FWcando. org网站与能源公司作战。FWcando. org的意思是“沃思堡市民反对采权条例”。当他邻近的一个草原保护区受到威胁的时候，他率先对勘探热潮发出了警告。沃思堡的这片土地是那么的古老而又令人魂牵梦绕。他开始以印刷传单并分发给邻居的方式进行反抗，并很快建了一个网站，保持信息的畅通。杨说，这个网站不但是沃思堡居民的交流平台，让他们关注后院天然气井的影响情况，而且每天还会收到全国不同群体发来的电子邮件。他的网站与新墨西哥州、怀俄明州、宾夕法尼亚州、阿肯色州和密歇根州的反钻井拥护者都有链接。

杨声称，他的一些邻居被编入沃思堡文化历史的德州神话吸引，包括《巨人》这类已经制成电影的传说，它讲述了詹姆士·狄恩饰演的一个阴郁而可怜的牧场雇工变成盲目开采油井的大富豪的故事。但是杨和其他的反对者却坚持认为，真正的得克萨斯州——城市里的旧街区和绿树成荫的小径，连绵起伏的草原和附近的小镇，这一切都受到了威胁。杨说：“石油公司觉得这里像西得克萨斯州一样，但它不是。我们正在努力限制事态的发展。”对他而

Worth neighborhood was threatened. He began the fight by printing flyers and distributing them to his neighbors, but he soon set up a website to keep the information flowing. It has not only been a clearinghouse for Fort Worth residents concerned about the impact of backyard gas wells, but it also attracts daily e-mail messages from groups across the country, Young says. His site links to other anti-drilling advocates from New Mexico and Wyoming to Pennsylvania, Arkansas and Michigan.

Young says some of his neighbors are attracted by the sort of Texas mythology that is woven into Fort Worth's cultural history, including legends portrayed in movies like Giant with the brooding poor ranch hand played by James Dean turning into a plutocratic① wildcatter②. But Young and other opponents insist the real Texas-the city's old neighborhoods and tree-lined trails, plus the rolling prairie lands and nearby small towns-are threatened. "The oil companies are acting like it's West Texas here, but it's not," Young says. "We're trying to put a brake on things." For him the fight is personal, sometimes sadly pitting neighbor against neighbor. Young has turned down a $25,000 signing bonus offered for his own land. With daily headlines proclaiming new exploration moves, Young is now committed to focusing his neighbors' attentions on the impact that the accompanying pipelines and service roads will have. Says Young: "The war is not won by them or lost by us yet."

(959 words)

---

① plutocratic [plʊtəˈkrætik] *adj.* 富豪的;有钱有势的

② wildcatter [ˈwaildˌkætə] *n.* 投机分子;盲目开采油井者

言，这是一场个人奋斗，甚至有时是可悲的邻里之争。杨已经拒绝了一份2.5万美元的签约红利，他不愿出售自己的土地。根据每日头条宣布的新一轮勘探行动，杨现在致力于吸引邻居的注意力，让他们关注附带管道和服务道路带来的影响。杨宣称："战争还说不准是他们赢了还是我们输了。"

知识链接

There Will be Blood 《血色将至》。美国电影《血色将至》由保罗·托马斯·安德森执导，丹尼尔·戴·刘易斯主演的电影。影片讲的是矿工丹尼尔·普莱恩维尤因井下作业事故摔断了腿，但他因祸得福，了解到秘密的石油信息，他利用聋童HW欺骗乡民赢得了石油地盘，一举成为石油大亨的故事。

Giant 《巨人》。美国电影《巨人》讲述了28岁的瑞典家具公司床垫推销员布莱恩(保罗·达诺饰)的故事。布莱恩是家里三个儿子中最小的一个，大哥是石油商人，二哥是外科医生，布莱恩显然是最没有出息的那个。为了给自己的生活找到一个目标，布莱恩决定领养一个中国孩子。而就在他计划着此事的时候，一位"快乐"小姐(佐伊·丹斯切尔饰)走进了这家家具店，并躺在了布莱恩卖的床垫上睡着了。这一瞬间，布莱恩坠入了情网，两人开始了吵吵合合的恋爱。

题　记

石油交易商艾伦·邓肯表示，商界的表述比政界更加诚实。用公司在证券交易所上市的相关文件和一个政党的竞选宣言相比，“一个是诚信的表现，另一个则经常是一种欺诈行径”。美国总统候选人麦凯恩要想赢得大选，就必须与投资人合作，运用商务交际的技巧，打破选举平衡，提升自己的高度。投资人阶层是一个庞大的投票集团，他们希望与政客们直接谈论税收，尤其是资本收益和股息。但麦凯恩却缺乏迎合投资人喜好的策略。他与投资人没有联系，他在某种程度上缺乏减税的激情，他忘了宣布企业减税实质上是消费者减税，他还需要提醒投资人高度警觉奥巴马的中产阶级减税政策。投资人的选票很可能左右总统大选日投票的平衡点，哪怕是杯水车薪，也可解救麦凯恩的燃眉之急。

Will McCain Make the Investor Connection?

If he does, it could well tip the balance of this election.

While the presidential candidates were debating in Nashville the Asian stock markets were selling off by 10 percent. Earlier in the day the U.S. market plunged by 500 points. These were big-time drops, yet presidential debaters never talk about the stock market. Nashville was no exception.

Roughly \$ 2 trillion in U.S. shareholder capital has been lost in the past 15 months. Stocks are down 20 percent over the last month alone. Those are nasty hits. Stock market people are very unhappy campers right now. And the bad-news financial statements are now either in the mail or on the kitchen table. But there were no references to investors either by McCain or Obama. This is nuts.

The investor class is a huge voting bloc. Shareholders in recent national elections represented nearly two out of every three votes cast. And most surveys① put the investor-class population at slightly over 100

---

① survey [ˈsəːvei] *n.* 调查

麦凯恩会和投资人合作吗?

如果他这么做，就会打破选举平衡，提升自己的高度。

虽然纳什维尔的总统候选人辩论正在紧锣密鼓地进行，但亚洲股票市场仍跌价 10%。今天早些时候，美国股票市场暴跌 500 点，这是大幅度的下跌，然而总统竞选人却从未提及股票市场。纳什维尔也不例外。

在过去的 15 个月内，美国股东大约有 2 万亿美元的资本消失了。仅上个月股票价格就下降了 20 个百分点。这些都是使人感到难受的打击。股民们现在成了伤心的露营者。无论是在邮件里还是在饭桌上，财政决算的坏消息无处不在。但是，不管是麦凯恩还是奥巴马，他们都没有关注投资人。这太疯狂了。

投资人阶层是一个庞大的投票集团。股东在近期的国民选举中占有约三分之二的选票。大多数调查认为，投资人阶层的人口略超过 1 亿。尽管投资人阶层中的大多数成员都拥有自己的个人退休账户，参与了 401（k）计划和养老金固定收益计划，如州、市的养老基金，但还要包括通过经纪账户的直接投资。

那么，为什么这些总统竞选人没有试图和投资人联系呢? 更显眼的是，为什么麦凯恩也没有做这方面的努力?

这场辩论之后，我咨询了技术计量市场信息公司的瑞格海文·

million. This includes direct investment through brokerage[1] accounts, although the vast majority of investor-class members own IRAs, 401(k)s, and defined-benefit plans, such as state and city pension funds.

So why aren't the presidential contenders trying to connect to investors? More glaringly, why isn't McCain?

After the debate I checked in with TechnoMetrica's Raghavan Mayur, who puts out the respected IBD/TIPP poll. Mayur consistently ranks among the top pollsters in terms of accuracy, including his work on investor preferences. Mayur's data show McCain with a small 45-41 lead over Obama among investors. That's roughly within the poll's margin of error, and for McCain it isn't enough.

Four years ago this September, George W. Bush had a 10-point lead over John Kerry among investors. In November Bush won investors by a 53-42 margin. By this measure, McCain is now way behind. And I suspect it may be a function of his reluctance to talk directly about investor taxes—especially on capital gains and dividends[2].

The Bush tax cuts in this area were very popular among shareholders since they reduced the cost of capital and raised after-tax investment returns. Of course, McCain has pledged to maintain President Bush's investor tax cuts at the current 15 percent rate, while Obama proposes to raise them to at least 20 percent. But McCain seldom talks specifically

---

① brokerage [ˈbrəukəridʒ] *n.* 佣金

② dividend [ˈdividend] *n.* 股息

梅尔，他公布了受人尊敬的民调结果。作为民意调查者，梅尔的准确性一直高居行业榜首，他的投资人参数选择也很精准。梅尔的数据显示，麦凯恩在投资人中的得票率以45：41小胜奥巴马。这个结果粗略包括民调的误差幅度，对麦凯恩来说，这还不够。

四年前，也是这样一个九月，乔治·布什在投资人中以10个点的得票优势领先约翰·克里。在十一月，布什赢得了投资人53：42的投票差额。用这种方式测量，麦凯恩现在已经落后。而且我怀疑，这正是他不愿直接谈论投资人的税收，尤其是资本收益和股息的原因。

布什在这个领域的减税政策很受股东们的欢迎，因为他们减少了资本的成本，增加了税后的投资回报。当然，麦凯恩已经保证维持布什总统目前执行的15%的投资人减税率，而奥巴马却计划至少增加20%的投资人税率。但是，麦凯恩极少提及资本收益和股息，民调数字给人以强烈的印象：他与投资人没有联系。

奥巴马不断地打压企业和成功的高端人群，人们可能认为，投资人会因此拒绝对他投票。但是，梅尔的民意调查并没有证明这一点，为什么呢？也许投资人意识到参议员麦凯恩缺乏减税的激情。

例如，在辩论期间，麦凯恩确实提到他是如何与奥巴马在税收政策上有所不同。麦凯恩甚至一度把奥巴马与胡佛相比。他说："我的朋友们，最后一位在经济困难时期提高税收的总统是赫伯特·胡佛，他还实施了保护主义措施。"麦凯恩后来又说："我要透露点信息，参议员奥巴马，这是个坏消息。因此，请不要增加任何人的税收。"

但是麦凯恩从来没有详细阐述资本收益和股息，他本想教育选

about capital gains and dividends, and the polling numbers strongly suggest he's not connecting with investors.

Obama constantly bashes businesses and successful high-end earners, and one would think investors would be totally turned off by this. But Mayer's polls don't confirm it. Why? Perhaps investors sense a lack of tax-cutting passion from Sen. McCain.

For example, during the debate, McCain did mention how he and Obama differ on tax policy. At one point McCain even compared Obama toHoover. "My friends," he said, "the last president to raise taxes during tough economic times was Herbert Hoover, and he practiced protectionism as well." McCain later said, "I've got some news, Sen. Obama—the news is bad. So let's not raise anybody's taxes."

But McCain never got specific on capital-gains and dividends, and he failed to educate voters on just how important investment is to healthy job-creating businesses.

Ditto for McCain's proposed corporate tax cut. The senator wants to slash the business tax rate from 35 to 25 percent. It's an excellent plan. But McCain doesn't explain how two-thirds of the benefits of a corporate tax cut go to the workforce through higher wages, with the rest then going to shareholders. He also doesn't point out that ordinary folks actually pay the corporate tax, since firms pass this tax cost along in the form of higher prices. So McCain could, in fact, call a corporate tax cut a consumer tax cut. But he's not doing this.

McCain also needs to put investors on red alert about Obama's

民，对合理创造就业机会的企业投资是多么重要，但是他失败了。

与麦凯恩提出的企业减税的做法一样。这位参议员要将商业税率从35%减至25%。这是一个完美的计划。但是麦凯恩没有解释，怎样通过更高的工资将企业税中扣除的三分之二的利润转移到工人手中，而剩余的部分转入股东手中。他也没有指出，实际上是平民百姓支付了企业税，因为企业通过税收成本转嫁带来了更高的价格。所以麦凯恩可以宣布，企业减税实质上是消费者减税。但是他没有这样说。

麦凯恩还需要提醒投资人高度警觉奥巴马的中产阶级减税政策。这位伊利诺斯州参议员的庞大的政府开支计划使他无法减免95%的民众的税收。事实上，麦凯恩应该提醒选民，1992年比尔·克林顿作为候选人时也做出了同样的承诺，但在1993年当上总统时，他食言了。

时间已所剩无几了。投资人阶层的选票看上去仍然待价而沽，如果麦凯恩在十一月胜出，就会让他占据优先权。瑞格·梅尔还没有公布十月份的民调结果，但是他认为，这场竞赛将比主流权威人士想象的更加紧张。给麦凯恩参议员提个醒：投资人的选票很可能左右投票的平衡点。

知识链接

TechnoMetrica 技术计量市场信息公司。全称为 TechnoMetrica Market Intelligence(TMI)，是美国权威的市场研究机构。

middle-class tax cut. The Illinois senator's huge government-spending plans will overwhelm his ability to cut taxes for 95 percent of the people. In fact, McCain needs to remind voters that Bill Clinton made exactly the same promise as a candidate in 1992 before he broke it as president in 1993.

Time's running out. The investor class vote — which still looks up for grabs — has simply got to be a McCain priority if he is to win in November. Rag Mayur doesn't have his October polling results in yet, but he believes the race will be much tighter than mainstream pundits believe. Message to Sen. McCain: The investor vote could well tip the balance.

(778 words)

Defined-benefit plans 养老金固定收益计划。养老金固定收益计划指雇主支持的养老金计划，员工退休或丧失就业能力后可按工龄、职位等因素，确定一个固定的（可按通货膨胀率调整）退休津贴数额，通常按月发放直至受益人去世。

题　记

有人说，“沉默是金”是人类为自己设下的一个怪圈，用语言否定语言的价值。沉默就像龙卷风，蕴藏着暴力杀手的力量，用各种手段遏制展开人际交往的会话。沉默有的时候是暴力，它使用绝对语言，不给人讲话的机会，或者打击人们公开参与谈话的勇气。沉默有的时候是怯懦，它缺乏向权威挑战的勇气，明知医生的处方错误也无人敢问津。沉默有的时候是虚伪，人们不愿开诚布公地谈论对方的表现，因为他们担心对友谊造成严重的危害。沉默有的时候是丑恶，那就是你可以整天与某人谈天说地，但从不谈论需要谈论的事情。沉默有的时候是奴性，美国航天局盛行的“沉默文化”甚至对员工产生了被胁迫感，它是哥伦比亚号航天飞机空难的罪魁祸首。沉默让人在真真假假、虚虚实实的世界中度日如年。沉默并不永远是金。

Silence Is not Always Golden

I grew up in "tornado alley," that stretch of geography up the midsection of Oklahoma and Texas that's a breeding ground for killer storms. The spring I turned 12 we had 63 consecutive days of tornado warnings. That's when a tornado is actually sighted on the ground. In those days, the TV weatherman was pretty good at reporting the weather that had already happened, but his predictions of weather-to-come were spotty at best.

Today's meteorologists are not only better trained, but they also have life-saving technology called Doppler radar. This marvelous tool enables them to track the earliest warning signs of a brewing storm, then predict with pinpoint accuracy when and where the storm will strike. You can do much the same with the storms of everyday relationships.

Good relationships are built on things like trust, caring, and follow-through. And the glue that holds it all together is dialogue. Real dialogue occurs when people feel safe in expressing their views without fear of being judged or ridiculed. Two competing monologues do not make for good dialogue.

So what does that have to do with tornadoes and Doppler radar?

Storms are the enemy of dialogue. Not the wind and rain variety. I'm talking about storms that are spawned① by our own behaviors. There are a

① spawn [spɔːn] *vt.* 造成，大量生产

沉默并不永远是金

我在地处俄克拉荷马州和得克萨斯州中部的“龙卷风之乡”长大，那里是杀手风暴的温床。我12岁那年的春天，我们连续63天在龙卷风的警报中度过。当时龙卷风实际上只是在地面上扫荡。在那些日子里，电视台的气象播报员非常擅长报告已经过往的天气，但预测未来的天气却极为力不从心。

现在的气象学家们不仅受过更专业的培训，还掌握了称为多普勒雷达的救命技术。这种神奇的工具使他们能够跟踪最早的风暴酝酿预警信号，然后精确预测风暴登陆的时间和地点。这样，你每天可以做很多与风暴相关的准备。

建立良好的人际关系需要一定的基础，如信任、关怀以及后期跟进工作。对话是联系这一切的纽带。当人们放心大胆地敞开胸怀表达自己的观点、无畏他人的评判或嘲笑时，真正的对话就应运而生。两段相互竞争的独白不利于造就良好的对话氛围。

那么这与龙卷风和多普勒雷达有什么关系呢？

狂风暴雨是对话的大忌。这里并不是指变化多端的风和雨。我谈论的是我们的行为举止引起的暴风雨。阻碍对话的方式有许多

number of common behaviors that get in the way of dialogue. These dialogue-snuffing behaviors fall under violence and silence.

Conversational violence is not necessarily mean-spirited, ill-intended or even loud. For instance, I recently overheard someone in a meeting say "As any smart manager knows, this is the best option. What do you think, Bob?" The unspoken implication was that if Bob disagrees he must not be "a smart manager."

Other forms of conversational violence include using absolute language, words like "every" and "always", or monopolizing the air time. On the surface, these practices may seem a bit annoying though relatively benign. But they still do violence to the dialogue by tending to shut people down or discourage them from open participation.

One form of conversational silence is "masking," which consists of understating or only selectively revealing our true opinions. Another form of conversational silence is "avoiding" or staying completely away from sensitive subjects. For example, only six people in a large organization received a "Needs Improvement" rating on their performance appraisals. The CEO said his people were pretty good at most everything except holding each other accountable. The problem was sugarcoating①. Rather than talking openly about performance issues that begged for honest discussion, people danced around the subject for fear of jeopardizing friendships.

An interesting thing about conversational silence is that you can talk all day long with someone and still be in silence. In this context, silence doesn't mean you're not talking. It means you're not talking about what needs to be talked about.

---

① sugarcoat [ˈʃugəkəut] *vt.* 裹以糖衣

共同的行为。这些扼杀对话的行为属于暴力和沉默。

会话暴力不一定要采取卑鄙无耻、心怀叵测以至高调喧闹的方式。举例来说，我最近无意中听到有人在会上说："任何聪明的管理人员都知道，这是最好的选择。你觉得呢，鲍勃？"这句话蕴涵的潜台词就是，如果鲍勃不同意，他肯定不是"一个聪明的经理"。

其他形式的会话暴力包括使用绝对语言，如"每一个"和"总是"这样的词汇，或垄断会话时间。从表面上看，这些做法虽然相对温和却似乎有点惹人反感。但他们倾向于不给人讲话的机会，或者打击人们公开参与的勇气，所以他们仍然是在实施对话暴力。

会话沉默的一种形式是"屏蔽"，包括轻描淡写的陈述或只是有选择性地泄露我们的真实意见。会话沉默的另一种形式是"回避"，或完全远离敏感议题。例如，一家大型机构只有 6 人收到"需要改进"的考核鉴定。首席执行官认为，他的下属各方面都很不错，就是缺乏对彼此的责任心。这是对问题的粉饰。人们不愿开诚布公地谈论表现问题，因为这需要诚恳地讨论；他们更愿意围绕主题打个漂亮的擦边球，因为他们担心对友谊造成严重的危害。

会话沉默有一个有趣的现象，那就是你可以整天与某人谈天说地，但还是在保持沉默。这种情况下，沉默并不意味着你不说话。它意味着你不是在谈论需要谈论的事情。

沉默的代价非常昂贵，甚至是致命的。有一个被广泛报道过的事件，一位女士住进医院，她需要做例行的扁桃体切除手术，但结果却是她的脚被截肢了一半。医院至少有 7 位工作人员已经意识到

Silence Is not Always Golden

Silence can be very expensive, or even deadly. In one widely reported case, a woman checked into a hospital for a routine tonsillectomy[①] but had half of her foot amputated. No fewer than seven hospital employees had sensed that something was amiss—for example, the person assembling the surgical instruments knew that an electric saw was not used to remove tonsils—but none of them spoke up to question the doctors giving the orders.

During a planned outage at a nuclear power plant I visited, crews worked two complete shifts before someone on the third shift challenged the supervisor and pointed out that work on a particular project wasn't scheduled until the following year. Oops. The error cost the company more than $ 2 million in lost revenue and outage expenses. Why did it happen? Workers on the first two shifts reported to supervisors who didn't welcome feedback. In other words, the workers simply didn't feel safe in.

And at NASA they have what has been dubbed the "culture of silence" in which some NASA employees felt intimidated[②] to the point of shutting down their repeated warnings of impending danger. This was famously apparent in the case of the Columbia space shuttle disaster.

Two competing monologues do not constitute dialogue. Genuine dialogue occurs when people are comfortable in putting their honest opinions and feelings on the table, when they aren't worried about being judged or ridiculed. In other words, dialogue flourishes only in a "safe" environment.

Genuine listening—with the intent to understand rather than with the

---

① tonsillectomy [tɔnsiˈlektəmi] *n.* 扁桃体切除术

② intimidated [inˈtimideitid] *adj.* 害怕的

有些不对劲，如组装手术器械的人知道，电锯不是用来摘除扁桃体的，但医生下单的时候他们谁也没有提起这个问题。

我参观过一个核电站，在一次计划停机的过程中，两个班次的工作人员已经全部完成了他们的工作，直到第三班才有人对主管提出质疑，指出一个特定的项目在来年的计划上也还没有被安排。真是令人匪夷所思。这个错误使公司损失了200多万美元的收入和停机费用。为何会发生这样的错误？前两班工人的报告交给了不喜欢下属提意见的主管。换言之，工人们只是没有安全感。

美国航天局盛行“沉默文化”，有些员工甚至产生了被胁迫感，关闭了即时预警的多次警告。哥伦比亚号航天飞机空难就是人人皆知的著名案例。

两个相互竞争的独白并不构成对话。当人们舒适地把诚实的看法和情感摆上桌面时，当他们不再担心遭受评判或嘲笑时，他们就开始了真诚的对话。换句话说，对话只有在“安全”的环境中才能畅所欲言。

真诚倾听的目的是理解，而不是试图判断或准备反驳，这是创造和维持会话的最好方式之一。另一个不错的安全手段是欢迎不同的意见。没错，欢迎分歧。许多人习惯性地避免分歧，甚至对有些问题采取完全逃避的态度。这样做就丧失了绝佳的学习机会。

我有一个朋友，各方面都非常有能力和创造力，他经常以这句话拉开话题："让我聪明一点。"他会问我最近读了些什么，发现了哪些有趣或有用的东西。他会问我对当前的新闻事件的看法，或对

intent to judge or to prepare your rebuttal[1]—is one of the best ways to create and maintain safety in a conversation. Another good safety tool is to welcome disagreement. That's right, welcome disagreement. Many people are conditioned to avoid disagreement, even to the point of evading some subjects altogether. Doing so forfeits[2] wonderful opportunities to learn.

I have a friend—exceptionally capable and productive in every way-who frequently starts a conversation by saying "Make me smart on something." He'll ask what I've recently read that I found interesting or helpful. He'll ask my view of current issues in the news, or my opinion on a hot social topic. If I express a view that's different from his he'll say something like, "Oh, that's great, you see it differently. Tell me more about your thinking." He's not only not threatened by disagreement, he recognizes disagreement as a great fulcrum[3] to learning.

One of the great joys of being a human being is the opportunity to interact with and learn from others. That opportunity is enhanced when we behave in ways that make it safe for people to express their true opinions and honest feelings.

Silence is not always golden.

(936 words)

---

① rebuttal [riˈbʌtəl] *n.* 反驳

② forfeit [ˈfɔːfit] *vt.* 丧失

③ fulcrum [ˈfʊlkrəm] *n.* 支点

社会热点话题的意见。如果我表达的观点和他的观点不一样，他就会这样说："噢，好极了，你的想法很不相同。把你的想法再多告诉我一点。"他不仅没有感到分歧的威胁，反而意识到分歧是一个很好的学习支点。

人类最大乐趣之一就是拥有与他人互动和学习的机会。当我们的行为方式使人们能够安全地表达他们的真实意见和诚实情感的时候，这种机会就会增强。

沉默并不永远是金。

知识链接

NASA 美国国家航空航天局（National Aeronautics and Space Administration）是美国负责太空计划的政府机构，总部位于华盛顿哥伦比亚特区。它拥有最先进的航空航天技术，在载人空间飞行、航空学、空间科学等方面为人类做出了巨大的贡献。

题　记

在世界经济长周期的下降通道上，欧洲正在采用工资津贴和失业福利的应对措施来扭转颓势，而美国似乎黔驴技穷，遏制需求和平抑通货膨胀的措施遭遇四面楚歌。欧洲大陆的就业保护法案使新的失业者受到保护，他们收到的津贴大约是工薪损失的三分之二；而美国则遭受了惨重的失业率打击，华尔街的金领们被迫走上街头杂耍卖艺。欧洲的公司利用工资津贴这种廉价的方式，保持在政府开支面前的开放选择权；而美国还在忙于逃离宽松的货币政策和金融衍生品所刺激起来的泡沫。欧洲缓解经济衰退的另一种方式是扩大社会福利制度；而美国政府仅提供6个月的失业福利。市场经济的力量已经显示：美国也许可以领导经济繁荣时期的富有世界，但欧洲已经显示出更强大的能力来应对经济衰退的冲击。

Wage Subsidies and Jobless Benefits

Wage subsidies and fatter jobless benefits have softened the impact of the recession but may yet hurt recovery.

America may lead the rich world in periods of prosperity, but Europe has shown a greater talent for dealing with recession. Unemployment in the euro area has risen by 30% from its pre-crisis levels. America's jobless rate has more than doubled. In Germany, the largest country in the euro zone, output fell far harder than America's during the worst months of the crisis but Germany's unemployment rate barely rose. Consumer spending has held up surprisingly well in a country where high saving is the norm even in good times. "Germany is calm," says one official with satisfaction. By comparison, America is deeply troubled.

What explains the resilience① of continental Europe? Some of it was already built-in. Job-protection laws make it costly for firms to lay off workers, and where posts are sacrificed, the newly unemployed are preserved from penury. They receive benefits worth around two-thirds of their lost salaries in most countries. Only in Italy are benefits anywhere

---

① resilience [riˈziliəns] *n.* 恢复力;弹力

工资津贴和失业福利

工资津贴和较丰厚的失业福利软化了经济衰退的影响，但仍有可能伤害经济的复苏。

在经济繁荣期，美国也许可以领导富有的世界，但欧洲已经显示出更强大的能力来应对经济衰退。欧洲地区的失业率相对危机前的水平已上升了30%。美国的失业率已经增加了一倍多。经济危机最恶劣的几个月里，作为欧元区最大国的德国，其产量下降远远多于美国，但它的失业率几乎没有上升。在这个即便是经济繁荣期高储蓄都很平常的国家里，消费性开支起着好得令人惊讶的作用。一位官员满意地说："德国波澜不惊。"相比之下，美国却深陷危机。

如何解释欧洲大陆的经济反弹？其中有一些约定俗成的因素。就业保护法案使公司裁员的代价很高，所以职位被放弃的地方，新的失业者会受到保护，不至于穷困潦倒。在大多数国家，他们收到的津贴大约是工薪损失的三分之二。只有意大利的补给津贴与美国和英国一样匮乏，那儿的新申请人只能得到其早前收入28%的津贴。欧洲政府对干预也较少疑虑。经济合作与发展组织的一份新报告确认，自衰退冲击以来，有14项提案已投放就业市场。法国比其他任何国家都多，参与了14个项目中的12个项目。

near as skimpy as in America and Britain, where new claimants[1] receive just 28% of their previous earnings. European governments also have fewer qualms[2] about intervention. A new report from the OECD identifies 14 kinds of job-market initiatives put in place since recession struck. France ticks 12 of those boxes, more than any other country.

One policy in particular has helped keep a lid on unemployment. Schemes that subsidize the wages of employees working fewer hours than normal were introduced or expanded in 22 of the 29 countries surveyed by the OECD. Germany had around 1.4m workers on its short-time working scheme, equivalent to a cull[3] of 400,000-500,000 full-time workers. That would add one percentage point to the jobless rate. Countries without these arrangements, such as America, Britain and Spain, have tended to suffer bigger rises in unemployment.

In normal times, wage subsidies would be frowned upon. But in a credit crunch they can be a smart use of fiscal resources. Firms worried about future sales, low on cash and deprived of credit, may too readily fire workers without a subsidy. That would only add to a downward spiral of confidence and spending. In Europe, the state funds generous jobless benefits in any case. Why not instead make it easier for firms to hoard workers and keep a skilled workforce intact for when the economy turns?

All policies have drawbacks, and those that help economies to absorb a shock will also tend to make the damaging effects linger. Subsidizing jobs that are no longer viable will hold back recovery. The flow of workers from

---

① claimant [ˈklemənt] *n.* [贸易] 索赔人;提出要求者

② qualm [kwɑm] *n.* 疑虑;不安

③ cull [kʌl] *n.* 剔除

一项特别的政策帮助掩盖了失业率。根据经济合作与发展组织的报告，该项目为那些工作时间比平时少的员工提供了津贴补助，并在29个国家中的22个国家得以引入或推广。德国约有140万名工人开始执行短工时工作计划，相当于裁员40万至50万全职工人。这将增加1%的失业率。美国、英国和西班牙等没有这些安排的国家往往遭受更惨重的失业率打击。

在正常情况下，工资津贴会引起反对。但在信贷紧缩之时，他们成了明智使用财政资源的方式。公司担心未来的销售，而现金不足和信贷损失又造成了工人被轻易解雇之后却领不到任何津贴。这只会造成信心和消费的螺旋式下降。在欧洲，不管发生什么情况，国家基金都会慷慨地补助失业者。公司要留住有技能的员工，完好无损地保持好劳动力，以备经济好转之用。为什么就不能让这一切变得更容易呢？

所有的政策都有弊端，那些帮助经济化解危机的政策同样也存在挥之不去的破坏性影响。为那些不切实际的工作进行补贴会阻碍经济复苏。从即将倒闭的行业流向新公司的工人也许会受阻。如果补贴的时间太长，短时工作计划对需要萎缩的行业来说可能成为矫揉造作的小道具。比如，西班牙计划付给建筑公司一笔钱，让他们留住工人，在西班牙空宅遍地之时还奢谈这种项目，简直是愚蠢至极。

公司也可以尝试利用工资津贴这种廉价的方式，保持在政府开支面前的开放选择权。可以用精心设计的方案抑制这种情况。在荷兰，公司如果在政策结束的三个月内解雇工人，就必须偿还一半的工资补助。公司注册资助的工人越多，津贴就消耗得越快。瑞

dying industries to new ones may be blocked. If sustained for too long, short-time working schemes can become artificial props[1] for industries that need to shrink. A scheme in Spain, say, to pay construction firms to hoard workers would be madness when there is a glut of empty homes.

Firms may also be tempted to use wage subsidies as a cheap way of keeping their options open at the government's expense. A well-designed scheme can curb this. In the Netherlands, businesses that lay off workers within three months of the scheme's end have to pay back half the subsidy. The more workers that firms register for support, the sooner the subsidy runs out. A Swedish policy to prevent lay-offs due to weak cash flow looks even smarter. Instead of wage support, Sweden gives its firms the option to delay their social-security contributions. A punitive interest charge for firms receiving such help would root out all but the truly distressed. Other countries have trimmed their taxes on jobs in addition to, or instead of, wage subsidies.

Another way of softening recession is to expand the welfare system. Around half of the rich countries in the OECD survey have done so since the crisis began—by raising benefits, making it easier to claim them or providing for longer. Extra money for the jobless is an effective stimulus measure since cash-starved households are likely to spend it. But if benefits are kept high for too long they will make the jobless less keen to search for work. One way of striking a balance between short-term stimulus and long-term incentives is to increase the value of benefits but withdraw them sooner. That is what Poland and the Czech Republic have done. The recession's length has forced America's government to do the opposite. It

---

① prop [prɔp] *n.* 支柱;支持者

典防止公司因资金流转疲软而裁员的政策看起来更加明智。瑞典没有工资津贴，而是给予企业选择权，延迟支付社会保障费用。除了真正受困的公司外，向这些寻找帮助的公司收取惩罚性利息可以帮助根除所有的不利因素。其他国家已经削减了工作税收，以抵消或代替工资津贴。

缓解经济衰退的另一种方式是扩大社会福利制度。根据经济合作与发展组织的报告，自金融危机开始以来，有一半的富裕国家采用这种政策，即通过增加福利，使他们更容易得到补助，或提供补助的时间延长。由于现金紧缺的家庭可能动用这笔资金，针对失业的额外资金是刺激消费的有效手段。但是，如果高额津贴持续的时间太长，又会使失业者不太愿意寻找新的工作。一种平衡短期刺激和长期激励的方式就是增加福利的价值，但必须尽快撤回。波兰和捷克共和国已经这么做了。漫长的萧条期已经迫使美国政府采取了相反的做法。它过去仅提供6个月的失业福利，但它已经扩大了资助面，以防人们陷入贫困。

政府为失业者提供太多的津贴、缺乏激励机制的行为遭到了反对。在失业率很高的时候讨论这个问题似乎显得冷酷无情。根据经济合作与发展组织的报告，在经济深度萧条期，富裕国家的公司提供了相当于员工总数14%~15%的就业职位。由于下岗的雇员增多，净职位数下降，更为慷慨的福利意味着职位空缺增补缓慢，从而推高了失业率。培训、咨询等服务积极帮助人们获得福利，但在经济萧条期也可能被忽视。瑞士和丹麦把失业率和消费政策联系在一起，以确保大量的失业者无法分享大量的定额支出。

来自过去经济严重萧条期的证据表明，失业率下降的速度不太

used to offer just six months of jobless benefits, but has extended its support to stop people falling into poverty.

It may seem heartless to counsel against too much support for the unemployed but incentives matter even when unemployment is high. Firms in rich countries make hires equivalent to some 14-15% of all employment in deep recessions, according to the OECD. Net job creation falls because there are more lay-offs. More generous benefits will mean vacanciesthat are filled less quickly, pushing up unemployment. Active help for those on benefits—training, counselling and so on—can also be neglected in recession. Switzerland and Denmark link spending on such policies to their jobless rates to ensure that a fixed amount of spending is not shared between a larger pool of unemployed.

Evidence from past deep recessions suggests that unemployment is unlikely to fall as quickly as it has risen. Indeed further increases seem likely in Europe, because jobs have not adjusted much to a lower level of GDP. In those circumstances, the temptation to prolong wage subsidies and buttress① benefits will be great. It should be resisted. The unemployment rate in the euro area has risen far less than America, but both are now close to 10% . Pre-crisis rates in Europe were higher precisely because of its rigid jobs markets. It would be a shame if measures that have helped mitigate crisis were left to spoil prospects for recovery.

(983 words)

---

① buttress [ˈbʌtrəs] *vt.* 支持

可能像失业率上升的速度一样快。事实上，欧洲失业率还会进一步攀升，因为就业岗位还没有按低水平的国内生产总值进行调整。在这种情况下，延长工资津贴和支持福利的诱惑也可能是强大的。它应该被抵制。欧元区失业率的上升远远低于美国，但双方现在都接近10%。正是因为其刻板的就业市场，欧洲危机前的失业率更高。如果帮助缓和经济危机的措施最终破坏了预期的经济的复苏，这将会非常遗憾。

知识链接

OECD 经济合作与发展组织(Organization for Economic Co-operation and Development)，简称经合组织，是由30多个市场经济国家组成的政府间国际经济组织，旨在共同应对全球化带来的经济、社会和政府治理等方面的挑战，并把握全球化带来的机遇。经合组织成立于1961年，目前成员国总数34个，总部设在巴黎。

题　记

苹果电脑公司曾经的首席执行官史蒂夫·乔布斯已经远离这个世界，但他创造的商务交际文化仍然渗透在苹果的每一个细胞。欣赏“伟大的威胁者”就是乔布斯留给苹果的思维方式之一。乔布斯本人就是一名“伟大的威胁者”。这位极富传奇色彩的人物20岁时与沃兹在父母的车库里创办了苹果电脑公司，10年后却离奇地被自己创办的公司解雇。经历了商海沉浮的乔布斯再次临危受命、重新执掌苹果之后，凭借独一无二的产品iPod数码音乐播放器令苹果起死回生。相比谷歌“远离邪恶”的广告语、拥抱开放的平台、信任由集体智慧做出的决定等多种理念，乔布斯从不循规蹈矩，他在独裁与个人魅力交织的平台上实现了“胡说八道的英雄过山车”式的平衡。不管是苹果成就了乔布斯，还是乔布斯成就了苹果，他的沉与浮、离与否都与苹果的前途和命运紧密地联系在一起。

An Appreciation of "Great Intimidators"

Despite flouting[1] all the rules of being "evil", Steve Jobs has built one of Silicon Valley's most successful companies. One Infinite Loop, Apple's street address, is a programming in-joke — it refers to a routine that never ends. But it is also an apt description of the travails of parking at the Cupertino, California, campus. Like most things in Silicon Valley, Apple's lots are egalitarian[2]; there are no reserved spots for managers or higher-ups. Even if you're a Porsche-driving senior executive, if you arrive after 10 am, you should be prepared to circle the lot endlessly, hunting for a space.

But there is one Mercedes that doesn't need to search for very long, and it belongs to Steve Jobs. If there's no easy-to-find spot and he's in a hurry, Jobs has been known to pull up to Apple's front entrance and park in a handicapped space. Sometimes he takes up two spaces. It's become a piece of Apple lore—and a running gag at the company. Employees have stuck notes under his windshield wiper: "Park Different." They have also

---

① flout[flaut] *v.* 嘲弄,轻视

② egalitarian [ˈgæliteəriən] *adj.* 主张人人平等的

欣赏"伟大的威胁者"

尽管视所有的规则为"邪恶"，斯蒂夫·乔布斯建立了硅谷最成功的公司之一——苹果电脑公司。苹果电脑公司的地址——"一个无限循环"——是一个编程笑话，它指的是没有尽头的日常工作，但这是对加利福尼亚州库布奇诺停车难的恰当描述。与硅谷的大部分情况相同，苹果的停车场奉行平等主义，经理和公司高层也不能预留停车位。即使开保时捷的资深主管，如果在上午10点后到公司，就得做好围停车场不停打转，找停车位的准备。

可是有一辆奔驰却不费吹灰之力就能找到停车位，这就是斯蒂夫·乔布斯的奔驰。如果停车场车位不好找，斯蒂夫又很着急的话，大家都知道他会把车开到苹果公司的前门入口，停在为残疾人准备的停车处。有时候占两个停车位。这成为苹果公司的轶闻——公司员工之间经常打趣的一件事。员工曾经在斯蒂夫汽车的风挡刮水器下粘贴"另类停车"的纸条。他们还常常把人行道上的最简轮椅标志修改成奔驰商标。乔布斯传说中有名的停车态度反映了他处理事务的方法：他不会循规蹈矩。所有人都熟悉谷歌那条醒目的广告语"远离邪恶"。"远离邪恶"已经成为硅谷的简短使命声

converted the minimalist wheelchair symbol on the pavement into a Mercedes logo. Jobs' fabled attitude toward parking reflects his approach to business: For him, the regular rules do not apply. Everybody is familiar with Google's famous catchphrase, " Don't be evil." It has become a shorthand mission statement for Silicon Valley, encompassing a variety of ideals that—proponents say—are good for business and good for the world: Embrace open platforms. Trust decisions to the wisdom of crowds. Treat your employees like gods.

It's ironic, then, that one of the Valley's most successful companies ignored all of these tenets. Google and Apple may have a friendly relationship—Google CEO Eric Schmidt sits on Apple's board, after all—but by Google's definition, Apple is irredeemably evil, behaving more like an old-fashioned industrial titan than a different-thinking business of the future. Apple operates with a level of secrecy that makes Thomas Pynchon look like Paris Hilton. It locks consumers into a proprietary ecosystem. And as for treating employees like gods? Yeah, Apple doesn't do that either. But by deliberately flouting the Google mantra, Apple has thrived. When Jobs retook the helm in 1997, the company was struggling to survive. Today it has a market cap of $ 105 billion, placing it ahead of Dell and behind Intel. Its iPod commands 70 percent of the MP3 player market. Four billion songs have been purchased from iTunes. The iPhone is reshaping the entire wireless industry. Even the underdog Mac operating system has begun to nibble into Windows' once-unassailable dominance; last year, its share of the US market topped 6 percent, more than double its portion in 2003. It's hard to see how any of this would have happened had Jobs hewed to the standard touchy-feely philosophies of Silicon Valley. Apple creates must-have products the old-fashioned way: by locking the doors and sweating

明，它包含多种理念——倡导者说——对企业、对世界有益的理念：拥抱开放的平台；信任由集体智慧做出的决定；员工就是上帝。

这简直是个极大的讽刺，硅谷最成功的公司之一却忽略了所有的这些宗旨。谷歌和苹果也许关系不错——毕竟谷歌的首席执行官埃里特·施密特是苹果的董事会成员——但按谷歌的定义，苹果无可救药地邪恶透顶，它更像一位过时的工业巨人，而不是具备另类思维的未来企业。苹果在一个保密的平台上运作，这使得托马斯·品钦看起来像帕里斯·希尔顿。它将顾客锁进私有的生态系统。像对待上帝那样对待员工吗？苹果也没有效仿。苹果刻意藐视谷歌的箴言，繁荣稳定地发展。1997年乔布斯再次执掌苹果之时，企业举步维艰。如今它的市值1 050亿美元，超过戴尔，排在英特尔之后。它的iPod音乐随身播放器占据MP3市场70%的份额。40亿首歌已经从iTune卖出。iPhone重塑了整个无线工业。就连名不见经传的Mac操作系统也打破由Windows一统天下的局面：去年，Mac的市场份额高达6%，比2003年翻了一倍多。如果乔布斯遵守硅谷的金科玉律，所有的这些成果都是难以想象的。苹果用老方法创造出必须拥有的产品：关起门来，流血流汗，直到产品完美地脱颖而出。很难想象MacOS和iPhone与微软的Vista操作系统或戴尔的口袋音乐播放器出自同一个委员会设计的流程。如果苹果同样地将iTunes-iPod的主宰权交给外部开发商，公司独一无二的整体服务就变成不受约束的应用软件大杂烩——互联网的剩余部分。想想这样

and bleeding until something emerges perfectly formed. It's hard to see the Mac OS and the iPhone coming out of the same design-by-committee process that produced Microsoft Vista or Dell's Pocket DJ music player. Likewise, had Apple opened its iTunes-iPod juggernaut① to outside developers, the company would have risked turning its uniquely integrated service into a hodgepodge of independent applications—kind of like the rest of the Internet, come to think of it.

And now observers, academics, and even some other companies are taking notes. Because while Apple's tactics may seem like Industrial Revolution relics, they've helped the company position itself ahead of its competitors and at the forefront of the tech industry. Sometimes, evil works. Over the past 100 years, management theory has followed a smooth trajectory②, from enslavement to empowerment. The 20th century began with Taylorism—engineer Frederick Winslow Taylor's notion that workers are interchangeable cogs—but with every decade came a new philosophy, each advocating that more power be passed down the chain of command to division managers, group leaders, and workers themselves. In 1977, Robert Greenleaf's Servant Leadership argued that CEOs should think of themselves as slaves to their workers and focus on keeping them happy.

Silicon Valley has always been at the forefront of this kind of egalitarianism. In the 1940s, Bill Hewlett and David Packard pioneered an approach what business author Tom Peters dubbed "managing by walking around," that encouraged executives to communicate informally with their employees. In the 1990s, Intel's executives expressed solidarity with the

---

① juggernaut [ˈdʒʌgənɔːt] *n.*世界主宰

② trajectory [ˈtrædʒiktəri] *n.*轨道,轨迹

的后果吧。

现在观察家、专家甚至其他公司都前往苹果取经。尽管苹果的战略像是工业革命的老古董，但他们帮助公司超越其竞争对手，跻身技术产业的前列。邪恶有时助你成功。在过去的一百年中，管理理论一直沿袭强制到授权的平稳轨道。20世纪开始实施泰勒主义——工程师佛莱德里克·温斯洛·泰勒的理念，即工人是可相互交换的齿轮——但是每10年就会产生新的管理哲学，全都倡导行政管理系统将权力下放给分管经理、团队领导者和工人。1977年，罗伯特·格林里夫的公仆式领导方式提倡，首席执行官应该把自己当成工人的奴仆，最主要的任务是让他们开心。

硅谷总是在这种平均主义的最前沿。20世纪40年代，比尔·休利特和戴维·帕卡德率先采用被管理学大师汤姆·彼得斯称为“走动管理”的方法，这种管理方法鼓励经理主管人员同员工非正式交谈。20世纪90年代，英特尔的主管们放弃豪华隐蔽的办公室，搬进出口便利的普通隔间，表达了与工程师们之间责任和利益的合伙关系。今天，如果谷歌没有把自己变成员工的格兰列式奴隶，至少也是一名导航者：这个山景区以其福利出名，谷歌有内部按摩，曲棍球比赛，员工随心所欲免费享用美食的自主餐厅。此外，谷歌的工程师有史无前例的自主权，他们可以选择自己想做的项目和合作伙伴。他们被鼓励启用20%的工作周实现自己的软件构想。结果如何？Gmail和Goole News之类产品均是从个人努力起

engineers by renouncing their swanky① corner offices in favor of standard-issue cubicles. And today, if Google hasn't made itself a Greenleaf-esque slave to its employees, it's at least a cruise director: The Mountain View campus is famous for its perks, including in-house masseuses, roller-hockey games, and a cafeteria where employees gobble gourmet vittles for free. What's more, Google's engineers have unprecedented autonomy; they choose which projects they work on and whom they work with. And they are encouraged to allot 20 percent of their work week to pursuing their own software ideas. The result? Products like Gmail and Google News, which began as personal endeavors.

Jobs, by contrast, is a notorious micromanager. No product escapes Cupertino without meeting Jobs' exacting standards, which are said to cover such esoteric details as the number of screws on the bottom of a laptop and the curve of a monitor's corners. "He would scrutinize everything, down to the pixel② level," says Cordell Ratzlaff, a former manager charged with creating the OS X interface. At most companies, the red-faced, tyrannical boss is an outdated archetype, a caricature③ from the life of Dagwood. Not at Apple. Whereas the rest of the tech industry may motivate employees with carrots, Jobs is known as an inveterate④ stick man. Even the most favored employee could find themselves on the receiving end of a tirade. Insiders have a term for it: the "hero-shithead roller coaster." Says Edward Eigerman, a former Apple engineer, "More

---

① swanky [ˈswæŋki] *adj.* 炫耀的,爱出风头的

② pixel [ˈpiksəl] *n.*像素

③ caricature [ˈkærikəˈtʃə] *n.*讽刺画,漫画

④ inveterate [inˈvetərit] *adj.* 根深蒂固的

步。

乔布斯则是一位恶名昭彰的微观管理者。达不到乔布斯的苛刻标准，任何产品难以离开古本蒂诺。规格精准到手提电脑底部的螺丝钉数量和显示器的拐角曲线。曾经负责研发 OSX 界面的前任经理科德·若查夫说，"他检查所有的一切，甚至显示器的像素标准"。在大部分公司，红脸的独裁老板是过时的形象，是对享受多层夹肉三明治生活的讽刺。在苹果却不然。其他技术公司用胡萝卜刺激员工，乔布斯是个顽固成性的人，即使最受欢迎的员工也发现自己在乔布斯长篇激烈的演说之后接受他的观点。内部人士对此有一个专用术语："胡说八道的英雄过山车。"苹果的前工程师爱德华·艾格曼说，"在苹果工作比在其他任何地方都更担心被炒"。但是乔布斯的员工很有献身精神。这是因为他的独裁与他的个人魅力实现了平衡——他可以让设计一个电源的工作感觉像是上帝赋予的神圣使命。麦金塔操作系统的首席设计师安迪·菲茨杰拉德说，乔布斯用"救世主似的热情"感染着他和他的同事。"他可以让每个人展现自己最好的一面"，与乔布斯在设计 OSX 时一起工作过 18 个月的若查夫说道，"我从他那里学到了极多的东西"。

苹果在乔布斯重新掌权后的一系列成功——iMac，iPod，iPhone——颠覆了"工人永远正确"管理流派的幻觉。在古本蒂诺市，创新不是来自娇惯员工和收集浮在表面的泡沫，它是一个激烈艰苦的过程，排斥任何个人感情。一些管理理论家正在接受苹果的

than anywhere else I've worked before or since, there's a lot of concern about being fired." But Jobs' employees remain devoted. That's because his autocracy is balanced by his famous charisma—he can make the task of designing a power supply feel like a mission from God. Andy Hertzfeld, lead designer of the original Macintosh OS, says Jobs imbued him and his coworkers with "messianic① zeal." And because Jobs' approval is so hard to win, Apple staffers labor tirelessly to please him. "He has the ability to pull the best out of people," says Ratzlaff, who worked closely with Jobs on OS X for 18 months. "I learned a tremendous amount from him."

Apple's successes in the years since Jobs' return-iMac, iPod, iPhone-suggest an alternate vision to the worker-is-always-right school of management. In Cupertino, innovation doesn't come from coddling employees and collecting whatever froth rises to the surface; it is the product of an intense, hard-fought process, where people's feelings are irrelevant. Some management theorists are coming around to Apple's way of thinking. "A certain type of forcefulness and perseverance is sometimes helpful when tackling large, intractable problems," says Roderick Kramer, a social psychologist at Stanford who wrote An Appreciation of "Great Intimidators"—including Jobs—for the February 2006 Harvard Business Review.

(1,174 words)

① messianic [ˌmesiˈænik] *adj.*救世主的

思维方式。斯坦福大学的社会心理学家罗德里克·克雷默认为，“在处理重大、棘手的问题时，某种形式的强制力和忍耐力有时发挥作用”。克雷默为2006年的《哈佛商业评论》写过一篇题为《欣赏“伟大的威胁者”》的文章，乔布斯包括在内。

知识链接

Taylorism 泰勒主义指美国著名的管理学家、经济学家弗雷德里克·温斯洛·泰勒(Frederick Winslow Taylor，1856—1915)在20世纪初创立的科学管理理论体系。泰勒认为，企业管理的根本目的在于提高劳动生产率，他指出：“科学管理如同节省劳动的机器一样，其目的在于提高每一单位劳动的产量。”而提高劳动生产率的目的是为了增加企业的利润或实现利润最大化的目标。泰勒被后世称为“科学管理之父”，其代表作为《科学管理原理》。

题　记

一场发源于美国的金融危机，使世界各国对全球化中的国际金融角色看得更加清楚，也使国际金融资本在全世界畅行无阻、自由自在、为所欲为的黄金岁月成为过去。曾几何时，国际金融资本明目张胆地利用全球化，大规模地洗劫那些经济获得了发展、刚刚富裕起来的地方。当国际金融资本在全球攻城略地的时候，世界各国开始了新一轮的顽强抵抗：有的国家严厉整治，有的国家举手投降，有的国家进退维谷。他们迫使国际金融大家改变靠金融洗劫而发财的一贯手段。金融危机减少了开放金融市场自由化的意愿，削弱了资本主义自由市场的信誉，加剧了全球经济的糟糕表现，但全球化也不得不调整近30年来由发达国家主导的模式，重新制定全球化金融规则。这同时也是金融危机对全球化的耐久性做出的最大贡献。

Financial crisis tests durability of globalization

Globalisation has been the great economic and political theme of the past three decades. It has brought the labour supplies of Asia into the world economy. It has transformed the operations of companies and financial markets. But will it survive the financial crisis? One precedent—that of the 1930s—is disturbing enough to give even the optimistic pause.

The first world war damaged, but did not destroy, the globalisation of late 19th and early 20th century. The world economy recovered its vitality in the 1920s. Then came the US stock market crash of 1929 and the financial melt-down of the 1930s. During the great depression, the world chose autarky①. By the late 1930s, the integrated global economy of half a century before was little more than a memory. Will today's prove more robust②?

The good news is that it has already survived terrorism, war and a series of devastating financial crises. As Carmen Reinhart of the University

① autarky [ˈɔːtɑːki] *n.* 自给自足

② robust [rəuˈbʌst] *adj.* 强壮的

金融危机对全球化的耐久性测试

过去30年来，全球化一直是经济和政治的伟大主题。它使亚洲的劳动力供应融入了世界经济。它已经改变了公司和金融市场的运作。但是，它能否在金融危机中生存呢？20世纪30年代有一个先例，它是那么的令人不安，足以使乐观的人窒息。

第一次世界大战破坏了但并未摧毁19世纪末和20世纪初期的全球化。在20世纪20年代，全球经济恢复活力，后来出现了1929年的美国股市崩盘和20世纪30年代的财政下跌。在经济大萧条期间，世界选择了自给自足。直到20世纪30年代末，半个世纪前的全球经济一体化也只不过是一场记忆。今天的情况会提供更有力的证明吗？

好消息是，全球经济一体化已经经受住了恐怖主义、战争和一系列毁灭性的金融危机的考验。正如马里兰大学的卡门·莱因哈特和哈佛大学的肯尼思·罗格夫在一篇开创性的论文中指出的，全球

of Maryland and Kenneth Rogoff of Harvard have shown in a seminal paper, the epoch of globalisation has been an epoch of banking crises. While most of these crises occurred in emerging economies, they also brought Japan and the Scandinavian economies low in the early 1990s. In the case of Japan, the financial crisis afflicted the economy for more than a decade.

Attentive readers will notice that the incidence of crises, measured by the proportion of countries affected, reached its apogee① in the late 1990s, whereupon it collapsed. This looked encouraging: Maybe, some hoped, the era of crises was coming to an end, as people learned how open financial systems should work.

The bad news is that this view now seems extremely naive. The current financial crisis affects the US and Europe, which account for more than half of world output measured at market exchange rates. Judged by the share of the world economy affected, this is the most significant financial crisis since the 1930s. This crisis also affects the world's most advanced economies and financial systems. This is no crisis of backwardness, but one of sophistication.

What then might such a crisis do to globalisation, which depends on the continuation of broadly liberal economic policies across the globe? While technology—particularly the reduction in the costs of information and communications—has played a big part, it does not drive globalisation on its own. Also important have been decisions to move towards open financial systems, accept inward direct investment and liberalise trade.

---

① apogee [ˈæpədʒiː] *n.*最高点

化的时代已经成为银行业的危机时代。虽然大多数危机发生在新兴的经济体，但它们仍然在20世纪90年代早期降低了日本和斯堪的纳维亚的经济发展速度。就日本而言，其经济受金融危机困扰的时间超过10年。

细心的读者会发现，以国家受影响的比例测量的危机发生频率在20世纪90年代末达到高峰，而后崩溃。这看起来令人欣慰：有人希望，也许当人们了解了开放的金融系统应该如何工作时，危机时代就该结束了。

坏消息是，这种观点现在看起来非常天真。目前的金融危机影响了美国和欧洲，按市场汇率计算，他们占据全球金融资本产出的一半以上。根据全球经济影响的份额判断，这是20世纪30年代以来最严重的金融危机。这场危机也影响了全球顶级发达国家的经济和金融体系。这绝不是一场倒退的危机，而是一场复杂的危机。

全球化取决于全球范围内广泛的自由经济政策的持续性，那么这样一场危机会给它带来什么样的影响呢？虽然技术、特别是降低信息和通信成本的技术发挥了很大一部分作用，但它自身并没有驱动全球化的进程。走向开放的金融系统、接受内部直接投资和贸易自由化的决定同样重要。

贸易似乎是全球化的发动机。在每一个连续的商业周期，贸易的增长速度高于全球的产出。以近年为例，按实际价值计算的全球

Trade seems to be the engine of globalisation. In each successive business cycle, trade has grown faster than world output. Recent years, for example, world exports of manufactures grew at a trend rate of 7.7 per cent a year, in real terms, while output of manufactures grew at 4 per cent. As the growth of trade accelerated, it seems to have pulled the world economy into faster growth, as well.

The financial crisis of today threatens globalisation in three ways. First, it will reduce willingness to liberalise financial markets. If even the US and Europe cannot manage liberalised financial markets, can emerging economies hope to do so? Second, it will undermine the credibility of free-market capitalism. This will affect not just finance, but, quite possibly, trade and direct investment as well. The more intrusive governments become in the high-income countries, the more unwilling the rest of the world will be to listen to their lectures on the virtues of free markets. Finally, it will worsen the performance of the world economy. If, as now seems plausible[①], the US and Europe go into a significant recession, a rise in economic nationalism is to be expected—and feared.

The failure of the Doha round of multilateral[②] trade negotiations must increase this danger. The 2000s have seen extraordinarily dynamic growth in emerging economies, driven by China and India. While these countries should continue to grow fast even in difficult times, their pace would probably slow. This then is, potentially, a turning point not just for the financial sector, but for financial globalisation and even globalisation as

---

① plausible [ˈplɔːzəbl] *adj.* 似乎是真的

② multilateral [ˌmʌltiˈlætərəl] *adj.*多边的

制造业出口的增长趋势达每年7.7%，而产品的输出量增长了4个百分点。由于贸易增长加快，这似乎也已经把全球经济推向更快的增长轨道。

目前的金融危机从三个方面威胁了全球化。首先，它将减少开放金融市场自由化的意愿。如果美国和欧洲无法管理自由化的金融市场，新兴的经济体可能希望这样做吗？其次，它会削弱资本主义自由市场的信誉。这不仅是对金融的影响，而且很可能还要影响贸易和直接投资。高收入国家政府插手的事务越多，世界其他国家就越不愿意理睬他们谈论的自由金融市场的优点。最后，这将加剧全球经济的糟糕表现。如果像现在这样似乎也合情合理，美国和欧洲进入了严重的衰退期，人们可以预料到经济民族主义的上升，但也不免忧心忡忡。

多哈回合多边贸易谈判的失败很可能增加了这种危险。21世纪已经见证了中国和印度推动的新兴经济体极富活力的增长。虽然这些国家即使在困难时期也应该继续快速增长，但他们的速度也有可能放缓。那么，这不仅对财政部门、而且对金融全球化和全球化这个整体，也是一个潜在的转折点。

这在很大程度上取决于如何迅速和有效地处理这一危机。

这在很大程度上也取决于相关的衰退会持续多久。

这在很大程度上至少还取决于世界距离自由化有多远。

a whole.

Much depends on how swiftly and effectively this crisis is dealt with.

Much depends, too, on how long the associated recession lasts.

Much depends, not least, on how far the world turns away from liberalisation.

With luck the excesses of the financial sector will not taint the market economy too much. But, at this moment, when the crisis is at its peak, this is but a hope. It is up to policy makers to ensure that it turns out to be a fact.

Lessons must indeed be learned. But among those lessons is not a need for self-sufficiency. That would add economic disaster to financial calamity①.

(788 words)

---

① calamity [kəˈlæmiti] *n.*灾难

幸运的是，金融部门的放肆行为不会过度染指市场经济。但在此时刻，当危机处于高峰期之时，这只不过为我们保留了一线希望。而实现希望则取决于政策制定者，他们应该确保希望变成事实。

一定要吸取教训。但狂妄自大并不在我们需要领悟的教训之中。那样做只会把经济浩劫强加给金融灾难。

知识链接

The Doha round of multilateral trade negotiations 多哈回合多边贸易谈判。多哈回合谈判的宗旨是促进世贸组织成员削减贸易壁垒，通过更公平的贸易环境来促进全球、特别是较贫穷国家的经济发展。谈判包括农业、非农产品市场准入、服务贸易、规则谈判、争端解决、知识产权、贸易与发展以及贸易与环境等 8 个主要议题。

题 记

丹麦模式一直是世人顶礼膜拜、虔诚仿效的无价之宝。丹麦凭借独特房贷模式保持房产市场稳定，房屋抵押债券已经成为美国次贷和欧债危机中投资人的避风港。丹麦的低碳经济发展创造了“减排和经济繁荣并不矛盾”的模式，在现代商业可持续发展的道路上实现了人文价值和生态文明的协调统一。丹麦的全球化模式更是独辟蹊径，即使公司裁员，工会也会支持企业将生产和制造外包给其他国家，使经济在走出去、请进来的全球化过程中充满生机。丹麦的免费教育、免费医疗保健，失业后保持良好的财务状况以及弹性的劳动力市场和丹麦公司的规模，若隐若现地向世人展现出生机勃发的全球化元素。丹麦的高端经济发展水平和高税率为全球的经济发展模式提供了一个全新的发展方向，证明了经济发展不只有华山一条路。

Why Denmark Loves Globalization

Last year Danish toymaker Lego announced plans to outsource most of its manufacturing to Eastern Europe and Mexico. Of 1,200 blue collar jobs at Lego's headquarters in the town of Billund, only about 300 would remain.

You might think this would make union leaders at Lego hopping mad[1]. You'd be wrong. "We thought it was the best way to keep as many workers' places in Denmark as possible," maintenance man and union shop steward Poul Erik Pedersen tells me. "We aren't against the management. We want to make sure that they make money and we make money." Then, unprompted, he takes the argument a step further: "There are some good things about outsourcing. Where the jobs go, the standard of living is growing, and then they can afford to buy more Legos or other things from the West."

In most of the developed world, globalization is a deeply fraught topic. Not in Denmark. There, 76% of respondents in a recent poll said

---

① hopping mad 非常生气的

丹麦为什么热爱全球化

丹麦的玩具制造商乐高去年宣布，计划将大部分生产外包给东欧和墨西哥。乐高在比隆小镇总部的1 200个蓝领职位只保留300个。

也许你会觉得这会让乐高的工会领导怒不可遏，那么你就错了。工会的工人代表保尔·艾里克·彼得森告诉我："我们认为，这是尽可能多地保持丹麦工作岗位的最好方法。我们不是反对管理层，我们要确保他们赚钱，我们也赚钱。"他后来自发地进一步阐明了这个观点："外包有一些好处。有工作机会的地方，生活水平相应增长，人们才能买得起更多的乐高产品，或者其他的西方产品。"

在大多数发达国家，全球化是一个深深令人担忧的话题，不只是在丹麦。在这些国家，最近的一项调查显示，76%的被调查者认为全球化是一个好现象。为什么不应该是好现象呢？丹麦是世界上生活水平最高的国家之一。虽然人均收入落后于美国，但它的分配更为平均。失业率仅为3.1%。丹麦的商品和服务出口大于进口。虽然只有A.P.穆勒-马士基集团和丹斯克银行两家丹麦公司具备足够的实力进入全球财富500强，但小规模、灵活敏捷和外向型

globalization was a good thing. And why shouldn't they? Living standards in Denmark are among the highest in the world. Per capita income trails that of the U.S. but is distributed far more equally. Unemployment is just 3.1%. The country exports more goods and services than it imports. And while only two Danish corporations, shipper A.P. Moller-Maersk and the Danske Bank, are big enough to make the FORTUNE Global 500 list, Denmark has more than its share of smallish, nimble①, outward-looking firms well positioned in growth areas ranging from alternative energy to health care to high-end furniture.

All that adds up, according to the latest rankings from the World Economic Forum (WEF), to the third most competitive economy on the planet. But while economic competitiveness has often been sold as something that requires long hours, low taxes and minimal government—a litany② often heard in the U.S.—Denmark doesn't fit that bill at all. Denmark has the second highest tax burden in the capitalist world after Sweden, which is just behind it in the competitiveness rankings, a generous welfare state, a heavily unionized workforce and at least five paid weeks off every year.

It's all part of a trade-off, the Danes say. By largely banishing③ the financial insecurity that plagues so many American workers, Danish politicians and business leaders have won public support for all manner of business-friendly policies. Corporate taxes are lower than in the U.S., and capital gains are taxed at a much lower rate than ordinary income. There

---

① nimble [ˈnimbl] *adj.* 敏捷的

② litany [ˈlitəni] *n.* 冗长而枯燥的陈述

③ banish [ˈbæniʃ] *vt.* 消除

的企业在丹麦的比例很高，他们位于经济增长地区，行业囊括可替代能源、医疗保健和高档家具。

根据最近的世界经济论坛排名，所有这一切直接导致丹麦成为全球排名第三的最具竞争实力的经济体。虽然经济竞争力经常被作为商品销售，需要长时间、低税收和极少的政府干预，但这只是美国人反复陈述的观点，丹麦的情况与之大相径庭。丹麦在资本主义世界的税收负担排名第二，仅次于瑞典，瑞典的竞争力排在丹麦之后，它是一个福利太过慷慨的国家，其劳动力受工会严格管理，雇员每年至少享受五个星期的带薪假期。

丹麦人认为，这一切还只是部分的权衡。通过大量消除困扰很多美国工人的财务不安全感，丹麦的政客和商界领袖在各种各样的商业友好政策方面赢得了公众的支持。企业税低于美国，资本增值收入的税率比普通收入的税率还低。丹麦几乎没有贸易限制。就因为如此，在丹麦解聘员工比欧洲其他任何地方更容易。

再次声明，上述大部分事情在14年前都是真实可靠的，丹麦的福利国家模型看起来已经精疲力竭，饱受增长停滞和高达两位数的失业率的困扰。一些政治上属于右翼的人确信，必须大幅削减税收和支出，甚至包括现任首相安德斯·福格·拉斯穆森，他是名为《从社会福利国家到小政府》一书的作者。从政治上讲，但是这从来不受政治的控制，社会民主党人士波尔·尼鲁普·拉斯穆森（丹

are few restrictions on trade. That, and it's easier to fire people in Denmark than anywhere else in Europe.

Then again, most of these things were true 14 years ago, and Denmark's welfare-state model seemed exhausted, beset by stagnant① growth and double-digit unemployment. Some on the political right—including current Prime Minister Anders Fogh Rasmussen, who wrote a book called From Social State to Minimal State—were convinced that taxes and spending had to be cut dramatically. But that was never in the cards politically, and Social Democrat Poul Nyrup Rasmussen (there are a lot of Rasmussens in Denmark), who became Prime Minister that year, crafted a compromise that kept the high taxes and most of the social protections but cut unemployment benefits, which replace about 90% of earnings, from nine years to four and beefed up job-retraining programs in a big way. This approach, which over the years came to be known as "flexicurity," seemed to work. Unemployment fell; the economy grew. There's still much debate over how effective Denmark's job-retraining programs really are, but it's undeniable that they foster the kind of political environment in which union workers like Pedersen at Lego advocate outsourcing even as their company cuts jobs.

And so when a right-leaning government led by the author of From Social State to Minimal State took power, it barely changed a thing. Says Employment Minister Claus Hjort Fredriksen, also a former advocate of big cutbacks in the welfare state: "I have to admit now, 15 to 20 years later, that the model we have found here—free education, free health care, a

① stagnant [ˈstægnənt] *adj*. 迟钝的

麦有很多姓拉斯穆森的）当年成为丹麦首相后，巧妙地达成了一项妥协，在保持高税率和大部分的社会保障的同时，将失业津贴从 9 年削减至 5 年，代之以 90% 左右的收入，并且大力度加强职业培训项目。这种多年来被称作“灵活保障制度”的方法似乎很有效。失业率降低了，经济增长了。丹麦的职业再培训项目究竟产生了什么样的效果，仍然存在很多争议，但不可否认的是，他们培养了一种政治环境，即使他们公司裁员，乐高的彼得森等工会职员也会提倡外包行动。

所以当《从社会福利国家到小政府》一书的作者领导的右翼政府掌权的时候，情况基本上没有什么改变。就业部部长卡洛斯·赫加特·弗兰德瑞克森以前也是一位大量裁减福利的拥趸者，他声称，“我现在必须承认，15 年到 20 年后，我们在这儿已经发现的模式，包括免费教育、免费医疗保健，失业后保持良好的财务状况以及弹性的劳动力市场和丹麦公司的规模，会以某种方式引人注目，这就是对全球化挑战的答案”。

丹麦模式已经取得了成功，它被欧洲社会民主党人和美国自由主义人士视为珍宝，来访的记者、学者和政客近来已经超出了国家可以接待的限度，他们期待寻找到真知灼见。一位游客发现了其中的一件事，即丹麦的规模和同种性对经济如何运转起着关键的作用。丹麦现有 540 万人，其中 47.8 万人是丹麦血统。汉斯·斯科

good financial situation if you lose your job, together with a flexible labor market and the size of Danish companies—somehow has struck something that is the answer to the challenges of globalization."

The way Denmark has achieved its success has made it a darling of European social democrats and American liberals, and the country has been overrun lately with visiting journalists, academics and politicians looking for insights. One of the things a visitor discovers, though, is that Denmark's size and homogeneity① —5.4 million people, of whom all but 478,000 are of Danish ancestry—are crucial to how the economy works. "We've been one small nation for 1,000 years," says Hans Skov Christensen, who as director general of the Confederation of Danish Industries negotiates the nationwide bargaining agreements between management and labor every few years. "We're basically a clan."

Informality, disputation and disrespect for authority are core Danish traits. But there are limits, and Danes seem to know in their bones just how far they can push them. The result is an economy that looks like something out of an enlightened management textbook. There are a few clear goals and lots of leeway② to achieve them. In one fascinating study, two American sociologists found that Danish line workers have nearly as much job autonomy as supervisors do in the U.S., while supervisors in Denmark have about as much autonomy as upper managers in the U.S. John Strand runs a consulting firm that does work for most of the world's big wireless carriers and gets 95% of its revenue outside Denmark. It could be based

---

① homogeneity [ˌhɔməudʒeˈniəiti] *n.* 同质性

② leeway [ˈliːwei] *n.* 回旋余地

夫·克里斯滕森认为，“一千年来我们都是一个很小的民族。从根本上来讲，我们是一个部落”。他是丹麦产业联合会的总经理，负责全国每隔几年的管理层和劳工之间的商讨谈判。

不拘礼节、争论和不尊重权威是丹麦人的显著特点。但有一定的限度，丹麦人似乎从骨子里知道，他们究竟能将这种限度推进到多远。结果他们发现了一种经济，看起来出自一本开明的管理教科书。有少数清晰的目标和很多回旋余地来达到目标。有一个引人入胜的研究，两个美国社会学家发现，丹麦流水线上的工人和美国的管理者拥有几乎一样的自主权，而丹麦的管理者和美国的高层管理者拥有几乎一样的自主权。约翰·斯特兰德经营着一家咨询公司，为世界上大多数大型无线传输公司工作，收入的95%来自于丹麦之外。公司本可以设在任何一个具备良好机场条件的城市。他说，他之所以坚持把斯特兰德咨询公司设在哥本哈根，主要是因为他的丹麦雇员愿意与他争论问题和挑战传统智慧。他认为，“丹麦人敢于跳出原有的思维定势”。

所以，丹麦的某些成功或许可以归结为丹麦特性。谁也不能保证这种状况的可持续发展。商业领袖认为，他们面临越来越恶化的人员短缺，不能吸引有技术的外国人，因为这个国家税率太高，更别提沉闷的天气和难以理解的语言了。丹麦已经将动态经济和一个几乎是美国两倍的税收负担结合在一起，这个事实揭穿了过去25年

pretty much in any city with a good airport. He says he keeps Strand Consult in Copenhagen largely because his Danish employees are so willing to argue with him and confront conventional wisdom. "Danes can think out of the box," he says.

So perhaps some of Denmark's success has to be chalked up to, well, Danishness. And there's no guarantee that it will continue. Business leaders say they face worsening labor shortages and can't attract skilled foreigners to a country that has such high taxes, not to mention dreary weather and an incomprehensible language. But the fact that Denmark has combined a dynamic economy with a tax burden almost double that of the U.S. gives the lie to many economic arguments made over the past quarter-century. There's more than one way, it turns out, to be competitive.

(1,089 words)

来很多经济论证的谎言。事实证明，并非只有一种方法具备竞争力。

知识链接

World Economic Forum “世界经济论坛”是以研讨世界经济领域存在的问题、促进国际经济合作与交流为宗旨的非官方国际性机构。由瑞士大学的施瓦布教授于 1971 年创建，原名“欧洲管理论坛”，1986 年起改名为“世界经济论坛”。

A. P. Moller-Maersk Group A. P. 穆勒-马士基集团成立于 1904 年。主要经营造船和集装箱航运、石油、天然气勘探与开发、航空运输、商品零售、数据处理、材料等。集团是欧洲最大的上市公司之一，有子公司 70 家，在世界 125 个国家设有办事机构。

From Social State to Minimal State 《从社会福利国家到小政府》是丹麦自由党(Venstre)领袖安德斯·福格·拉斯穆森的成名作。他在著作中宣扬丹麦的福利国家古典自由主义路线改革，包括低税和政府减少干预政府与个人的事务。

题　记

信托这个穿梭在信贷紧缩灰色地带的“托儿”，在商业银行的规范操作之下，既达到了贷款规模控制的要求，又帮助客户完成了融资。可是我们会发觉自己生活在这样一个世界：贷款人囤积资本，借款人空手而归，经济齿轮慢慢停了下来。J. P. 摩根曾信誓旦旦：“作为基督徒，我不会贷款给我不信任的人。”他的信托理念其实既简单又重要：信贷体系依赖于信任。只有当金融机构和企业互相信任时，资金流动才能平稳地从贷方转向借方，新企业开始起步，现有企业得以扩大，日常交易畅通无阻。商业票据在短期内给企业注入了活力，金融机构放心大胆地投资信用评级优良、财务稳健的公司。但雷曼兄弟的破产却让金融机构陷入了极度的恐慌。也许我们还是应该按照那句古老的格言行事：我们相信上帝，所有其他人请付现金。

The Trust Crunch

In December, 1912, J. P. Morgan testified before Congress in the so-called Money Trust hearings. Asked to explain how he decided whether to make a loan or investment, he replied, "The first thing is character." His questioner skeptically suggested that factors like collateral① might be more important, but Morgan replied, "A man I do not trust could not get money from me on all the bonds in Christendom." Morgan's point was simple but essential: systems of credit depend on trust. When trust is present, money flows smoothly from lenders to borrowers, allowing new enterprises to start, existing ones to expand, and daily business to move along without a hitch. When it's absent, we find ourselves in a world where lenders hoard capital, borrowers are left empty-handed, and the economy's gears grind to a halt—a world, in other words, like the one we're now living in.

A few years ago, banks and other lenders seemed indifferent to risk, as they doled out② loans to people with dubious incomes and poor credit records. Today, they are positively paranoid③, distrusting even the best

---

① collateral [kɔˈlætərəl] *n.* 附属担保品

② dole out 少量地发放

③ paranoid [ˈpærənɔid] *adj.* 多疑的

信托紧缩危机

1912年12月，J. P. 摩根在国会所谓的货币信托听证会作证。当被要求解释他如何决定是否贷款或投资时，他回答道："首要的事情是品质。"发问者提出质疑，认为抵押之类的因素也许更为重要，但摩根回答道："作为基督徒，我不会贷款给我不信任的人。"摩根的观点既简单又重要：信贷体系依赖于信任。当大家互相信任时，资金流动平稳地从贷方转向借方，新企业开始起步，现有企业得以扩大，日常交易畅通无阻。当信任空缺时，我们会发觉自己生活在这样一个世界：贷款人囤积资本，借款人空手而归，经济齿轮慢慢停了下来，换句话说，这与我们现在生活的世界如出一辙。

几年前，银行和其他放贷机构对风险漠不关心，他们对那些收入不稳定和信用记录差的人少量地发放贷款。现在，他们又过分地疑神疑鬼，即使是最好的借款人也无法获得他们的信任，并强行提高了公司的借款利率。尽管政府债券的利率已经下跌，利率评价最高的两年期公司债券在过去的一个月中已经上升了50%。

比起近期股票下跌形成的震动，信贷冻结对稳定美国经济的伤害更大。所以，美国财政部和美联储在过去几周内不遗余力地试图

borrowers and forcing companies to pay far more interest on money borrowed. The interest rate on the most highly rated two-year corporate bonds has risen by fifty per cent in the past month, even as the interest rate on government bonds has fallen.

Shocking as the current stock-market drops have been, the freezing up of the flow of credit is far more damaging to the health of the U. S. economy. So, during the past few weeks, the Treasury Department and the Federal Reserve have been desperately trying to fight that freeze. Scarcely a day goes by without some dramatic new initiative, even as market chaos makes each new idea soon seem like ancient history. It's been just over a week since the Treasury's plan to buy seven hundred billion dollars' worth of "toxic assets" became law, but already it feels like a year. Last week, in a potentially crucial move, the Fed announced that it would start buying billions of dollars in commercial paper—which means that it will be issuing short-term unsecured loans① to corporations. The Fed has historically been the lender of last resort to banks. Now it's becoming the lender of last resort to everyone.

Commercial paper is the name for short-term promissory notes that companies sell to raise money for daily operations, to meet payroll②, and to bridge the gap between when they spend and when they get paid, while keeping their own cash in higher-yield investments. Commercial paper is not a new innovation—Goldman Sachs actually started as a commercial-

① unsecured loan 无担保贷款

② payroll [' peirəul] *n.* 工资总支出

对抗这种状况。几乎每天都有一些戏剧性的新举措，即使市场的混乱让每一个新想法看起来像古老的历史。财政部计划购买价值7 000亿美元的“有毒资产”一周前刚刚拍板，但感觉好像已经过去了一年。上周，美联储提出了一个潜在的关键举措，宣布购买数十亿美元的商业票据，这表明它将向企业发行短期无担保债券。美联储历来都是银行的最后贷款人。现在它变成了所有人的最后贷款人。

商业票据是一种短期期票，公司出售短期期票以筹集日常运营资金，支付薪酬，填补收支空白，同时维持他们在高收益投资中的现金。商业票据并不是一个新的创新，戈德门·萨克斯实际上在19世纪成立时就是一个商业票据公司，但自1980年以来，商业票据已经在美国的日常交易中变得不可或缺，商业票据的年度发行量从1 240亿美元增加到16 000亿美元。这些贷款的大部分没有担保，公司并不提供抵押，只是承诺偿还现金流外的贷款。因此，只有成熟、财务稳健的公司才可以利用商业票据市场。

由于商业票据贷款期短，只是用于信用评级优良的公司，所以它们一直被认为几乎没有风险，贷款人（最明显的是货币市场资金）也愿意以低利率贷款。然而，去年已经有人对低风险贷款概念提出了质疑。当雷曼兄弟带着数十亿美元的商业票据破产时，信用评级竟然还保持在A2。自雷曼兄弟破产以来，贷款人目光敏锐地盯着每个人，致使一些重量级的企业无法进行基本交易，从而加剧了市场恐慌。像美国长途电话通信公司这样的企业在可预见的近期内根本不可能破产，但是在雷曼兄弟倒下之后，贷款人是如此惊慌，以至于美

paper firm, in the late nineteenth century—but it has become essential in day-to-day business in the U. S. Since 1980, annual commercial-paper issuance has gone from $ 124 billion to $ 1.6 trillion. Most of these loans are unsecured—companies don't put up collateral but simply promise to pay the loans back out of cash flow—so only well-established, financially solid companies can tap the commercial-paper market.

Because commercial-paper loans are short-term and are made only to companies with sterling credit ratings, they've always been assumed to be practically riskless, and lenders (most notably money-market funds) have been willing to lend at low interest rates. But the past year has called into question the very idea of a low-risk loan. Lehman Brothers, after all, still had an A2 credit rating when it went under, taking down with it billions in commercial paper. Since its failure, lenders have adopted a gimlet-eyed approach to everyone, making it hard for key companies to perform basic transactions, and thereby exacerbating① the market panic. A company like A. T. & T. is hardly likely to go bankrupt in the foreseeable future, but, after Lehman's collapse, lenders were so skittish② that A. T. & T. couldn't get commercial-paper loans that lasted longer than overnight.

The fear that has overpowered lenders is not just about the current market chaos. It also reflects their lack of faith in the models and systems that they rely on to evaluate risk. For Morgan, that process of evaluation was all about relationships. In the modern financial system, by contrast,

① exacerbate [eksˈæsəbeit] *vt.* 使加重

② skittish [ˈskitiʃ] *adj.* 易惊慌的

国长途电话通信公司也无法获得超过隔夜的商业票据贷款。

让贷款人极度恐慌的不仅是当前市场的混乱，这也反映出他们对用于评估风险的模型和体系缺乏信任。对摩根而言，评估过程完全凭借人际关系。与此相反，在现代金融体系中，风险评估涉及两个方面：客观分析和外部采办。个人对借款人可靠性的判断，这种摩根或小镇银行机构的做法，已经被数学模型所取代。贷方将评估借款方的责任委托给其他参与者，如信用评级机构。在许多情形下，AA 信誉等级是公司获得贷款的必要条件。

毫无疑问，这个体系已经具有很多好处，它使借贷双方更容易通过货币取得联系。它消除了一种个人偏见，让资本掌握在批准 J. P.摩根贷款的人手中。它还广泛地扩大了贷款的额度。然而，所有这些好处都以高昂的价格为代价。客观体系的问题是，当模型失效、公司信用等级令人怀疑时，任何事都要遭到质疑。贷款人不能依靠自己对特定的公司或个人做出判断，因为这种判断在部分程度上并不具备决策过程的代表性。相反，他们顽固地怀疑所有的借款人，甚至是财务安全的借款人。如果美联储现在收取公司白条，那就是因为所有其他人都在按照那句古老的格言行事：我们相信上帝，所有其他人请付现金。

知识链接

Commercial paper 商业票据。商业票据指发行体为满足流动资金需求所发

risk evaluation involves two things: impersonality and outsourcing. Personal judgments about the reliability of a borrower—the sort of judgment that Morgan, or a small-town banker, would make before issuing a loan—have been replaced by mathematical models. And lenders have delegated much of the responsibility for evaluating borrowers to other players, such as credit-rating agencies. In many cases, an AA rating was all a company needed to get a loan.

There's no doubt that this system has had huge benefits. It has made it easier for money to connect lenders and borrowers. It has removed the kinds of personal bias that kept capital in the hands of people whom men like J. P. Morgan approved of. And it has vastly expanded the amount of lending as well. But all those benefits have come at an exorbitant① price. The problem with an impersonal system is that when the models fail, and when companies' ratings become suspect, everything is called into question. Lenders can't fall back on their own judgments of a specific company or individual, because such judgments aren't part of their typical decision-making process. Instead, they've adopted a deep-seated distrust of all borrowers, even financially secure ones. If the Fed is now taking corporate I.O.U.s, it's because everyone else is acting according to that old motto: In God we trust—all others pay cash.

(916 words)

① exorbitant [ig'zɔːbitənt] *adj.* 过分的,过度的

行的、期限为2天至270天的、可流通转让的债务工具。一般是指商业上由出票人签发，无条件约定自己或要求他人支付一定金额，可流通转让的有价证券，持有人具有一定权利的凭证。

Credit rating 企业信用等级。按照信用程度，企业信用等级原则上从高到低分为A、B、C、D四等。每等可进一步细分为级。每个信用等级的细分差别，可用表示字母的数量来区分。在同一等中，字母数量越多(最多三个)，表示信用程度越高。

题记

进行一场球赛，管理一个团队；训练球员的教练，挖掘人才的领导。这看似毫无关系的两个事物却在层层类推之下相呼相应，相寓相随，堪称一绝。领导者为何方神圣？他们是当时间接近尾声、比赛进行到紧要关头之时想要控球的运动员；他们是招揽客户的销售人员，希望为这个孤注一掷的交易完成关键性的投掷；他们是律师，当委托人的命运吉凶未卜之时，渴望进行结案陈词。商界有三种不同类型的领导者：从不传球的领导者，笨手笨脚地传球导致失败的领导者和传球流畅并取得胜利的领导者。商业公司培养球员的策略同样与篮球运动息息相关：发现有潜力的球员，从带球上篮开始，在下半场开始前传球，在非关键球赛结束时传球，以及时机成熟时传球。作为一个商人，应该志在建立相当于一个商业王朝的球队。

It's Time to Pass the Ball

If you want your team to succeed, you need to develop others to "take the last shot" when the game is on the line.

One of the lessons on teamwork that I enjoy teaching is the Law of the Catalyst①, which states, "Winning teams have players who make things happen." Look at any highly successful team—business, sports, volunteer, or otherwise—and you'll find people who perform at a seemingly superhuman level to help the team succeed. To such people, losing is simply unacceptable, and they find a way to win, no matter what.

When crunch② time comes, catalysts want to take control. They are the athletes who want the ball in their hands when the clock is winding down and the game is on the line. They are the salespeople who want to make the critical pitch③ to the client for the make-or-break deal. They are the lawyers who want to make the closing arguments when the fate of their client hangs in the balance.

When I talk about this idea to a room full of leaders, they immediately connect with it. Why? Because most good leaders possess this catalytic

① catalyst [ˈkætəlist] *n.* 催化

② crunch [krʌntʃ] *n.* 危机

③ pitch [pitʃ] *n.* 程度

该是传球的时候了

如果你希望你的团队取得胜利，当比赛命悬一线的时候，你需要帮助其他人“出手绝杀”。

“催化剂法则”是我喜欢教授的有关于协同工作的课程之一，课程规定：“获胜的团队拥有促成事情发生的成员。”看看任何成功的团队，不管是在商界、体育界、志愿者还是其他人，你总会发现，人们发挥了看似超人的水平，帮助团队取得成功。对这种人来说，失败明显不可接受，他们会不惜一切代价寻找成功之道。

当关键时刻来临的时候，有感染力的人应该控制局面。当时间接近尾声、比赛来到紧要关头之时，他们是想要控球的运动员。他们是招揽客户的销售人员，希望为这个孤注一掷的交易完成关键性的投掷。他们是律师，当委托人的命运吉凶未卜之时，渴望进行结案陈词。

当我与满屋子的领导人谈论这个问题时，立即引起了他们的共鸣。为什么？因为大多数优秀的领导者都拥有这种催化剂的品质。他们拒绝失败，他们在艰难的逆境中取得胜利。哪怕面对压倒性的困难，他们也能转败为胜。

教会他人做同样的事情。这个夏天，我给一群在国家橄榄球训练场参加高级领导层会议的企业家做了一场报告。在我即将结束演

quality. They refuse to lose, and they pull out victories when the odds are overwhelmingly against them.

Teaching Others to Do the Same. This summer I spoke to a group of entrepreneurs who were gathered for an exclusive leadership conference held at an NFL training facility. At the end of my session, a sharp businessperson asked a question related to this issue. "I always feel like nobody else can deliver the way I can," he said. "When you're a leader who wants the ball in his hands at crunch time, how do you know when to pass the ball to another leader to develop him or her?"

It's a good question, one that may determine whether a leader can go to the next level, because good leadership is about developing other leaders who can deliver, not just delivering yourself. It's my observation that there are three different kinds of leaders when it comes to passing the ball.

Leaders Who Never Pass the Ball: Some people never consider passing the ball to another player, which would give someone else a chance to win the game or clinch the contract. They've always been the go-to person, and they want to keep it that way because it feeds their egos or because they're afraid to let go of control.

Leaders Who Botch① the Pass and Lose: Other leaders, like the one who asked the question, recognize the value of developing other leaders and team members by passing the ball. However, they think of passing the ball as a single event, not a long-term development process, so they pass the ball poorly. They pick the wrong player, choose the wrong time, or neglect to properly develop and empower the person. As a result, they lose.

---

① botch [bɔtʃ] *vt.* 拙笨的修补

讲之时，一位言辞犀利的商人提出了一个与之相关的问题。他问道：“我总觉得没有人可以按我能做的方式把球传出去。当你是一名在关键时刻想控球的领导者时，你怎么知道什么时候把球传给另外一名领导者，传给他还是她？”

这是个好问题，它可能决定着一名领导者是否能够进入一个更高的境界，因为优秀的领导者要善于激发其他能够传球的领导者，而不仅仅是传球给自己。据我的观察，在提到传球的时候，有三种不同类型的领导者：

从不传球的领导者。有的人从不考虑把球传给别的球员，其实这样做可以给他人一个机会，赢得比赛或敲定合同。他们永远是不可或缺的重要人士，他们想维持这种方式，因为这样可以满足他们的虚荣心，或者是因为他们害怕失去控制权。

笨手笨脚地传球导致失败的领导者。还有一类领导者，就像前面提问的那位一样，他们认识到通过传球培养其他领导者和团队成员的重要性。但是他们认为传球只是一个简单的事件，而不是一个长期的发展过程，所以他们传的球很差。他们选择了错误的球员，选择了错误的时间，抑或忽略了正确地激励球员和授权给球员。结果，他们失败了，于是，很多人发誓再也不传球了。

传球流畅并取得胜利的领导者。最后一群人包括对过程心领神会、在关键时刻传球给能够得分的领导者，为整个团队创造了胜利。

我们还是继续篮球运动的类比，下面要讨论在你的商业公司步入正轨时，你如何培养球员接球。

发现有潜力的球员。篮球运动的整个过程始于天赋，你不可能

And many vow never to pass the ball again.

Leaders Who Pass the Ball Well and Win: The final group consists of leaders who understand the process well, develop leaders who can score during crunch time, and create wins for the entire team.

Continuing the basketball analogy, here's how you can prepare a player to accept the pass when everything is on the line in your business.

Find a player with potential. The entire process begins with talent. You cannot turn a below-average person into the corporate equivalent of Michael Jordan. The skills need to be inherent in the person. Look for people who are intuitive①, passionate, influential, creative, and responsible.

Begin with layups②. Most young, hungry leaders picture themselves winning the game by making a three-point shot from the parking lot under huge pressure. Don't let them start there. Begin with layups, the easiest shot to make. Simpler tasks not only instill confidence, they also show you that someone has the character, responsibility, and focus to deliver under ordinary circumstances.

Pass the ball before the half-time buzzer. You want to ease players with potential into pressure situations. The best way to do that is to give them responsibility in situations that feel critical to them but still give you the ability to recover if they make mistakes.

Pass the ball at the end of noncritical games. Once they're ready, let them have the ball when their actions really do count. Just don't make it a situation that will make or break the organization. Give them minor

---

① intuitive [in'tjuitiv] *adj.*有直觉力的

② layup ['leiʌp] *n.* 上篮得分

把一个低于平均水平的人培养成迈克尔·乔丹那样的企业版球员。精彩的球技需要球员的禀赋。寻找那些有直觉、富有激情、有影响力、有创造力、敢于承担责任的人。

从带球上篮开始。许多年轻、渴望成功的领导者在巨大的压力之下，想象自己在停车场投中三分球取胜。不要让他们从三分球开始，应该从带球上篮开始，这是最容易的得分方式。更简单的任务不仅可以增强信心，而且向你展示了人的品质、责任心以及一般情况下能否专心地传球。

在下半场开始前传球。要帮有潜力的球员缓解压力，做这件事的最好办法就是让他们感到在关键的时刻承担责任，但是如果他们犯错，你要有能力补救。

在非关键球赛结束时传球。一旦他们准备好了，在他们真能胜任的情况下让他们控球。不要在决定团队生存命运的时刻把球交给他们。先给他们一些小项目，较小的账户等。

时机成熟时传球。在你认为他们已经准备好了，在时机成熟之时把球交给他们。即使在这个时候，也应该循序渐进：何时争取一场比赛、何时争取一个赛季以及何时争取夺冠，都需要合理的策划。

何必要这么麻烦呢？保持控球不是更简单吗？是的，短期来说是这样的，但是长期来说并非如此。假如你学会了把球传给其他的领导者，就会使你自己的领导水平上升到一个更高的层面。在你帮助有潜力的领导者从普通的球员转型为关键球员、并最终成为核心球员的过程中，你也成功地转型为胸怀全局的教练，而不只是局限于当前的一场比赛或者是一个赛季。

projects, smaller accounts, etc.

Give them the ball when it really counts. When you think they're ready, give them the ball when it really counts. But even this should be done in a progression: when the game is on the line, when the season is on the line, when the championship is on the line.

Why go to all this trouble? Isn't it easier to retain control? Yes, in the short run it is. But not in the long run. If you learn to pass the ball to another leader, it frees you up to take your own leadership to a higher level. As you help a potential leader make the transition from practice player to game player to go-to player, you will be undergoing your own transition to coach and developer who has the whole organization in mind, not just the current game or season.

As a businessperson, winning a few games or a season isn't enough. You want to build the sports equivalent of a dynasty, a team that keeps performing at the highest possible level and keeps winning.

(937 words)

作为一个商人，赢得几场比赛或者一个赛季是不够的。你应该志在建立相当于一个王朝的球队，它尽可能发挥出最高的水平，并一直保持胜利。

知识链接

NFL 美国国家橄榄球联盟(National Football League)是美国一个庞大的橄榄球联盟。联盟中共有32支队伍，被分为两大联合会：美国橄榄球联合会(American Football Conference，简称AFC，美联)和国家橄榄球联合会(National Football Conference，简称NFC，国联)。每个联合会有16支队伍，又分成4个分赛区：东部、南部、西部和北部。每个分赛区有4支队伍。

题　记

人们通过一系列的思维模式来达成对世界的认知，领导者的魅力通过五个关键特征展现出艺术的认知美感。优秀领导者的首要特质是远见卓识，他们时时刻刻在脑海中保持着公司的愿景，不定期地重新评估公司的愿景，使它跟上不断变化的时代。优秀的领导者拥有激情，能点燃雇员的心中之火，使他们像当年跟随克里斯多佛·哥伦布或莱弗·埃里克松探索新大陆的水手，在商界摸爬滚打，矢志不渝。优秀的领导者是伟大的决策制定者，他们使用 QACT 体系，与管理团队共同酝酿公司的最佳方案。优秀的领导者是团队的建造者，无论顺境还是逆境，都是公司的中流砥柱。优秀的领导者具有独特的魅力，他们既是冷兵器时代的项羽，沧海横流，方显英雄本色；又是互联网时代的乔布斯，用创新和孤独打造超越于产品之上的艺术和人文结合的生态系统。

The Traits of Great Leaders

It's very difficult to lead today when people are not really truly participating in the decision. You won't be able to attract and retain great people if they don't feel like they are part of the authorship of the strategy and the authorship of the really critical issues. If you don't give people an opportunity to really be engaged, they won't stay. As an entrepreneur with employees, one of your primary goals is most likely to attract and keep motivated workers. So let's explore the five key traits that will help you become the kind of leader people love working for.

Key Trait 1: You must have a vision. We've all heard the saying "You must stand for something, or you'll fall for everything." But what does that really mean? Standing firm when it comes to your company's policies and procedures is all well and good, but it doesn't speak to having a vision. As a leader, you have to learn to communicate your vision or the vision of your company to the people you want to follow you. But how can you do that?

Learn to paint a picture with words. Speak it, write it, draw it, touch it. Whatever methods you can use to create a picture, do it. As they say, "A picture is worth a thousand words."

Ask each of the other managers in your company to tell you, in their own words, about the vision of the company. How close is it to what you

优秀领导者的特征

在人们并不能真正参与决策的今天，领导他们是件很困难的事。如果他们没有感觉到自己的决策者身份、是关键问题的真正领导者，你就不可能吸引和留住优秀的人才。如果你不能给他们提供真正参与的机会，他们就不可能留下。作为一个拥有雇员的企业家，你的主要目标之一最有可能是吸引和留住有活力的工人。因此，让我们来探索五条关键的特征，它们能帮你成为员工愿意为你工作的那种领导者。

关键特征 1：远见卓识。我们都听说过这样一句话："你必须立场鲜明，否则就会随波逐流。"但它的真正含义是什么呢？就公司的政策和程序而论，稳定固然很好，但这并不能表示公司的远景规划。作为领导者，你必须学会与那些追随你的人交流你的想法或公司的发展愿景。但是你如何做到这一点呢？

学会用文字绘画。说出它，写下它，描绘它，触摸它，不论你用什么方法作画，动手吧。正如人们所说："一画抵千言。"

向公司的每一位管理人员请教，请他们用自己的语言描绘公司的愿景。你认为他们的理解与你的想法有多么接近？你的团队是

thought they understood? Is your team on the same page as you?

As you work, your company's vision should be in your mind every day, and you should reevaluate① it occasionally so that it stays current with the changing times in which we live. And remember, your staff needs to be just as involved as you in keeping it up to date if you truly want them to buy in on the vision. Be sure to keep your key players involved.

Key Trait 2: You must have passion. Your employees want passion; in fact, they'll go to the ends of earth because of it, live and die for it. Think of the sailors who traveled with Christopher Columbus or Leif Ericsson to explore uncharted② territory. Their leaders' passion inspired them to take on new and very dangerous challenges.

To build an extraordinary management team, you've got to light the "fire in their bellies," to get them to feel passion about the company and connect to the leader's vision. Passion is such a key part of being a great leader that if you don't have it, you simply can't be a great leader. Think of all the great leaders throughout the ages and try to name one that did not have passion.

And passion is infectious: When you talk about your vision for the company, let your passion for your vision shine through. Others will feel it and want to get on board with you. If you don't have passion for your vision, you need to recreate your vision or reframe your description of your vision so it's connected to your passion.

Key Trait 3: You must learn to be a great decision maker. How are major decisions made in your company? What is your process for making

---

① reevaluate [riːiˈvæljʊeit] *vt.* 重新评价

② uncharted [ˌʌnˈtʃɑːtid] *adj.* 地图上没标明的

否与你达成了共识?

随着工作的深入，公司的愿景应该每天都在你的心中，你应该不定期地重新评估公司的愿景，使它跟上我们身处其中的不断变化的时代。同时要记住，如果你真的希望员工拥有公司的愿景，他们需要像你一样参与其中，使之不断更新，跟上时代的步伐。一定要确保核心团队成员的参与。

关键特征 2：拥有激情。你的员工需要激情。事实上，他们会出于激情而走遍天涯海角，为激情而生，为激情而死。想想那些跟随克里斯多佛·哥伦布或莱弗·埃里克松探索新大陆的水手。他们的领导者的激情鼓舞他们接受了全新的、充满危险的挑战。

要打造一支非凡的管理团队，你应该点燃“他们的心中之火”，让他们感受到公司的激情，与领导者的视野相连。激情是伟大领导者的核心元素，如果你不具备激情，你就不可能成为伟大的领导者。回想一下历史上各个时期的伟大领导者，有哪个不满怀激情。

激情是有感染力的。当你谈论公司的愿景时，让你的激情渗透你的愿景。其他人会感受到这一点，和你一起起航。如果你对自己的想法没有激情，你需要重新制定你的愿景，或重新构思对愿景的描述，使之与你的激情连在一起。

关键特征 3：你必须学会成为一名伟大的决策制定者。你公司的重大决策是如何制定的？制定过程是怎样的？例如，你与管理

them? For instance, do you talk to your management team and create a list of pros and cons to help you make the best decision? Maybe you conduct a cost analysis. Or do you create a timeline① for the implementation② strategy, process and timing?

Some leaders have a set process, and others fly by the seat of their pants. But you don't want to be one of those leaders who consults no one before making a decision, announces the change the next day and then gets frustrated when no one follows it. If you're one of those, I urge you to implement a set process.

In fact, here's a system you can use to become a better decision maker. It's called the QCAT:

· Q=Quick. Be quick but not hasty.

· C=Committed. Be committed to your decision but not rigid.

· A = Analytical. Be analytical, but don't over-analyze (Too much analysis can cause paralysis.)

· T = Thoughtful. Be thoughtful about all concerned, but don't be obsessive.

When you use the QCAT, it'll help you to decide when to bring others into the process and what steps need to be taken to help you make better decisions.

Key Trait 4: You must be a team builder. To become a great leader, you must develop a great team or, one might say, a well-oiled machine. But how do you do that? You can start by handing off responsibility to your team and letting your team to run with it. Don't breathe down their necks

---

① timeline [ˈtaimlain] *n.* 时间轴

② implementation [implimenˈteiʃən] *n.*实行

团队商量过创建一份利弊清单、以帮你做出最佳决策吗？ 也许你会进行成本分析。 或者你会为执行策略、进程和耗时安排时间吗？

有些领导者有一套固定的过程，而有些领导者则是随心所欲。有些领导者不和任何人商量就做出决策，第二天又宣布变动，没有人附和时就会感到沮丧，希望你不会成为他们中的一员。 如果你真是这其中的一个，我会敦促你执行一套程序。 事实上，这是一套你可以采用并成为优秀决策人的体系。 这套体系被称为 QCAT：

Q＝快。 迅速但不草率。

C＝承担责任。 对你的决定承担责任但不要死板。

A＝分析。 要分析决策，但不要过度（过度分析会引起停滞）。

T＝思考。 要对相关事件考虑周全，但不要沉迷其中。

使用 QACT 体系时，它会帮你决定何时把其他人带入这一过程，需要采取哪些步骤使你做出更好的决策。

关键特征 4：你必须是团队的建造者。 要成为一名伟大的领导者，你就必须组建一个伟大的团队，或者说，一台润滑良好的机器。 但你要怎样做？ 你可以先将职责交给团队，并让团队围绕它开展工作。 不要管得太严、太细，但是如果出现问题或麻烦时，你要亲自处理。 教会团队使用 QCAT 决策体系，并放手让他们根据自己的决策工作。

项目未能步入正轨或不能按期完成时，如果你指手画脚，对任何人都于事无补。 这时需要你挺身而出，激励员工的信心，让他们

and don't micromanage①, but make yourself available if questions or problems come up. Teach your team to use the QCAT decision-making system and give them the freedom to work through their own decisions.

When projects aren't on track or your team is falling behind on deadline, it serves no one if you start pointing fingers. This is when you need to rise to the occasion and inspire confidence in your employees, to let them know you support them and ready to help. Be ready to alter plans and make new ones. Don't forget to use humor to keep your team's spirits up during a crisis. When an emergency hits, your team will look to you to be a tower of strength and endurance.

Key Trait 5: You must have character. Without character, all the other "keys" are for naught. That's because your innate character strengths and limitations play a critical role in your leadership style. The real question is, are you aware of just what role they play? All great leaders have taken steps to learn about their individual personality and what part it plays in their leadership style.

So what's your leadership style? If you don't know, there are many leadership style assessments available on the market. Two popular ones that have been around for many years are the Myers-Briggs assessment and the "360-Degree Feedback" model. It's a good way to do a "character check" on yourself and your leadership skills.

Then, once you've done the assessment, the question to ask yourself is, do you feel your character matches what the assessments are pointing out to you? If you feel the traits don't match who you think you are, then look a little deeper and be honest with yourself. Sometimes our first response is

① micromanage [maikrəʊˈmænidʒ] *n.* 微管理

知道你支持他们，并准备帮助他们。随时准备改变计划和制订新计划。在危机期间，不要忘记用幽默鼓舞团队的士气。当紧急情况出现时，团队会期待你成为中流砥柱。

关键特征 5：一定要有性格。没有性格，所有其他的“关键”特征都没有意义。这是因为内在特征的力量和局限性在领导风格中起着关键作用。真正的问题是，你是否已经意识到了他们起的什么作用？所有的伟大领导者已经采取了步骤，了解自己的独特个性，以及他们在领导风格中扮演的是什么角色。

你的领导风格是怎样的？如果你不知道，市场上有许多领导风格评估方法。两种流行多年的方法是迈尔斯·布里格斯评估法和“360 度反馈”模型。对自己和领导艺术做一个“个性检测”是一种很好的方法。

那么，一旦完成评估后，你要问自己的问题是：你觉得你的性格与评估中指出的相符吗？如果你觉得这些特征与自己想象的原型不一样，那就对自己了解再深入、再真实一点。有时，我们的第一反应是抵触。你可能想从不同的方面评估一下自己，然后再比较结果。

在“360 度反馈评价模型”中，你也有机会了解员工和同事对你的看法。在学会成为一名伟大的领导者的过程中，第一步就是公开接受对你这个领导者的反馈，并把它与你本人分开。

你是伟大的领导者吗？或者你希望成为伟大的领导者吗？请

defensive. You might want to assess yourself with a different type of profile and then compare the results.

Within the 360 Degree Feedback model, there's an opportunity to see how your employees and peers view you, too. In learning to be a great leader, the first step is to be open to feedback about yourself as a leader and separate it from you the person.

So are you a great leader? Or do you have the desire to become one? Remember, a great leader is someone who has a clear vision and can turn that vision into a vivid picture that others can see. When you speak about your vision, it should be with a passion you feel in your heart, a passion that creates so much enthusiasm that your team will want to jump on board. When major decisions need to be made, you should encourage everyone to use the QCAT system and be responsible for his or her own actions. And you should be continually assessing your own character and never stop growing, personally or professionally.

If you can apply the five keys to great leadership, you'll be well on your way to becoming a great leader surrounded by great employees!

(1,306 words)

记住，伟大的领导者具有清晰的愿景并把它转变成其他人能够看得见的生动的画面。当你陈述你的愿景时，应该感到心中充满激情，这种激情能创造如此大的热情，以至于你的团队也会随声附和。在需要做出重大决定时，你应该鼓励所有人都使用QCAT体系，并对他或她自己的行为负责。你应该不断地评估自己的个性，在个性化或专业化的道路上勇往直前。

如果你能把这五个关键特征运用于伟大的领导工作之中，在这条道路上你会感觉良好，它使你成为一个伟大的领导者，周围还有优秀的员工。

知识链接

The* 360 *Degree Feedback model 360度反馈评价模型。该模型以其民主参与、多源反馈的特点成为一种新型的人力资源管理的评价方法，被许多知名企业所尝试。360度评价从不同层面的群体中评价信息，如同事、下属、客户，同时也包括本人自评，这样就保证了所获得信息的全面性和准确性。同时，360度的实施，给被评价者提供了一面“镜子”，可以提高自我知觉、自我评价和自我管理的效能，促进员工自身能力的进步和业绩的提高。

题　记

一个不断取得成功的领导者，其天才之处在于能感知环境的变化。沃伦·本尼斯对领导者决策能力的精辟论断至今仍然发人深省。战略性选择、人力资源选择和在危机情况下做出的选择是测量领导者能力的三个举足轻重的领域。20世纪的美国总统中唯一没有接受过大学教育的哈里·杜鲁门制定出最具深远影响决策，多数的学者至今仍视他为最出色的美国总统之一。星巴克的创建人兼首席执行官霍华德·舒尔茨是一位能做出良好判断的现任领导者，他伸缩有度，知道如何拿捏时机。弗洛伦斯·南丁格尔的变革型领导风格非常成功，其原因就是她熟谙官吏的社交礼仪，可以想象判断的后果。伟大的领导者是风云瞬息万变的商海的弄潮儿，但是，“只有当浪潮消退时，你才可以看到谁在赤裸着身体游泳”。

Great Minds Judge Alike

Warren Bennis is one of the world's foremost thinkers and teachers on the subject of leadership. From his early works, including On Becoming a Leader, to his more recent publications, such as Geeks and Geezers, Transparency and Judgment (co-authored with Noel Tichy), Bennis explores the subject of organizational leadership with precision, insight, compassion, and, well judgment.

My life's work has focused on leaders and leadership. What role does judgment play in this realm? I believe that the essence of effective leadership is judgment and taste. And where judgment really counts is in consequential① decisions made in three areas-strategic choices, people choices and choices made in crisis situations. When I want to take the measure of a leader, I always look at their decisions in these three areas.

As we speak, we're in the midst of a political campaign that has inevitably become, at least in part, about differing qualities of leadership. What else besides judgment seems essential to us? The key issue facing most leaders today is figuring out what's really relevant given the kinds of changes organizations, markets and economies are experiencing. In a way, with the proliferation② of C-Suite officers, it surprises me that we don't

---

① consequential [ˌkɔnsiˈkwenʃəl] *adj.* 有重要性的

② proliferation [prəuˌlifəˈreiʃən] *n.* 增加

智者所见略同

沃伦·本尼斯是世界上领导力学科最著名的思想家和教师之一。他早期的著作包括《如何成为领导者》，他的最新著作包括《极客与怪杰》、《透明度和判断力》(与诺埃尔·蒂奇合著)，在这些书中，本尼斯从精确度、洞察力、同情心和良好的判断力等角度探讨了组织领导力的话题。

我终身的工作就是关注领导者和领导力。在这个领域判断起着怎样的作用呢？我认为，判断和鉴赏力是有效领导不可或缺的因素。判断真正起作用的地方在三个举足轻重的领域——战略性选择、人力资源选择和在危机情况下做出的选择。我在测量领导者的能力时，经常考察他们在这三个方面的决策。

正如我们所说的，我们处于不可避免地形成的政治活动的漩涡，这至少部分地区分了不同的领导品质。除了判断之外，还有别的什么看上去对我们很重要呢？考虑到各种组织变化、市场和经济正在经历的发展，大多数领导者目前面临的关键问题是需要思考领导力究竟与什么相关。在某种程度上，我对企业最高管理层人员的增加感到吃惊，我们找不到首席相关性官员来问这样一个问题："如果环境发生彻底的改变，我们必须确保企业从现在开始能够再发展两年，那么我们该如何知道那些真正的相关因素呢？"以我的经验来

have a chief relevance officer to ask, "with all that's changing in our environment, how do we know what's really relevant to make sure we are going to exist two years from now?" In my experience, every senior leader has to include "chief relevance officer" in their leadership portfolio. No leader can ignore the question of relevance. And in addition, top leadership should create a focal point for this ongoing inquiry within their organizations.

With the compression① of time we are all experiencing today, speed is also going to be an important determinant. The capacity to make quick decisions is going to be an increasingly important aspect of leadership. It seems to me that one of the primary tasks of any leader is to keep reminding people what's important. One of the great dangers of especially successful organizations is that they stop asking what's really important and so keep doing the same things over and over again.

One of the major flaws of most human systems today is absence of reflection. Now there is one exception to that-the military. That's where they invented the word "debriefing②." Organizations and teams need to make time and space where they routinely look at decisions, even small ones. Where they ask, what was the process like? What were the failures? What should we have done differently? What kind of information didn't we have that we should have had? Beyond that, organizations also need to ask broader questions, like, what are we doing? Does it make sense? What if we were taken over? Or what should we be doing that we are not doing? Those are kinds of questions we should ask on a regular basis, but don't.

---

① compression [kəm'preʃən] n. 压紧

② debriefing [di'bri:fiŋ] n. 任务报告

看，每一位高级领导者必须在领导力投资组合方面纳入“首席相关性官员”。任何领导者都不可忽视相关性问题。另外，最高领导层应该为此创建一个汇聚点，在组织内部不间断地探讨这个问题。

由于我们现在都体验到了时间的紧迫感，速度也就成为一个重要的决定性因素。迅速做出决策的能力将会成为领导力越来越重要的方面。在我看来，任何领导者面临的主要任务是不断提醒员工什么是重要的。特别成功的组织面临的最大危险之一就是他们不再问员工什么是真正重要的，我们需要一而再、再而三地重复同样的事情。

当今大多数人文系统的主要缺点之一就是缺乏反省。对此，现在有一个例外——军人。他们在军事领域发明了“任务报告”这个词汇。组织和团队需要抽出时间和空间，考虑日常的决策，哪怕是细微的决策。他们对哪里有疑问，过程进行得如何？存在哪些失败？我们应该做哪些不同的处理？哪些应该了解的信息我们还不知道？除此之外，组织还需要回答更广泛的问题，例如，我们正在做什么？这样做有意义吗？如果我们被接管了会出现什么情况？我们应该做哪些我们还没有做的？这些是我们应该定期扪心自问的问题，但是都还没有做到。

我们花了很多时间研究领导者行为，帮助他们深入了解向外发展所面临的挑战。如果你发现与你一道工作的人没有表现出良好的判断力，你会怎么做呢？你不能让这种情况继续下去。比如说，你一直在试图帮助某人，观察他先前做出的决策，但他的决策并不太行得通。领导力包括了解这些信息、请求辞职和寻找构建终端，或许他并不适合这个职位，另换职位可能会更好。

We spent many hours with leaders helping them to develop outside insight on the challenges they face. What do you do if you find that someone you are working with is not exercising good judgment? You can't let that continue. Let's say you've been trying to help that person look at the decisions previously made that didn't work out very well. Leadership involves knowing this, and asking for the resignation, looking for some kind of constructive termination, or maybe it's a matter of a bad fit in that role and that another role would be much better.

There are a few leaders who exemplify great judgment. It's always easier to talk about greatness or badness through time. Harry Truman is a very good example. He was the only non-college educated U.S. president of the 20th century and made some of the most far-reaching decisions of any of our presidents. We went through a time when he was not thought to be very impressive-in fact, in 1948, when he was running for re-election, people said, "To err is Truman," but now historians view him as a credible president.

A current leader that I think makes good judgment calls, even with the current setbacks he faces, is Howard Schultz, founder and CEO of Starbucks. He keeps learning. He uses a wide network of people that he talks with before he makes decisions. He knows when to fold and when to hold-he's enough of a gambler, but he knows the difference between bold and reckless. When Shakespeare's Henry IV wanted to be sure that his son Prince Hal was ready to lead, he sent Falstaff to mentor him. Falstaff said to Prince Hal, "If you want to lead people, you've got to enter their world." I think that's a profound remark. That's what Howard does. He goes into all those Starbucks and he smells the coffee! He gets down into the customer's mind. He enters their territory. I think that's key.

有少数领导者是伟大判断力的典范。穿越时光谈论伟大与糟糕总是会更容易。哈里·杜鲁门就是一个很好的例子。他是20世纪的美国总统中唯一没有接受过大学教育的总统，但他是所有总统中制定出最具深远影响决策的总统。曾经有一段时间，我们认为这些决策没有太大的影响力。事实上，当他在1948年再度当选为总统时，人们声称："杜鲁门总是犯错误"，但历史学家现在认为，他是一位值得信赖的总统。

我认为，星巴克的创建人兼首席执行官霍华德·舒尔茨是一位能做出良好判断的现任领导者，即使现阶段他遇到了一些挫折。他坚持不断地学习。在做决策前，他广泛结交志趣相投的人，和他们进行交谈。他伸缩有度，知道如何拿捏时机。他是一个十足的赌徒，但是他知道冒险和蛮干的区别。在莎士比亚戏剧中，当亨利四世确认他的儿子哈尔王子准备称王时，便打发福斯塔夫去做儿子的私人教师。福斯塔夫对哈尔王子说："如果你要领导人民，就必须融入你的子民的世界。"我认为，这是一句经典的语录。霍华德就是这么做的。他走进每一家星巴克，品尝咖啡的味道。他亲自了解消费者的想法。他融入他们的生活。我认为这就是秘诀。

我想说一下弗洛伦斯·南丁格尔。众所周知，她的变革型领导风格非常成功，其原因就是她能深刻理解官吏的社交礼仪。真正了解组织复杂性的领导者可以想象判断的后果，包括对外部的股东、内部的员工和自己的团队。我认为，这种想象力对任何组织的成功领导力都有必要。

我们有时在危如累卵之际做出个人决策，而且是真正改变世界的决策。我曾经做过的最艰难的决策是我任辛辛那提大学校长的时

And I'd like to mention Florence Nightingale. It has been said of her that the reason she was so successful in transformational leadership was that she had a deep understanding of the social etiquette of bureaucracy①. Leaders who really know the intricacies② of their organization can picture the consequences of judgments on the stakeholders outside, on the people within, on their own team. I believe that power of imagination is essential to successful leadership of any organization.

We sometimes made a personal decision where our judgment was at stake, one that made a real difference in the world. The hardest decision I ever had to make was when I was president of the University of Cincinnati. It was a decision that I think only an outsider could have made: changing a city university to become a state university. There was enormous local pressure to maintain the mythology that the University of Cincinnati was a city-supported university when in fact the city was supplying only 5% of the revenue. That meant we had to keep raising tuition for people who couldn't afford to pay it, because it is basically a blue-collar school. It took three years of work to get this to happen—at which point, the new governor was going to bring in a new board that would ask for my resignation. It was hard, controversial and I didn't do it all correctly. But in the end, it was the right judgment. It was a fine moment for all when I was granted an honorary degree recently at the University of Cincinnati, now proudly a state school, 30 years after that judgment.

(1,093 words)

---

① bureaucracy [bjuə'rɔkrəsi] *n.* 官僚机构

② intricacy ['intrikəsi] *n.* 错综复杂

候。我认为，只有局外人才能做出这样决策：将一所城市大学改变成州立大学。维持这个神话要承受巨大的地方性压力，辛辛那提大学是一所城市支撑的大学，实际上，这座城市只供给5%的税收。这就意味着，我们必须对那些交不起学费的人不断涨学费，因为它本质上还是一所蓝领阶层的学校。我们花了三年的时间实现这个计划，在某种程度上，新州长打算引进一个新的董事会，这样就可以要求我退休。这件事很艰难，争议颇多，我也没有做到全对，但它最终被证明是正确的决策。当我最近获得辛辛那提大学的荣誉学位时，对所有人来说，那都是一个美妙的时刻。这个决策已经过去了30年，令我感到自豪的是，辛辛那提大学现在是一所州立大学。

知识链接

Warren Bennis 沃伦·本尼斯是领导力之父，组织发展理论的先驱，四任美国总统顾问团成员，多家《财富》500强企业的顾问。他两度被《华尔街日报》誉为“管理学十大发言人”，他使领导学成为一门学科，为领导学建立了学术规则。他是XY理论创始人麦格雷戈、经济学泰斗萨缪尔森的学生，管理大师汉迪的老师。

C-Suite “C型雇员”，指企业最高管理层。即首席执行官CEO（Chief Executive Officer），首席财务官CFO（Chief Financial Officer），首席运营官COO（Chief Operations Officer），首席信息官CIO（Chief Information Officer），首席技术官CTO（Chief Technology Officer），首席风险官CRO（Chief Risk Officer）等。由于每个主管都是以C开头，所以称为C-Suite。

题　记

内部竞争是把双刃剑，它既可以产生“鲶鱼效应”，使得竞争的参与者去寻找更低成本的供方、管理成本以及更为积极的渠道建设；又可以产生“山包效应”，使得在企业内部形成了一个个利益小主体，子公司与事业部之间不能形成良好的协作与配合关系。美国情报界的混乱可归咎于它的历史，官僚地盘战、职业保密和兄弟姐妹间的竞争造成了一种功能紊乱。安然公司的倒塌在某种意义上也是末位淘汰、内部竞争的恶果，公司职员个个心怀鬼胎，质疑身边的合伙人是私家侦探和蓄意破坏者。拥有多个标签的唱片公司经常开展标签之间的互相竞争，以抬高唱片的价格。事实证明，处理好企业内部的竞争与合作的动态协调平衡关系才能有效地规避风险。如果你必须吃掉你所杀死的猎物，至少试着不要咬伤你捕猎的手。

Trying Not to Bite the Hand That Feeds You

Amid the contentiousness① and acrimony② of the debate over September 11th and the war in Iraq, the one thing that almost everyone seems to agree on is that the American intelligence community is a mess. We have fifteen agencies responsible for gathering and analyzing intelligence, and they are not exactly a band of brothers. On a good day, they duplicate each other's efforts, leaving important work undone. On a bad day, they hoard information and undermine their cohorts③, seeming at times more preoccupied with reputations, budgets, and internal power struggles than with the nation's security.

The intelligence community owes its failings to a history of bureaucratic turf wars, occupational secrecy, and sibling rivalry—a kind of dysfunction that seems typical of the public sector. But its chaotic structure resembles something else: the ideal corporation, as envisioned by management gurus, when tight-knit, top-down organizations bound together by a common purpose fell out of fashion. Bandying coinages like

---

① contentiousness [kən'tenʃəsnəs] *n.* 争论

② acrimony ['ækriməni] *n.* 尖刻

③ cohort ['kəuhɔːt] *n.* 同伴

不要咬伤捕猎的手

在对9·11事件和伊拉克战争无休止的争吵和尖酸刻薄的讽刺声中，有一件事几乎得到了所有人的一致认同，那就是美国的情报界一团糟。我们有15个部门负责收集和分析情报，他们并不完全像乐队的兄弟那样紧密合作。风平浪静的时候，他们分享彼此的成果，搁置重要的工作。形势恶劣的时候，他们封闭信息，伤害同伙，有时候仿佛更关注声誉、预算和内部权力斗争，而不是国家的安全。

美国情报界的混乱可归咎于它的历史，官僚地盘战、职业保密和兄弟姐妹间的竞争造成了一种功能紊乱，这似乎是公共部门的典型现象。但是，管理领袖们推测，它的混乱结构类似于一家理想的公司，关系紧密、自上而下的组织为了过时的共同目标捆绑在一起。他们散布“内创业”和“达尔文革命”这样的新造词，认为公司员工彼此之间的竞争应该和他们与其他公司之间的竞争一样激烈。人们鼓励企业“引入市场机制”，即培养内部竞争，独立和分权。只有最强的公司才能取得胜利，走势较弱的公司要么改善状况，要么灭亡。一个备受推崇的格言是“各食其利”——泰德·努金似的光环笼罩着汤姆·彼得斯。瑞士巨头A. B. B集团被大家捧为未来的“组织形式”，它是一个由数千相互竞争的小公司组成的联

"intrapreneurship" and "Darwinian revolution," they argued that people in a corporation should compete as hard against each other as they do against other companies. Businesses were encouraged to "bring the market inside"—to foster internal competition, independence, and decentralization. May the strongest division win; let the weaker ones improve or die. A favorite maxim was "Eat what you kill"—a sort of Ted Nugent gloss on Tom Peters. The Swiss giant A.B.B., a confederation of thousands of small competing companies, was hailed as the "organizational form" of the future. Enron's survival-of-the-fittest model—in which divisions openly worked at cross-purposes—attracted wide acclaim as well. Internal competition is, of course, inevitable. But, where previously it had been seen as something to be counteracted or, at least, carefully managed, in the new world it was to be stirred up and cheered along.

In the economy as a whole, competition generates innovation and creates wealth. We pit companies against each other, and trust that the strongest will prosper and that society will benefit. The pied pipers believed that what worked in the world should work on the job, too. To be sure, there were sound ideas buried in the buzzwords. Decentralization is often good: it encourages people to specialize, and it gives them more say in solving the problems they're most familiar with. Independence encourages responsibility. And competition can be a useful prod for making people work and think harder.

But there are some things that people can do better together than they can apart. Companies, in theory, anyway, are a way to make it easier for people to cooperate, to share information, to learn from each other, and to

邦。安然公司的适者生存模型也得到了广泛的认同，它的每个子公司在工作目标上形成了相互交叉。当然，内部的竞争不可避免。但是，之前被人们认为可以抵消或者至少经过认真经营的东西，在新的环境中一定会被激发，受到人们的欢迎。

就整体经济而言，竞争带来了改革，创造了财富。我们促使公司相互竞争，期待最强大的公司繁荣，社会受益。善于开空头支票的领导者认为，世界上发生的事情也应该发生在工作上。当然，有些术语隐含着合理的想法。分权制通常还不错：它鼓励人们专业化，给予他们在处理自己最熟悉的事情时更多的发言权。竞争可以称为一种有效的办法，使人们工作更努力，思维更活跃。

但是，有些事情如果一起完成会比单枪匹马做得更好。不管怎么说，公司在理论上是易于人们相互合作、分享信息、相互学习、共同努力的一种方式。它们也能帮助减少经济学家罗纳德·科斯广为人知的言论“交易成本”，即交易竞价成本，监督人们确保他们正在做自己应该完成的工作。过度的内部竞争抵消了这些好处。它鼓励人们封闭信息，背叛同事，追逐个人私利。在安然公司，员工们锁住他们的门，犹豫不决地离开办公室，因为他们担心，他们的同事是私家侦探和蓄意破坏者。当公司的能源交易部指出，他们如何通过操纵加州的能源市场赚取巨额利润时，却没有将此事告知由于能源成本暴涨而濒临破产的安然能源供应子公司。同样的，拥有多个标签的唱片公司经常开展标签之间的互相竞争，以抬高唱片的价格，尽管协作能节约公司的成本。通用汽车公司的前主席曾经描述过制造新车的过程，工程师与装配工之间常有一些恶意的交流：“好吧，如果你可以，你自己造吧。”

coordinate their efforts. They can also help to mitigate[①] what the economist Ronald Coase famously called "transaction costs," the costs of haggling[②] over deals and monitoring people to make sure they're doing what they're supposed to. Excessive internal competition eliminates these advantages. It encourages people to hoard information, betray their colleagues, and pursue their own ends. At Enron, employees locked their doors and hesitated to leave their desks because they were afraid their associates were snoop[③] and saboteurs[④]. When the company's energy-trading division figured out how to make huge profits by manipulating the California energy market, it did so without telling Enron's energy-providing division, which got crushed as power costs soared. Similarly, record companies that own multiple labels often allow them to bid against each other, driving up prices, when collaboration would almost certainly save money. A former chairman of General Motors once described the process of building a new car there as a series of spiteful exchanges between the engineers and the assemblers: "O.K., you build it if you can."

It turns out that cooperation, not competition, is the real management challenge. Jeffrey Pfeffer, a Stanford business professor, has pointed to a series of studies that demonstrate how seldom rival divisions in corporations share information with each other. At one food manufacturer, the best factory was a hundred and twelve per cent more productive than the worst, even though the factories were using the same machines. At

① mitigate [ˈmitigeit] *vt.* 减轻

② haggle [ˈhægl] *vi.* 竞价

③ snoop [snuːp] *n.* 到处窥视人

④ saboteur [ˌsæbəˈtəː] *n.* 从事破坏活动者

事实证明，合作而不是竞争才是真正的管理挑战。斯坦福大学商学院教授杰弗·里佛指出：一系列的研究表明，企业中能够相互分享信息的竞争部门是如此之少。在一家食品制造公司，尽管各家工厂使用同样的机器设备，但最好的工厂比最差的工厂产量高出112%；在另一家公司，最好的工厂能比最差的工厂产出多300%。你当然可以马上关掉这些效益差的工厂。但是，分享那些效益好的工厂的技术信息却通常更便宜和更有效。纽柯钢铁公司一直在这么做，因而产生了巨大的效益。在纽柯钢铁公司，各家工厂以自负盈亏为主，不需要总公司告诉他们做什么，公司的每个人都能知道各厂的运作情况，这样落后者就无法隐藏。当时，纽柯钢铁公司没有关闭最差的工厂，或者任其发展，而是将强者做得好的经验告诉弱者，用以帮助弱者发展。

我们不想回到过去的时光：总部下达旨意，奴才不假思索地服从。但如果人们相信，他们受到激励后能够相信，组织作为一个整体能比微不足道的个体创造更多的价值，分权和内部竞争才会发挥作用。在这种情况下，知识——任何公司最重要的资源，就会很便宜。毕竟，雇佣成百上千的人找出问题，然后又敦促他们不要对外声张毫无意义。竞争暴露问题，合作解决问题。如果你必须吃掉你所杀死的猎物，至少试着不要咬伤你捕猎的手。

知识链接

Intrapreneurship 内创业指企业发展到一定阶段后，为了提升核心竞争力并获得创新性成果而做出的组织允诺、授权和资源保证的一系列内部创业

another, the best plant was three hundred per cent more productive. You could just shut down the weak plants. But usually it would be far cheaper and more efficient to get the strong ones to share their techniques. That's what the steel company Nucor has done, to great effect. At Nucor, individual factories essentially run themselves, without the home office telling them what to do, and everyone in the company can see how each plant is doing, so that the laggards can't hide. Then, instead of purging the weak factories or leaving them to flounder①, Nucor takes what the strong are doing well and employs it to help the weak.

We don't want a return to the days when headquarters handed down edicts and minions mindlessly obeyed. But decentralization and internal competition work only if people believe, and if they're given incentives to believe, that the organization as a whole matters more than their little part of it. When that's the case, knowledge, the most important resource any company has, is cheap. It is senseless, after all, to hire hundreds of thousands of people to find stuff out and then urge them to keep what they know to themselves. Competition reveals problems, and cooperation solves them. If you must eat what you kill, at least try not to bite the hand that feeds you.

(903 words)

① flounder [ˈflaundə] *vi.* 挣扎,困难地往前走

行动。

A. B. B. 该集团是一家瑞典跨国公司，总部设在瑞士苏黎世，主要经营机器人技术和自动控制技术，在全球100多个国家设有分公司。ABB是三位公司创始人各自的首字母。

Nucor 纽柯钢铁公司总部设在美国北卡罗来纳州夏洛特市，主要制造和销售钢铁制品。产品包括普碳钢、紧固件、合金钢、不锈钢等。同时公司在美国17个州设有钢材生产地，全球产量排名第11位。

题　记

出生在20世纪80年代左右的年轻人被称为“Y代”，他们是“高峰期人口的回音”——娇生惯养但充满自信，最有特权并富有洞察力。相比“生活是为了工作”的婴儿潮人口，X代人崇尚“工作是为了生活”，而Y代比婴儿潮人口和X代更为乐观。Y代人持有一套全新的价值观念，他们从工作之中以及工作之外追求生活的实现，他们习惯于高水平的富裕生活，他们不再对长期的工作关系感兴趣。他们不要控制，要引导；不要指派，要解释；不要发号施令，要恳求；不要忽略，要回应；不要隐瞒，要沟通。当企业对接受过良好教育、并且具备一定技能的劳动力资源的需求在不断地增大之时，顺应和引导“授权予我一代”已成为企业应对激烈的全球竞争、造就经济腾飞的历史重任。

Communicating with "Empower-ME Generation"

Here are five ways to successfully engage with Gen Y, whose members want to add meaning to their lives and to the world. Gen Y is gaining attention for its participation in the 2008 Presidential primaries, voting in numbers not seen in decades. But the group's influence obviously isn't limited to politics. Some 30 million young people in their late teens to early 30s are expected to join the U.S. workforce by 2010. Effectively communicating with them will be crucial to your company's success.

Empowerment is what young people crave①. I have spent the last two years interviewing dozens of business leaders who run companies that rely on employees in their teens and 20s. To a person, these leaders have learned that it's important to offer young people more than a paycheck and a free on-site massage. This group wants to know that its work is adding up to a great cause. They want to add meaning to their lives and to the world. The old command-and-control style of managing won't work with this generation. Lip service won't fly. I've distilled five ways to engage

① crave [kreiv] *vt.* 渴望

与“授权予我一代”沟通

有五种方法可以使你成功与Y代人沟通，Y代人希望为自己的生活和世界增光添彩。Y代人参与了2008年的总统初选，赢得了大众的关注，他们投出了近几十年来前所未见的大量选票。但是，这个群体的影响力显然并不只是限于政治。大约3000万十八九岁到三十出头的年轻人有待在2010年进入美国劳动力市场。如果贵公司想取得成功，那么与他们进行有效的交流真是至关重要。

年轻人渴望授权。过去两年，我花时间采访了许多商界领袖，他们经营的公司主要依靠十几岁到二十几岁的年轻人。对自然人而言，这些领导人已经意识到，重要的是不能只为年轻人支付薪酬和免费上门按摩。这个群体希望知道他们做的这份工作为某一项伟大的事业做出了贡献。他们渴望自己的生活和世界变得更有意义。陈旧的指挥和控制管理模式对这代人不起作用。空头支票也不会奏效。我精挑细选了五种与他们打交道的方法。

不要控制，要引导。时尚新闻收集网站DIGG的共同创办人杰森·阿德尔森认为，年轻的员工对自己和管理人员都抱有很高的期望值。这个群体渴望为具有丰富经验的管理者工作，以期这些管理

them.

Don't manage, mentor. Jason Adelson, co-founder of the popular news gathering site Digg, says young employees have high expectations for themselves and their managers. Members of this group want to work for highly engaged managers who help them grow and develop their professional skills. "Younger workers are transforming the workplace from the get-rich-quick attitude to a culture of empowerment① and contribution," Adelson told me. "At the end of the day, these employees want to feel as if they are part of something extraordinary, and, more important, have contributed to its achievement." While your primary goal might be to get projects accomplished on time and on budget, young people want to learn from you. Allocate more of your time to developing staff. Ask your younger employees about their goals and career ambitions. Is their position helping them achieve those dreams? If not, it is a manager's responsibility to help employees find the right roles where they have the best chance of success.

Don't assign, explain. Cold Stone Creamery is one of the largest franchises② in the U.S. What sets it apart from other ice cream chains is simple. When customers throw a tip in the jar, employees sing a song. While the chain offers high-quality ice cream, its attraction is the experience. Most of its employees are teenagers. When I spoke to leadership at Cold Stone, they acknowledged that a 16-year-old doesn't dream of scooping③ ice cream into her 30s. The Cold Stone approach is to

---

① empowerment [imˈpauəmənt] *n.* 授权

② franchises [ˈfræntʃaiziz] *n.* 特许权

③ scoop [ˈskuːp] *vt.* 舀取，掘

人员帮助他们成长和培养他们的专业技能。德尔森告诉我："年纪较轻的员工正在改变职场，使之从快速致富的态势转变为一种赋权和奉献的文化。这些员工在一天工作结束时，感觉自己仿佛是非同寻常的事业的一部分，更重要的是，他们对取得的成就做出了贡献"。虽然你的首要目标也许是在预算内按时完成项目，而年轻人的目标则是想向你学习。分配更多的时间培养员工吧。了解年轻雇员的目标和职业抱负，他们的职位有助于他们实现这些梦想吗？如果不是，那么作为一个经理，有责任帮助员工找到正确的职位，使他们最有可能获得成功。

不要指派，要解释。"酷圣石"冰淇淋是美国最大的特许经营商之一。公司与其他冰淇淋连锁店的区别很简单。客人往罐子里扔一枚小费，员工就会唱一首歌。虽然连锁店提供高品质的冰淇淋，但它的吸引力其实是体验。它的大多数员工是十几岁的青少年。我和"酷圣石"冰淇淋的领导人谈话时，他们承认，16岁的年轻人并不想到三十多岁时还在舀取冰淇淋。"酷圣石"冰淇淋的方法是鼓励他们利用现在的职位学习生活技能，忽略所选择的职业。特许权所有者和管理者都要接受培训，以强化这样一个观念："酷圣石"冰淇淋是他们迄今得到的"最好的第一份工作"。指派不会对Y代人起作用，除非他们另有目的。

不要发号施令，要恳求。谷歌公司的马里萨·梅耶毕业于斯坦福大学的计算机科学专业，她将学术界的思想引入了自己的新职位，即充分利用办公时间。每天下午4点开始，在持续90分钟的时

encourage them to use the position to learn life skills regardless of their chosen careers. Franchise owners and managers are trained to reinforce the idea that Cold Stone is "the best first job" they could ever have. Assignments don't work with Gen Y unless there's a reason behind them.

Don't dictate, solicit. Google's Marisa Mayer studied computer science at Stanford and brought an idea from academia to her new position: office hours. For 90 minutes each day beginning at 4 p.m., her staff can sign a sheet outside her office for a 15-minute impromptu meeting. At these meetings, staffers voice opinions or pitch new ideas. Mayer says some of Google's most innovative features have come from these office hours. Although these employees may have spent only a few minutes with Mayer, they leave knowing they have been heard and that their opinions matter.

Don't ignore, respond. Recently a reporter from the Newark, N.J., newspaper The Star-Ledger asked me to talk about New York Giants head coach Tom Coughlin. Coughlin had come close to being fired early in the season but ultimately led his players to a Super Bowl upset victory over the undefeated New England Patriots. How did Coughlin turn everything around? He did something that is absolutely critical to get buy-in from young people: He empowered them and made them feel as though they were part of the building process. Instead of ignoring the criticism leveled against him, Coughlin began to talk to his players with no clipboard and no agenda—just to listen. He also set up a council of veteran① players to improve communication and to bring issues to his attention. According to defensive player Michael Strahan, Coughlin "adjusted" to his team by

---

① veteran [ˈvetərən] *n.* 经验丰富的人；老兵

间内，员工可以在她的办公室外签一张纸条，申请参加15分钟的临时会议。在这些会议上，员工们要么发表自己的意见，要么提出新的观点。梅耶说，谷歌有些最具创新力的项目就是在这些办公时间的会议上产生的。虽然这些员工可能只和梅耶相处了几分钟，但他们离开时已经知道，有人听取了他们的意见，而且这些意见很有价值。

不要忽略，要回应。最近，一位来自新泽西州纽瓦克“明星纪事报”的记者请我谈论一下纽约巨人队总教练汤姆·库格林。库格林在本赛季早期险些被开除，但最终带领他的球员在超级碗上取得了颠覆性的胜利，战胜了新英格兰的爱国者队。库格林是如何扭转这一切的呢？他做了一件至关重要的事，那就是赢得年轻人的支持：他授权给他们，使他们觉得自己好像是球队构建过程中的组成部分。库格林没有忽略针对他提出的批评，开始与球员交谈，既不用写字板，也不用记事册，而是倾听球员的意见。他还成立了老球员委员会，以改善交流，让问题得到重视。据防守球员迈克尔·斯特拉恩透露，科格林“调整”了他的团队，使他们成为决策过程的参与者。

不要隐瞒，要沟通。今天，年轻人在生意场上渴望获得同僚和管理人员的反馈和相互交流，这种感觉比前辈更为强烈。研究人员对专业的猎头公司哈德森事务所的2 000多名雇员进行了一项调查，他们发现，在对待老板和同事的态度上，几代人之间有明显的区别。属于Y群体的25%的员工希望，有必要至少每周一次从老板那

making them part of the decision-making process.

Don't conceal, communicate. Young people in business today crave feedback and interaction with their peers and managers, more so than previous generations did. When researchers at professional staffing firm Hudson (HHGP) conducted a survey of 2,000 employees, they found striking differences between generations in their attitudes toward their bosses and co-workers. Twenty-five percent of workers who fall into the Gen Y category consider it important to get feedback from their bosses at least once a week. However, only 11% of baby boomers① desire that level of communication. Young employees also want greater social interaction with their peers and supervisors. Maintain an open, consistent dialogue and you will win their loyalty.

Young people fall into a category I call the "Empower ME Generation" because that is exactly what they are asking from their employers—to be empowered. The 2008 election is proving that young people can be engaged when they feel as though they are making a difference. The same holds true in the workplace.

(888 words)

① boomer [ˈbuːmə] *n.* 婴儿潮时代出身的人

里获得反馈。然而，婴儿潮时期出生的人中，只有 11%渴望同等水平的交流。年轻员工还希望与同事和管理人员有更多的社会交往。维持开放、一致的对话平台，他们会对你忠心耿耿。

年轻人属于我称之为的"授权予我一代"人，因为这正是他们要求从他们的雇主那里得到的——自主权。2008 年的选举证明，年轻人感觉自己已经有了重要的影响力时，就会身体力行。职场也同样如此。

知识链接

Cold Stone Creamery "酷圣石"冰淇淋是世界知名的时尚冰淇淋品牌，第一家门店在 1988 年诞生于美国的亚利桑那州。它在短短的时间内，以独一无二的"欢乐满溢"（Always Happy）创新品牌理念风靡全球，迅速成为全球年轻一族的心头所好，每天有超过 40 万人在世界各地超过 2000 家的"酷圣石"门市中体验极致完美的冰淇淋假期。"酷圣石"冰淇淋用纯正的美国鲜奶做原料，坚持每天在门市新鲜制作，拥有超过 30 种丰富自选配料，在零下 9 摄氏度的花岗岩石板上拌制而成，不仅如此，在您享受纯正美式冰淇淋的同时，更能听到店内伙伴欢乐的歌声和抛冰淇淋球的特技表演，给顾客完全不同的冰淇淋体验！

题　记

在一个过分拥挤的救生艇里，为了救出其他人，船里最强硬的老兄要扔出三个弱小的成员，让他们淹死……你该怎么做？这是在全球化进程中，跨国公司必须面对的现实。联合国把跨国公司恰当地描述为“世界经济全球化的生产力核心”；与此同时，各国政府的边界和监管机构却在为全球化的新秩序妥协或买单。跨国公司通过一系列的政府间贸易和投资协定，正在重组世界经济结构，从而维持政治权利的平衡；而这些国际贸易和投资的协定又允许企业规避国家政府和地方社区的权力和权威，从而危害了工人的权利、环境和民主的政治进程。全球化看起来确实像一个伟大的平均主义者，但跨国公司的物质贪婪和权力欲望却让人们宁愿相信这是一个轻率而且危险的错误。

The Performance of Transnational Corporations

Transnational corporations—those corporations which operate in more than one country or nation at a time—have become some of the most powerful economic and political entities in the world today. From Joshua Karliner, in his book, The Corporate Planet: Ecology and Politics in the Age of Globalization, we can gleam a host of fundamental realizations, including the fact that many of these companies have far more power than the nation-states across whose borders they operate.

For example, the combined revenues of just General Motors and Ford—the two largest automobile corporations in the world—exceed the combined Gross Domestic Product (GDP) for all of sub-Saharan Africa. Overall, fifty-one of the largest one-hundred economies in the world are corporations. The revenues of the top 500 corporations in the U.S. equal about 60 percent of the country's GDP. Transnational corporations hold ninety percent of all technology and product patents worldwide, and are involved in 70 percent of world trade. More than thirty percent of this trade is "intra- firm"; in other words, it occurs between units of the same corporation.

跨国公司的表演

跨国公司是那些同时在一个以上的国家或民族运作的公司，它们已经成为当今世界上一些最强大的经济和政治实体。从约书亚·卡令那的《公司星球：全球化时代的生态和政治》一书中，我们可以隐约意识到大量的基本现实，其中包括这样一个事实，即许多此类公司的效率远远高于跨界经营的民族国家企业。

例如，通用汽车和福特汽车是世界上两家最大的汽车公司，他们的综合效益超过了所有撒哈拉以南非洲国家的国内生产总值（GDP）的总和。总体而言，世界上最大的一百家经济实体中有五十一家是跨国公司。美国跨国公司500强的收入相当于整个国家国内生产总值的60%。跨国公司拥有全球90%的科技和产品专利，并参与了70%的全球贸易。超过30%的交易属于“公司内部交易”，也就是说，在同一公司、不同部门之间的交易。

联合国把这些跨国公司恰当地描述为“世界经济全球化的生产力核心”。跨国公司的外国子公司拥有全球绝大部分的产业能力、技术知识、国际金融贸易和最终控制权。在能源方面，它们从地面

The United Nations has justly described these corporations as "the productive core of the globalizing world economy." Their foreign affiliates account for most of the world's industrial capacity, technological knowledge, international financial transactions, and ultimately the power of control. In terms of energy, they extract most of the world's minerals from the ground. They manufacture and sell most of the world's automobiles, airplanes, communications satellites, computers, home electronics, chemicals, medicines and biotechnology products. They harvest much of the world's wood and make most of its paper. They grow many of the world's major agricultural crops, while processing and distributing much of its food. Given their dominance of politics, economics and technology, it is not surprising to find the big transnational deeply involved in most of the world's serious environmental crises. Indeed, the interests of the most powerful governments in the world are often intimately intertwined① with the expanding pursuits of the transnationals that they charter. At the same time, transnational corporations are moving to circumvent② national governments. The borders and regulatory agencies of most governments are caving in or being paid off to the New World Order of globalization.

These corporations, together with their host governments, are reorganizing the world economic structures—and thus the balance of political power—through a series of intergovernmental trade and investment accords. These treaties serve as the frameworks within which globalization is evolving—allowing international corporate investment and

---

① intertwined [intəːˈtwaind] *adj.* 互相交织的，错综复杂的

② circumvent [səːkəmˈvent] *vt.* 回避

提取了世界绝大部分的矿产。它们制造和销售世界上绝大多数的汽车、飞机、通信卫星、计算机、家用电子、化工、医药和生物技术产品。它们砍伐世界上大量的树木并生产最多的纸张。它们种植世界上的很多主要农作物，同时加工和分配大量的粮食。由于其在政治、经济和技术上的主导地位，不难看出这些大型跨国公司造成了世界上大多数严重的环境危机。事实上，世界上最强大的政府的利益往往与得到特许的跨国公司追求扩张密切交织。与此同时，跨国公司开始设法规避国家政府。大多数政府的边界和监管机构都向全球化的新秩序妥协或被收买。

这些公司，连同它们的东道国政府，通过一系列的政府间贸易和投资协定，正在重组世界经济结构，从而维持政治权利的平衡。这些条约作为不断发展的全球化的框架，允许国际合作投资和贸易在全球蓬勃发展。它们包括：乌拉圭回合关税及贸易总协定（GATT）、为强制执行关税及贸易总协定的准则成立的世界贸易组织、拟定的多边投资协定（MAI）、北美自由贸易协议（NAFTA）和欧盟（EU）。这些国际贸易和投资的协定允许企业规避国家政府和地方社区的权力和权威，从而危害了工人的权利、环境和民主的政治进程。

但是，还有个小问题，跨国公司和国内大型企业已经控制了美国政府和大多数工业化国家。这是通过企业政治和进行批发购买的政客完成的。拥有财政经济实力的企业王国已经上位。顺便说一

trade to flourish across the Earth. They include: The Uruguay Round of the General Agreement on Tariffs and Trade (GATT); The World Trade Organization, which was created to enforce the GATT's rules; The proposed Multilateral Agreement on Investment. (MAI); The North American Free Trade Agreement (NAFTA) and The European Union (EU). These international trade and investment agreements allow corporations to circumvent the power and authority of national governments and local communities, thus endangering workers' rights, the environment and democratic political processes.

There is a slight problem, however. The TNCs and domestic major corporations already control the governments of the United States and most of the industrialized nations. This is done by Corporate Politics, and the wholesale purchase of politicians. Already in place is a Corporate State, which wields① the economic power of Money. This, by the way, is not a new development. Even in the United States, the dye was cast by the Fourteenth Amendment to the Constitution for the United States of America, whereby private corporations were given the status of persons—and thus allowed to enjoy the benefits of the Bill of Rights, without the commensurate② unlimited liabilities of life. In other words, it's pretty much a done deal.

The problem, of course, is not merely the greed, power-hungry, and irresponsible actions of certain CEOs and the elite of the TNCs—but also those who support them. The latter clearly includes bribed governments,

---

① wield [wiːld] *vt.* 使用,行使

② commensurate [kəˈmenʃərit] *adj.* 相称的

下，这并不是一个新的发展过程。即使在美国，美利坚合众国宪法第十四修正案也摒弃了对肤色的歧视，并凭此给私营企业提供了法人地位，从而享有权利和自由法案的权益，没有与生命相当的无限责任。换言之，这是一个很值得做的交易。

当然，这个问题不仅仅是跨国公司中某些首席执行官和精英贪婪、渴望权力和不负责的行为，还包括支持他们的人。后者显然包括接受贿赂的政府，但也包括普通人，他们购买和使用这些公司提供的产品和服务。由于政府的干预，这一事实似乎别无选择，使之较少指责普通个人的过失。但是，这些相同的个人往往会选择阻力最小的路径，选择生活的质量，包括电话、网络连接、任由自己摆布的公用事业和服务，方便的交通，在偏远地区休假，等等。这种观念引发了一场讨论，包括几个感兴趣的观察家提出的“统一世界秩序”——一种能量守恒。

例如，“统一世界秩序”的一个显著特征在于，一些所谓的“高级别”个体已经明确表示，可能在过去的数百年间，世界上有一些力量控制着星球的命运。统治集团超越了世俗，成为世界强国。这些力量开始发起各种各样的可疑行动：从发起战争和饥荒到纵容瘟疫以及四骑士的其他成员。虽然他们只是回应这些事件，但在某种程度上，世俗的伦理和道德规范也许已经发现了令人震惊的事实。

如果我们假定跨国公司仅仅是问题的一部分，假定这些权力事

but they also include the average person who buys the products and uses the services that these corporations provide. The fact that there is seemingly little choice—due to governmental intervention-makes it less of a charge of negligence to the average individual. But these same individuals also often take the path of least resistance, and choose the quality of life which includes telephones, Internet connections, utilities and services at their beck① and call, easy transportation, vacations at remote locations, and so forth and so on. An intriguing discussion of this idea is included in One World Order—a conservation among several interested observers.

For example, one highlight of the One World Order is the number of allegedly②"high-ranking" individuals who have made it clear that there are forces in the world, potentially for the last several hundred years, that control the destiny of the planet. That there's a hierarchy which far transcends the mundane③, worldly powers. These forces may have initiated all manner of questionable acts—from initiating wars and famines to encouraging plagues and other members of the Four Horsemen. Are they have simply responded to these incidents, but in a way that mundane ethics and morality might have found shocking.

If we assume TNCs are simply a portion of the problem, that there are in fact powers far in excess of the average multi-billion dollar corporate CEOs, and that these higher powers are intent upon a One World Order, then we have to wonder if perhaps, just perhaps, this is a good thing in the grander scheme of things. If one was in an overcrowded lifeboat, for

---

① beck [bek] *n.* 招手

② allegedly [əˈledʒidli] *adv.* 依其申述地

③ mundane [ˈmʌndein] *adj.* 世俗的

实上远远超过平均价值数十亿美元的公司首席执行官，假定这些高级权威人士下定决心要实行“统一世界秩序”，那么我们不得不思考这样一个问题，在这些事情的宏大计划中，或许，只是或许，这是一件好事。例如，在一个过分拥挤的救生艇里，为了救出其他人，船里最强硬的老兄要扔出三个较弱的成员，让他们淹死……你会怎么做?

承担责任有时需要做出艰难的决策，关键是谁在主宰那些更深层次的意图。举例来说，如果某人或某个团体比乔治·布什总统的权力更大，这会那么糟糕吗？这也许是个好消息吗？这取决于那位更强硬的老兄的意图吗？这些如何掺和到布什的意图中去？让我们面对现实吧：还有什么比让约翰·阿什克罗夫特当司法部长更糟糕的事情了？阴谋在平均个体之间通常不会有很高的可信度。但是，“阴谋之源”有成为并不那么糟糕的议事日程的可能性。也许，在我们的创造现实中，可以准确地证明这种形势。

知识链接

GATT 关税及贸易总协定(General Agreement on Tariffs and Trade)是一个政府间缔结的有关关税和贸易规则的多边国际协定，简称关贸总协定。它的宗旨是通过削减关税和其他贸易壁垒，削除国际贸易中的差别待遇，促进国际贸易自由化，以充分利用世界资源，扩大商品的生产与流通。

example, and in order to save everyone else, the toughest dude in the boat tossed three of the weaker members overboard and allowed them to drown... what would you do?

Being in charge sometimes requires tough decisions. The key is the deeper intentions of whoever is in charge. If, for example, someone or some group has much more power than President George Bush, would this be all that bad? Would that perhaps be wonderful news? Doesn't it depend upon what the tougher dude's intentions are? And how those stack up to Bush's intentions? Let's face it: Could things be worse than having John Ashcroft as Attorney General? Conspiracies do not generally have a great deal of credibility with the average individual. But there is just the possibility that the "Mother of Conspiracies" may be one that has an agenda that is not all that bad. Perhaps, in our Creating Reality, we can manifest exactly that sort of situation.

(1,076 words)

NAFTA 北美自由贸易协议(North American Free Trade Agreement)是美国、加拿大及墨西哥在1992年8月12日签署的关于三国间全面贸易的协议。

MAI 多边投资协定(Multilateral Agreement on Investment)是国际经济合作组织曾经组织拟定的一个关于促进与保护国际投资发展的国际条约，由于各国分歧较大，最终没能达成一致。

Four Horsemen 四骑士。这一典故取自《圣经》，指战争、饥荒、瘟疫、死亡四大灾难。

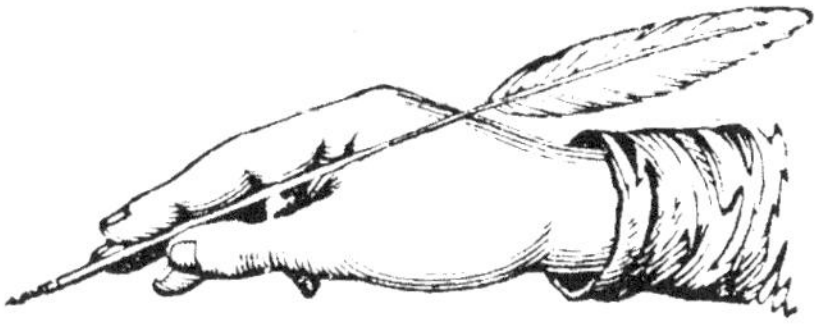

题　记

贸易全球化导致了资本技术的快速流动，以跨国公司为主体、以世界市场为依托、以全球生产为基础的开放式生产结构改变了以国家为主体的国际产业分工和贸易，新的判断标准和游戏规则在验证亚当·斯密自由贸易命题的同时，接受了美国人莱·特维的经济全球化概念。贸易全球化共识既让美国人获利匪浅，也让美国人忐忑不安。他们担心发展中国家追求的经济战略只指财富积累和建立地理政治权势，而不是提高居民的生活质量；他们担心石油价格上涨使大量的资本净值从新兴的边缘地区流向工业中心，造成不可收拾的地理政治原因和经济后果；他们担心美国会成为最后贷款人的进口商，对本国生产的商品价格削减加剧经济衰退。贸易全球化的阴谋与爱情让美国人倍感纠结。

The Global Consensus on Trade

With two wars still continuing and violence in Georgia dominating the foreign policy debate; and with the financial crisis and economic insecurity for families dominating the domestic debate, US international economic policy is receiving less attention in this presidential election year than usual. The limited attention it has received has focused on concerns about specific trade agreements, not broader questions of international strategy. That is unfortunate. The next administration faces the prospect of having to make the most consequential international economic policy choices in a generation at a time when the confidence of governments in free markets is being increasingly questioned.

The current distribution of regional economic power is unlike anything that was predicted even a decade ago. The rise of the developing world, its growing share in global output and far greater share of global growth, is perhaps a quantitative but not a qualitative surprise. The qualitative surprise is this: with almost all the industrial world in or near recession, much of the momentum① in the global economy is coming from countries with authoritarian governments that are pursuing economic

① momentum[məu'mentəm] *n.* 势头

贸易全球化共识

在这个总统选举年，美国国际经济政策受关注的程度较之平时更加不容乐观，这些政策包括仍在继续的两场战争、控制外交政策辩论的格鲁吉亚暴力以及金融危机和家庭经济不安全感等国内主要的辩论话题。人们对特别贸易协定趋之若鹜，对国际战略等更广泛的问题置之不理，这真是很不幸。当政府在自由市场上的自信受到越来越多的质疑时，下届政府不得不面临制定最重要的国际经济政策的前景，这就是一代人在一段时期中的选择。

目前的地域经济实力分布与十年前的预测不同。发展中国家正在崛起，他们在全球出口份额的增长远远高于全球经济份额的增长，这或许是一种数量，而不是一种定性，并不令人感到惊讶。但定性分析的结果却让人感到突兀：即使全球工业临近或者正在衰退，全球经济的势头还是主要来自独裁政府的国家，他们追求的经济战略只指财富积累和建立地理政治权势，而不是提高居民的生活质量。这种趋势出现在亚洲国家、俄罗斯和其他石油输出国。

strategies directed towards wealth accumulation and building up geopolitical strength rather than improving living standards for their populations. The tendencies, however, can be seen in Asia, Russia and other oil exporting countries.

Even before the slowdown in the industrial world, a striking feature of the global economy was the substantial net flow of capital from the emerging periphery① to the industrial centre. Rising oil prices have geopolitical as well as economic consequences. The run-up in oil prices over the past year has generated more than $ 10bn a week in extra revenues for Opec members. Asian export powers and oil exporters have enjoyed a vast accumulation of wealth, adding about $ 1,000bn a year in assets.

These shifts have affected almost every global economic issue. The pressure created by the investment of these surpluses was one of the big factors driving the excesses that preceded our financial problems. Concern about the flow of imports from countries that have pursued a strategy of export-led growth is a big reason for the protectionist backlash② now being seen in the industrialized world. It is now recognised that meaningful efforts to address climate change require a framework that induces China and other emerging markets to co-operate.

It has become a cliché to suggest that the world's institutional approaches to economic co-operation need overhauling③ to take into

---

① periphery [pəˈrifəri] *n.* 外围

② backlash [ˈbæklæʃ] *n.* 对抗性反应

③ overhaul [ˌəuvəˈhɔl] *vt.* 大修,翻修

工业国家经济发展减缓之前，大量的资本净值从新兴的边缘地区流向工业中心，形成了全球经济的一个显著特点，所以提高石油价格既是地理政治原因也是经济后果。油价在过去几年持续走高，石油输出国组织成员每周可多赚100多亿美元。亚洲出口巨头和石油输出国因此聚集了大量的财富，每年增加的资产约达1万亿美元。

这些转变几乎影响了全球所有的经济事件。这些过剩投资产生的压力是导致早前发生财政无度放纵的主要因素之一。有些国家奉行以出口为主导的增长战略，关注进口流通成为贸易保护主义的对抗性反应，这在很大程度上解释了工业化国家目前出现的问题。人们普遍认为，应对气候变化的有效努力需要一个构架，其中包括与中国和其他新兴市场的合作。

全球经济合作的制度方法需要彻底改革，考虑新兴市场日益增长的经济影响力和七个工业化集团国家主导地位的下降，这种建议已经成为陈词滥调。这是正确的。迄今为止采取的步骤即使存在不足也弥足珍贵，它包括在20世纪90年代开始行动的20国集团和调整国际金融机构表决权份额。

但是问题比坐在谈判桌边讨论的问题更加深入。在商谈国际经济政策的背后，过去几十年所有的意见分歧存在一个共同的前提，

account the rising economic clout[①] of emerging markets and the decline in dominance of the group of seven leading industrialized nations (G7). This is correct. The steps taken so far—the initiation of the G-20 during the 1990s and the adjustments of voting shares in international financial institutions—are valuable if insufficient.

But the problems are much deeper than the question of who sits around the negotiating tables. For all the disagreements over the past decades, there has been a shared premise behind international economic policy discussions—the goal of increased economic integration, the spread of market institutions and more rapid growth for all nations. While companies may compete, the premise has been that nations co-operate to build a stronger economy in the interests of all.

It is no longer clear that this premise remains valid. Nations are increasingly preoccupied with their relative economic standing, not the living standards of citizens. Issues of strategic leverage and vulnerability[②] now play a bigger role in economic policy discussions. At the same time, it is unclear which underlying driver of global growth will replace the one in place for the past decade—the US as importer of last resort. Global growth has depended on US growth, which has depended on the US consumer; and the US consumer has depended on rising asset values first of stocks and more recently of real estate. With falling house prices and a challenged financial system, US consumer spending is falling. The US is no longer in a position to be a net source of demand for the rest of the world. Indeed,

① clout [klaut] *n.* (尤指政治上的) 影响

② vulnerability [ˌvʌlnərəˈbiləti] *n.* 易损性;弱点

即已经增长的经济一体化目标、市场机构的分布和所有国家经济更快速的增长。虽然公司之间可以竞争，但前提是国家之间开展合作，建立一个符合所有国家利益的、更强大的经济体。

这个前提是否有效不再明确。各个国家越来越关注彼此相对的经济地位，而不是市民的生活标准。策略的杠杆作用和脆弱性问题在经济政策讨论中占据越来越重要的位置。同时，哪一个全球经济增长的潜在驱动力将取代过去十年已经在位的驱动力尚不明显，美国将成为最后贷款人的进口商。全球的经济增长依赖于美国的经济增长，美国的经济增长依赖于美国的消费者，美国消费者首先依赖于股票的增长价值，近期则依赖于房地产增值。随着房价下跌和金融系统的挑战，美国消费者的开支下降。美国不再是世界其他国家需求的净资源。实际上，随着美元的贬值，美国的经济增长已是今日黄花，美国的经济增长过去一直依赖进口，从而促进了其他国家的出口导向型增长。欧洲和日本已经处于或非常接近经济衰退。

现在的全球经济政策争论出现了不和谐的声音。提倡增加美国储蓄和削减美国经常性的账户赤字当然很好，但实现这一进程意味着减少美国对外国产品的需求。如果没有实施到位的弥补性措施，这将造成其他国家就业和产量增长的压力。相反，没有其他政策改变的美元强势回归，将会增加美国对出口的需求，而对国内生产的

with the drop in value of the dollar, US growth—which had been focused on imports and which had enabled the export-led growth of other countries—is a thing of the past. Already, Europe and Japan are in or are very close to being in recession.

The current global policy debate is a cacophony①. It is all very well to advocate increased US saving and a cut in the US current account deficit but the process for bringing it about will mean less US demand for foreign products. That will put pressure on jobs and output growth in other countries if no countervailing② measures are put in place. Conversely, the return of a stronger dollar without other policy changes will raise US demand for exports but at the price of cutting demand for domestically produced goods and compounding the recession.

These problems will be with us for some time. They may not be at the top of anyone's agenda right now. But the success of the next administration could depend on its ability to engage with a wider range of global economic stakeholders, on a broader agenda, at a time when disagreements are increasing not just about means but also about ultimate ends.

(877 words)

---

① cacophony[kəˈkɔfəni] *n.* 不和谐的声音

② countervailing [ˈkauntəˈveiliŋ] *adj.*弥补的,抵消的

商品却存在价格削减需求和加剧经济衰退。

这些问题在一段时间里会存在于我们的周围，他们不会被立刻提上紧急议事日程。但是，下一届政府的成功依赖于其交际能力，要与更广泛的全球经济利益相关者在更广泛的议题上进行交流，在这个分歧越来越多的时代，不仅要有手段，还要关注最终的结果。

知识链接

OPEC 石油输出国组织（Organization of the Petroleum Exporting Countries，也称为“欧佩克”）成立于1960年9月14日，1962年11月6日在联合国秘书处备案，成为正式的国际组织。其宗旨是协调和统一成员国的石油政策，维护各自和共同的利益。现有11个成员：沙特阿拉伯、伊拉克、伊朗、科威特、阿拉伯联合酋长国、卡塔尔、利比亚、尼日利亚、阿尔及利亚、印度尼西亚和委内瑞拉。

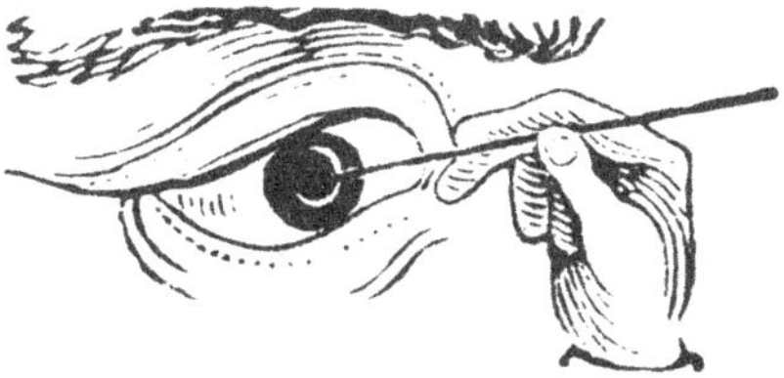

题 记

恺撒·博尔吉亚是文艺复兴时期的一个反面人物。他是罗马教皇亚历山大六世的私生子，他掠夺了北意大利，攻占城池，谋杀阻挡他去路的人。连他的盟友也没有安全感。如果恺撒·博尔吉亚是你的公司领导，你该如何与他打交道呢？马基雅弗利的《君主论》从人性的角度探讨了对权力的追求和行使，给你提供了点石成金的启示。如果你拒绝承认公司领导滥用权力的真相，就容易成为他捕获的猎物；如果你误判你与领导的关系，则会危及你的职业生涯、健康和银行存款余额；如果领导仗势欺人，你必须保持坚强、冷静和自信。有效领导的关键在于自知之明和自我接纳，永远虔诚地观察别人，审视自己，培养你的内在能量。古代的领导者是令人恐惧的神话，现代的领导者是善于运用威胁利诱的现实。这世界已经是比任何时候都更在乎马基雅弗利的世界。

Why Machiavelli Matters

How would you respond if Cesare Borgia invited you to dinner?

Cesare Borgia was the bad boy of the Renaissance. The illegitimate son of Pope Alexander VI, he ravaged northern Italy, seizing towns and murdering those who stood in his way. Not even his allies were safe. A dinner invitation could be your death sentence. He stabbed, strangled and poisoned with impunity.

Cesare Borgia died in 1507, so he won't be inviting you to dinner. But his spirit lives on. We will all, at some point in our lives, meet our very own Cesare Borgia. He—or she—may not be obvious at first. A new manager, a work colleague, a community leader, maybe even a pries—it doesn't matter which disguise he wears. Before you meet your Cesare Borgia, you had best be prepared.

As a Florentine diplomat, Niccolò Machiavelli spent four months in Borgia's court. The behavior he observed there inspired The Prince. At first glance, The Prince may seem irrelevant to our lives today. After all, the book is almost 500 years old! But the abuse of power is not peculiar to Renaissance politics. It can occur at any time, in any workplace, in any relationship. The principles Machiavelli discovered apply equally to our lives today.

In popular culture, Machiavelli is synonymous with deceit and

马基雅弗利启示

如果恺撒·博尔吉亚邀请你参加他的晚宴，你该如何回复呢？

恺撒·博尔吉亚是文艺复兴时期的一个反面人物。他是罗马教皇亚历山大六世的私生子，他掠夺了北意大利，攻占城池，谋杀阻挡他去路的人。连他的盟友也没有安全感。受邀出席的晚宴有可能是鸿门宴。他可以刺伤你、扼死你、毒死你而不受惩罚。

恺撒·博尔吉亚在1507年寿终正寝，所以他不会邀请你出席晚宴。但他的灵魂仍在游荡。我们所有人在生命中的某个时刻，都会遇到自己的“恺撒·博尔吉亚”。起初，他或她也许并不显眼。新经理、同事、社区领导、甚至是一名牧师——他穿什么装着来掩饰自己并不重要。在遇到自己的“恺撒·博尔吉亚”之前，你最好做好准备。

作为佛罗伦萨的外交官，尼科罗·马基雅弗利在博尔吉亚法院度过了四个月。他在那儿观察到的言行举止为他创作《君主论》提供了灵感。乍一看，《君主论》似乎与我们的生活没有多大关系。毕竟，这本书距离现在已有500多年。但是，滥用权力不是文艺复兴时期政治的特殊表现，它可以发生在任何时代、任何场合，纠缠于任何关系之间。马基雅弗利发现的原理同样适用于我们今天的生活。

treachery. However, Machiavelli's main concerns were the security of the state and the welfare of its people. Much of his leadership advice is plain common sense. In Chapter 21 of The Prince, he explains what leaders must do to be esteemed. Presidents who attend the Olympics and CEOs who act as philanthropists are simply following his counsel.

Philanthropy, of course, is far less interesting than a good old-fashioned murder. While Machiavelli admired Borgia, he also recognized his weaknesses. Here, Machiavelli is brutally honest. He identifies some unpalatable① truths about human nature and gives them to us straight. If we refuse to acknowledge these truths, we become easy prey for the first Cesare Borgia to happen our way. Powerful people do not always play nice.

These days, of course, our leaders are far less bloodthirsty than Borgia. If you cross your manager, he probably won't have you drowned in the Tiber. Backstabbing is not what it used to be; usually there's no funeral involved. Even so, misjudging your relationship with powerful people can jeopardize② your career, your health and your bank balance. Open any newspaper and you will find the stories of those who abused their power and those who became their victims. Power is most often abused when both the perpetrator③ and the victim share dysfunctional beliefs about power. Both act out of fear. The perpetrator fears losing power, or being exposed as a fraud. The victim fears humiliation and ridicule. In the end, both reap what they fear most.

The sad fact is very few people know how to lead. This was as true

---

① unpalatable [ʌnˈpælətəbl] *adj.* 令人不快的

② jeopardize [ˈdʒepədæiz] *vt.* 危及

③ perpetrator [ˈpɜːpətreitə] *n.*作恶者

在通俗文化中，马基雅弗利形同骗子和叛徒。然而，马基雅弗利对国家安全和人民福利尤为关心。他的大部分领导建议是简单明了的普通常识。在《君主论》的第二十一章，他解释到，领导者必须受到尊重。参加奥林匹克运动会的总统和装扮成慈善家的首席执行官们只是机械地听从他的忠告。

当然，慈善事业远比不上优秀、守旧的谋杀者有趣。尽管马基雅弗利仰慕博尔吉亚，但他也意识到博尔吉亚的弱点。马基雅弗利在这方面近乎残忍地诚实，他指出了一些令人不快的真相，然后把这些真相直接呈现在我们面前。如果我们拒绝承认这些真相，我们就成为出现在我们生命中的第一个恺撒·博尔吉亚容易捕获的猎物。有权势的人的表演并不总是尽如人意。

当然，在现代，我们的领导者远不如博尔吉亚残暴。如果你冒犯了上司，他不会把你淹死在台伯河。卑鄙的陷害手段不再像以前那样，常常连葬礼都不举行。即使如此，误判你与领导的关系仍然会危及你的职业生涯、你的健康和你的银行存款余额。打开任何一张报纸，你会发现关于那些滥用权力者以及成为滥用权力受害者的报道。当作恶者和受害者分享权力功能失调的信仰时，权力最有可能被滥用。双方都是出于恐惧心理，作恶者害怕失去权力，或害怕骗局被揭穿；受害者害怕受到侮辱和嘲笑。最终，双方都吞噬了他们最害怕的恶果。

可悲的是，几乎没有人知道如何当领导，今天的这种情形与文艺复兴时期如出一辙。领导者从精神上引导臣民奔赴共同的目标。他们调控自身利益。他们建立人际网，而不是构筑堡垒。大多数人缺乏这些技巧，而他们则善于运用威胁利诱的方式。这不是领

during the Renaissance as it is today. Leaders channel the energies of their people toward a common goal. They temper their self-interest. They build networks, rather than fortresses. Most people lack these skills. Instead, they cajole①, criticize or threaten. This is not leadership; this is bullying. It is the only strategy they know.

Bullies are essentially weak. The best defense against a bully is not to cringe②, nor to fight back. The best defense against a bully is no defense at all. Bullies are not attracted to people who are strong, calm and self-confident. We may be tested, however. Any decent bully knows how to press our buttons. We all have self-doubts, and bullies can sense these instinctively. If we cower③, we become victims. If we fight back aggressively, we become bullies. Neither stance will bring us happiness. Once we begin bullying others, we must always watch our backs. The vast majority of Roman Emperors cited in The Prince died violently, before their time. Every time we bully someone, we create an enemy.

How we respond to those more powerful than us shapes our treatment of those who are weaker. We will all be given the opportunity to lead others. It might be at work, in politics, in our community, or even within our family. Families can be the most dangerous of all-Cesare Borgia is said to have murdered his brother. Those whom we know intimately are best attuned④ to our frailties⑤.

---

① cajole [kəˈdʒəul] *vi.* 劝诱
② cringe [krindʒ] *vi.* 畏缩
③ cower [kəuə] *vi.* 畏缩
④ attuned [əˈtjuːnd] *adj.* 熟悉的
⑤ frailty [ˈfreilti] *n.* 弱点

导，这是威胁恐吓，但这是他们所知道的唯一策略。

仗势欺人者本质上软弱无能。最好的防范方式既不是畏缩，也不是抵抗。对待仗势欺人者的最佳防范方式也不是完全不抵抗。坚强、冷静和自信的人对仗势欺人者不屑一顾。然而，我们也许还会受到考验。任何有分寸的仗势欺人者都知道如何向我们施压。我们都缺乏自信，仗势欺人者可以本能地意识到这一点。如果我们退缩，我们就成为受害者。如果我们积极地反击，我们就变成恃强凌弱者。两种姿态都不会给我们带来幸福。一旦我们威吓他人，我们就会永远担心腹背受敌。《君主论》所引用的大部分罗马统治者都死于暴力。我们每次伤害一个人，我们就树立了一个敌人。

我们如何回应这些，比我们强大得多的人给我们提供了对付那些弱者的处理方式。我们都会获得机会领导他人。机会也许就会在工作中，在政治事务中，在我们的社区，甚至在我们的家庭里。家庭可能是所有机会中最危险的处所——据说恺撒谋杀了他的兄弟。那些我们认识的亲密朋友是最熟悉我们弱点的人。

当我们变成领导者时，我们将受到挑战，如果我们有任何的自我怀疑，就会把弱点暴露给别人。我们既有优点又有缺点。如果我们试图隐藏缺点，他们就会暴露出来。

有效领导的关键在于自知之明和自我接纳。当大多数人想起马基雅弗利时，这并不是他们脑海中的形象。但是，博尔吉亚这类人由于缺乏自知之明也遭到了严重的毁灭。如果博尔吉亚能够认识到自己的弱点，他可能会有另外一种人生。但是只有品格坚强的人才会承认自己的缺点。自我接纳同样重要。一旦我们接受了自己的缺点，他们就失去了权势，其他人也不可能用这些缺点来操纵我

When we become leaders, we will be challenged. If we have any self-doubts, they will become obvious to others. We all have strengths and weaknesses. If we try to hide our weaknesses, they will be exposed.

The key to effective leadership is self-knowledge and self-acceptance. This is not what most people imagine when they think of Machiavelli. But men like Borgia were destroyed precisely because they lacked self-knowledge. Had Borgia recognized his weaknesses, he would have taken a different path. But only strong people can acknowledge their weaknesses. Self-acceptance is equally important. Once we accept our imperfections, they lose their power and others cannot use them to manipulate us. We find the courage needed to speak the truth to power. And we find it easier to accept the imperfections in others. Whether we lead or follow, self-knowledge and self-acceptance are indispensable.

Machiavelli teaches us to take responsibility for our relationship with power. This is not obligatory, of course, but merely wise. Understanding Machiavelli gives us a richer appreciation for human nature. It allows us to foresee problems, defuse dangerous situations and make wiser decisions.

To learn the inner workings of power, read The Prince. Observe others with unfailing honesty. Look within yourself. Identify and acknowledge your weaknesses. Cultivate your inner strengths. Then, when the Cesare Borgia in your life invites you to dinner, you will be able to respond with clarity and confidence.

(959 words)

们。我们找到了需要向权势讲真话的勇气，我们发现自己更容易接受别人的缺陷。不论我们是领导还是下属，自知之明和自我接纳都是必不可少的。

马基雅弗利教导我们，要对我们有权势的领导承担责任。当然，这不是强制性的，只不过是明智的。理解马基雅弗利让我们对人性有了更加深刻的认识。它让我们能够预见问题，化解危险的形势，做出更明智的决策。

要了解权力的内部运作，请读《君主论》。永远虔诚地观察别人，审视自己，识别并承认你的弱点，培养你的内在能量。那么，当出现在你生命中的恺撒·博尔吉亚邀请你参加晚宴时，你就可以清楚并自信地回复他了。

知识链接

Niccolò Machiavelli 尼科罗·马基雅弗利(1469–1527)是意大利著名的政治思想家、外交家和历史学家。他是一位深受文艺复兴影响的法学思想家，他主张建立统一的意大利国家，摆脱外国侵略，结束教权与君权的长期争论。他的名著《君主论》(The Prince)写于1513年，旨在根据史实及当时的事件，揭明公国是怎样得来的、怎样保住的、怎样失掉的。这本书对现代公司治理和商务交际也起着画龙点睛的作用。

The Tiber 台伯河。意大利中部的一条流程约406公里(252英里)的河流，向南和西南方向流经罗马，并在奥斯蒂亚市附近注入第勒尼安海。